WORLD CLASS

WORLD CLASS

Peggy Shinn

THE
MAKING
OF THE
U.S.
WOMEN'S
CROSS-
COUNTRY
SKI
TEAM

*

ForeEdge

ForeEdge

An imprint of University Press of New England

www.upne.com

© 2018 Peggy Shinn

Manufactured in the United States of America

Designed by Eric M. Brooks

Typeset in Quadraat by Passumpsic Publishing

For permission to reproduce any of the material
in this book, contact Permissions, University Press
of New England, One Court Street, Suite 250,
Lebanon NH 03766; or visit www.upne.com

Library of Congress Cataloging-in-Publication Data
available upon request

Paperback ISBN: 978-1-5126-0065-0
Ebook ISBN: 978-1-5126-0181-7

5 4 3 2 1

To my teammates,

Andy and Sam Shinn

CONTENTS

Color photos follow
page 110

PREFACE

The idea for this book began to hatch in late February 2012, when I interviewed four ebullient women who had just finished a World Cup cross-country ski relay race in fifth place—better than any American women before them. They then carried that momentum into the next season, winning their first World Cup medal in a relay the following November. In a sport where American women had toiled for decades mostly in the middle of the pack or the back, it was unprecedented—as if a Norwegian baseball team began hitting home runs against the Red Sox.

When I asked the women what was behind these improved results (better fitness? faster skis?), they did not credit their individual strengths. To a person, they credited teamwork—even though cross-country skiing is an individual sport. In the months and years that followed, the women on the U.S. cross-country ski team began to finish better than they ever had before against the world's best skiers, and they still credited teamwork. Although they were each competing against the clock and everyone else, including their teammates, it was these same teammates who were lifting them up.

This concept intrigued me. Over the past thirty-plus years, I have competed in a handful of individual sports, from my high school's cross-country running team to my college's alpine ski team, a regional women's cycling team, and most recently, a women's tennis team. None had a healthy dynamic. Personal insecurities were never addressed and jealousy festered. We focused on the negatives that each person brought to the team, not the positives. The coaches and/or team captains did little to change the dynamic; they tended to focus most of their attention on the best runner/skier/cyclist on the team. When they did turn their attention toward the more mediocre team members (of which I was one), they mostly told us what we were doing wrong and very little of what we did right. It undercut my self-confidence, and thus, my performance. I found it more constructive training with men than with women. Men tend to beat each other up on the field of play —in a tennis match or on a training ride—then put aside hostilities when the competition ends and gather for a beer. They don't usually judge each other by poor performances, only by poor sportsmanship. We women tend to take our poor performances personally, as if they reflect our self-worth.

As a journalist covering Olympic sports, I expected to encounter female athletes with their claws out. Although I have encountered a few, I have also witnessed how athletes have fared on teams with a positive dynamic, where they cheered each other on and seemed genuinely happy for each other's successes. The U.S. swim team competing at the 2012 and 2016 Olympic Games exemplified such a dynamic. They almost literally danced their way to London (making a music video during a pre-Olympic training camp) and Rio, and even unheralded athletes, such as Katie Ledecky in 2012 and Maya DiRado and Katie Meili in 2016, won Olympic medals. Women's rowing at the 2012 and 2016 Olympics also exhibited a similar dynamic. Although rowing is a team sport, the women spent four years competing against each other for seats in the Olympic boat classes, from the eight to the pair. Rather than tearing each other apart, they pushed each other in training and made each other better. USA Luge also benefitted from a solid team dynamic, winning more World Cup medals in 2016 and 2017 than they ever had before. Even my daughter's U14 alpine ski team (for kids under age fourteen) thrived on good teamwork. They skied their individual races, then stayed in the finish area or headed back to the start to cheer for each other. After the races, no one was judged by how he or she had finished. They gathered almost every weekend for dinner or a movie. Every kid was included, from the fastest on the team to the slowest. A mother from an opposing team once asked me, "Do they always get along so well?!"

As I watched the athletes on these "good" teams, I thought about how women's sports have changed since I first competed in the late 1970s. In the forty years since Title IX was enacted, had women learned how to compete in a more positive environment? The landmark legislation requiring federally funded educational institutions to provide fair and equal treatment of both genders in all areas, including athletics, was enacted by Congress in 1972, and it had an immediate impact on college sports, with participation filtering down to the local level. Women's sports began to proliferate and gain acceptance in the United States. But this did not necessarily mean that women were taught *how* to compete. Coaches—almost all male at the time—were capable of teaching women the biomechanics of the various sports. But sportsmanship, as I found out, would be harder to learn. Women tend not to compartmentalize their lives the way that men do, making it challenging for women to go head-to-head with friends in competition, then maintain those friendships off the field. If one person on a team excels, women often default to a sense of defeat: her win is my loss. While men typically welcome the challenge—a rising tide raising all boats—women can view that same rising tide as an imminent threat of drowning.

But here in the twenty-first century were women who were now rising with the tide, and I began considering the ingredients that went in to making a positive team dynamic. On these "good" teams, how had these women learned to be good teammates? Was it the coach? Or the personality of the team leader/captain? Or the personality of each team member? And what did each person on a team do to keep a good dynamic?

I began researching teamwork but found surprisingly few books that specifically addressed the topic. Most tried to take teamwork learned on the field and apply it to business. I also read academic papers and found this compendium enlightening: *Group Dynamics in Exercise and Sport Psychology*, published in 2007 and edited by Mark R. Beauchamp and Mark A. Eys, professors of human kinetics at the University of British Columbia and Laurentian University, respectively. Several of the papers resonated both with my experience as an amateur athlete and with what I was witnessing on the elite level. One paper explored coach-athlete relationships and suggested that "when coaches have the interpersonal skills and resources to connect with every athlete on the team, close coach-athlete relations can in turn ignite a sense of togetherness among team members" ("Coach-Athlete Relationship Ignite

Sense of Groupness," by Sophia Jowett). Another looked at the role of personalities and how they blend in groups, suggesting that teams with agreeable, conscientious, emotionally stable people tend to integrate more effectively around a team goal and that "energy sappers" who can't be directed to become "energizers" can destabilize teams ("Personality Processes and Intra-group Dynamics," by Mark R. Beauchamp, Ben Jackson, and David Lavallee). A paper titled "Transformational Leadership in Sport" (Colette Hoption, John Phelan, and Julian Barling) highlighted how a humble, modest, enthusiastic leader can inspire and motivate a team.

I also read a *New York Times Magazine* story titled "What Google Learned from Its Quest to Build the Perfect Team," by Charles Duhigg (February 25, 2016). The article detailed how researchers at Google determined that a good team dynamic is not created by focusing on the team's efficiency but instead is fostered by a sense of psychological safety among team members. Psychological safety is achieved when members share who they are as people in a supportive environment. What the Google researchers discovered is that the best teams are not simply a collection of people with specific skills. To work most effectively together, these people should care about each other as humans. This makes work more than labor, wrote Duhigg.

It's easy to see how this finding can apply to sports. When team members who care about one another get into competition, they are more apt to dig deeply for an outcome that the team can share. It will be a success that they can all celebrate together, and good teammates know their value to the team and to one another.

But rather than make this book an academic tome about creating effective teamwork, I wanted to tell the story of a team that's making it work. And the U.S. women's cross-country team that began to come together in 2012 is a perfect example. They have everything from the transformational leader, to the coach who connects with his athletes, to the agreeable, conscientious, energizers who comprise the team.

To witness them in action away from the field of competition, I traveled to Alaska in July 2016 and spent a week at their training camp in Anchorage, when team leader Kikkan Randall was returning after the birth of her first child. As a group, they roller skied or did hill-bounds (intervals with their ski poles up hills) in Anchorage neighborhoods in the mornings, then ran or hiked with their coaches for hours in the mountains of Chugach State Park right outside Anchorage in the afternoons, gathering at their large rental house in the evenings for dinners that they took turns preparing. They invited me to run and dine with them (I was more successful at eating with them than keeping up with them in the mountains), and I spent hours between training sessions talking to each of them. I also spent four days with the team in Park City, Utah, at their final off-season training camp before the 2016–2017 World Cup season started. They roller skied in the mornings on mountain roads in the Wasatch Mountains or on paved paths at Soldier Hollow (the 2002 Olympic Winter Games Nordic venue) and did strength training in the afternoons at the U.S. Ski Team's Center of Excellence. In the evenings, they had team meetings, at one point trying to come to terms with the previous season, when the team had frayed a bit at the edges. Then I traveled to Lahti, Finland, for the 2017 FIS Nordic World Ski Championships, and Quebec City for the 2017 World Cup Finals.

I also interviewed as many U.S. Ski Team veterans as I could, as well as iconic coaches such as Marty Hall, the first U.S. women's cross-country ski coach; John Caldwell, known as the father of cross-country skiing in America who helped initiate women's cross-country skiing in this country; and Pete Vordenberg, a two-time Olympian and U.S. Ski Team coach from 2002 to 2011, who helped create the structure that would launch this team. I chatted on the phone with Bill Marolt, who was CEO of the U.S. Ski & Snowboard Association (now called U.S. Ski & Snowboard) from 1996 to 2014 and raised the funds needed for success. At U.S. Ski & Snowboard's headquarters in Park City, I sat down with Tiger Shaw, who took over U.S. Ski & Snowboard's reins in 2014, and even though he is an Olympic alpine skier, he is also a fan of Nordic skiing; Luke Bodensteiner, also a two-time Olympic Nordic skier who started the SuperTour series of elite races in this country in 1996, then moved through the ranks at U.S. Ski & Snowboard; and Tom Kelly, who worked in public relations at the Telemark Resort, home of the United States' first women's cross-country World Cup in 1978, and is now vice president of communications for U.S. Ski & Snowboard. And I chased down parents, husbands, friends, and former coaches of the women portrayed in this book. They all helped paint a vivid picture of the obstacles that female athletes had to overcome in the mid-twentieth century just to ski with the world's best—let alone beat them. And they gave me insight into why this particular group of women is clicking.

What I learned is that there is an "I" in team—a collection of the right individuals who work well together. They have figured out how to bring the best of themselves to this team, and they have created an environment where they feel at home, even when they are on the road for almost half of each year. They are inherently optimistic and happy for each other, where one person's success is not everyone else's loss. As coach Matt Whitcomb likes to say, "You don't have to be best friends with everyone on the team, but you have to be best teammates."

They have come to know each other like sisters, celebrating birthdays with homemade cupcakes concocted from whatever ingredients they can find on the road (chocolate chip cookie dough cupcakes?), or wearing stick-on mustaches and singing country songs in the van driving from races in Italy to more races in Switzerland. From dragging their suitcases through the snow and slush at 3 a.m. in the grim city of Rybinsk, Russia, to hugging each other through pre-race breakdowns of confidence, they have learned to focus on the positives and help each other through the negatives of careers in a sport that garners few headlines in the United States. It's a sport where they really could view the glass as half empty—having had to overcome funding issues and injuries and illnesses in a brutally hard sport in which it takes decades to develop, and to compete against countries where doping has been rampant. But these women perpetually see the glass as half full. Through many ups and downs, they have had one goal in mind—to win an Olympic medal, especially in the team relay. But should they fall short of this goal, they know that the journey of creating this team has been worth it. It's a dynamic that we all could learn from.

This is the story of how Kikkan, Liz, Holly, Jessie, Ida, Sadie, Sophie, Rosie, and their coach Matt made the perfect team.

WORLD CLASS

THE RELAY

On November 25, 2012, a gray afternoon in Gällivare, Sweden, a smiling thirty-year-old from
Alaska named Holly Brooks lined up at the
start of a World Cup cross-country ski relay.
The leadoff skier for the U.S. women's relay
team, she looked relaxed. And why not? No one
expected the U.S. team to finish in the medals of
a cross-country ski race. They hadn't yet. In the
sixty years that women had been competing in
the Olympic Games and world championships
in cross-country ski racing, skiers from Russia,
the Scandinavian countries, Germany, and Italy
had most often claimed all the medals, especially
in the relays—where a team of four takes turns
racing around a 5-kilometer racecourse. At the
time, the Norwegians were the reigning world
and Olympic relay champions, and the depth of
their team always showed in the relays. Although
the Soviet Union and then Russia had had an iron
grip on the women's cross-country ski podium
from the early 1950s through the early 2000s, the
Norwegian women had more recently become
the team to beat. At the Vancouver Olympic Winter Games in 2010, the Norwegians won more
Olympic medals in cross-country skiing than
any other country, including three of the six gold
medals available in the women's races.

But in the past year, the Americans had been
showing signs of life. For the first time ever, five
women had committed to competing on the full

Teamwork is the ability
to work together toward
a common vision. The
ability to direct individual
accomplishments toward
organizational objectives.
It is the fuel that allows
common people to attain
uncommon results.

*

Andrew Carnegie, American
industrialist who amassed
a fortune in the nineteenth-
century steel industry

World Cup tour: about thirty races, mostly held in Europe, extending from late November to mid-March. From 2006 to 2011, Kikkan Randall, a muscular Alaskan with a dimpled smile and pink streaks dyed in her blonde hair, was usually the only American woman to represent the U.S. at World Cup races—and she was the first American woman to stand on a World Cup podium and win a World Cup race. Other U.S. women had skied in a few World Cups here and there, but Kikkan— by then a three-time Olympian and a sprinting specialist—had been competing in almost the full schedule of races since 2007. The U.S. Ski Team only fielded a full team (of more than four women) for the Olympic Games and the world championships, which are held every other year on odd years.

For this reason, the U.S. women had usually skipped competing in World Cup relays, where four women per team each ski 5 kilometers (it's referred to as the 4 x 5-kilometer relay), with the first two skiers racing in the classic kick-and-glide technique and the final two competing in the freestyle or skating technique (like speed skating, but with skis and poles). Kikkan simply had no other teammates to hand off to in the relays.

In November 2011, however, at new women's head coach Matt Whitcomb's insistence, three other women joined Kikkan on the full World Cup tour: 2010 Olympians Holly Brooks and Liz Stephen, and Ida Sargent, a Dartmouth College student who had been runner-up to Kikkan in a U.S. SuperTour sprint race the previous spring. Then in January 2012, a recent high school graduate named Jessie Diggins joined them. At age nineteen, Jessie had just won three national titles (in the freestyle sprint, 10-kilometer freestyle, and 20-kilometer classic mass-start race). Now with five women competing in Europe, the Americans could field a relay team, even if the best they had finished to date was ninth. The relay, Matt always said, was the true test of a team's success. To win, or even make it into the medals, required four talented skiers —not just one—to keep the team out front. In the Americans' case, they had yet to show this depth.

Their chances had looked especially dismal for a World Cup relay the previous season. In mid-February 2012, in a World Cup stop in Nové Město na Moravě in the Czech Republic, the races featured a

15-kilometer event in the classic technique on the first day of competition, then a relay the following day—4 x 5-kilometers for the women, 4 x 10-kilometers for the men. With Kikkan on the sidelines nursing a cold and the entire team fatigued after the brutal 15-kilometer race, where none of them had finished in the top thirty, it looked like the team would again finish somewhere near the back in a World Cup relay.

Rather than grimly accepting their fate, on the morning of the relay Holly, Ida, Liz, and Jessie cranked up the music, applied face paint and glitter to their cheeks, and pulled on red, white, and blue striped socks over the legs of their speed suits. Kikkan had picked up four pairs of these striped socks at a German convenience store earlier in the season. She thought they might help with some good ol' U-S-A team spirit so far from home. As the U.S. women warmed up for the relay, the other teams looked at them as if they had lost their minds. Who were these clowns with paint on their faces and crazy socks on their feet?

On the course, the four American women were all business. With Kikkan cheering from the sidelines, the women ended up finishing fifth in the Nové Město relay, the best finish by a U.S. team in a World Cup relay to date. And Jessie skied the fastest freestyle leg that day— even faster than Olympic champion Charlotte Kalla from Sweden.

Now, nine months later, the U.S. women had traveled to Gällivare in the snowy reaches of Lapland for the start of the 2012–2013 World Cup season. The weekend's races featured a 10-kilometer freestyle race and another 4 x 5-kilometer relay. One hundred kilometers north of the Arctic Circle and home to about 8,500 people, Gällivare did not attract a huge crowd for the World Cup. But the thousand or so fans who did show up—some clad in red Santa suits with elf-like fur-trimmed hats—bordered the racecourse and cheered on the Swedish skiers like Kalla, hopeful that home course advantage might help them beat the dominant Norwegians. This far north, the sun hardly rose this time of year, making it feel more like evening, but a few stadium lights in the start/finish arena fought off the Arctic gloom. The small Dundret alpine ski area, with its handful of tree-lined trails strung with lights, served as a backdrop—a reminder that skiing of all forms is a way of life this far north in Sweden.

But it was the Americans who were really enjoying the Gällivare racecourse. In the 10-kilometer freestyle race, Kikkan finished third, her best-ever result in a distance race. Holly took fifth, a personal best for her too, and Liz finished twenty-first after falling early in the race. Crucially, she scored World Cup points—given to those finishing in the top thirty. Skiers ranked in the top thirty, called the red group, start near the front in World Cup mass-start races, and near the back in interval-start races (where they can chase the times of those who started earlier). But perhaps more important, the International Ski Federation (FIS) pays for the red group's travel costs, which amount to around 125 euros per day. On the U.S. Ski Team, only the A-team skiers' costs are fully covered by the U.S. Ski & Snowboard Association (USSA, now called U.S. Ski & Snowboard). And during the 2011–2012 season, only Kikkan was on the A team.

For Kikkan, third place in a 10-kilometer race was remarkable—and not just because she had suffered a stress fracture in her foot earlier in the fall. A twenty-nine-year-old veteran of six world championships and three Olympic Games, she already had fifteen World Cup medals in her collection, and a silver medal from the 2009 FIS Nordic World Ski Championships. But to date, all her medals were won in sprint races —fast dashes around 1-kilometer (or so) racecourses. Distance races of 10 or 15 kilometers require a different set of skills—namely, more endurance and less brute power. By finishing third in the 10-kilometer race at Gällivare, Kikkan showed that she was incredibly fit, and also that her physical talents were broadening. Perhaps one day she would contend for an overall World Cup title, given to the skier who accumulates the most points in races throughout an entire season.

After such a strong showing in the 10-kilometer race, the U.S. women's hopes were high for the Gällivare relay. But expectations were measured. After all, they had only finished in the top five once—at Nové Město the previous February. As the British Eurosport announcer speculated before the relay's start, "We could see America finishing in the top five today. That would be a good achievement."

Back on the starting line, Holly Brooks was smiling, as if she were about to head off into the Arctic twilight on a ski tour with friends. When the starter fired the pistol, she quickly found her rhythm. Looping through the forest, the racecourse was particularly hilly and re-sembled cross-country terrain typical of northern New England. On each 5-kilometer leg of the relay, each skier would have to climb 525 feet—the equivalent of ascending about halfway up the Empire State Building. But Brooks—a mediocre junior ski racer turned ski coach who burst onto the scene a month before the 2010 Vancouver Olympics when she was twenty-seven years old—stayed with the leaders for most of the race. She fell near the end of her second lap but quickly regained her footing. When she tagged Kikkan after 5 kilometers, she was in eighth place but only 11.7 seconds out of first place. Norway's two teams, labeled Norway I and Norway II, were leading, with Sweden and Italy in hot pursuit. Russia and Finland I and Finland II were just ahead of the U.S. women.

Kikkan took off after the leaders like a woman possessed. Practically running up the hills on her classic skis, rather than gliding and poling her way up at a slower tempo more fitting a longer ski race, she passed the Russians and Finns within the first kilometer, then fearlessly flew by Italy on a steep downhill—a reminder that Kikkan was an alpine skier in her youth. Now the U.S. team was in fourth.

"Randall is possibly starting too quickly," warned the Eurosport commentator to the television audience, but then added that he admired her tenacity.

Kikkan was not slowing down. She was skiing as fast as Norway I's skier, Therese Johaug, who, in 2010 at the Vancouver Olympic Winter Games, had anchored Norway's relay team to an Olympic gold medal and who, at the time, was a reigning world champion. In the Gälli-vare relay, Johaug was way out in front, and Kikkan had little chance of catching her. But skiing at the same fast pace as the Norwegian, Kikkan was catching everyone else. Scampering up a steep hill on the second lap, the American moved into second place. By the time she tagged Liz Stephen at the relay's halfway mark, Kikkan was only 8.2 seconds off Johaug—and a whopping 18.9 seconds ahead of Sweden and 19.5 seconds ahead of Norway II.

Could Liz hold them off? Barely 100 pounds, the twenty-five-year-old had also started her career on alpine skis, switching to cross-country in 2002 while a sophomore at Burke Mountain Academy, a prep school for talented ski racers in northern Vermont. An endurance sport, cross-country skiing suited both her temperament and her physiology. Rather than skiing solo through slalom gates, Liz liked training side by side with her teammates as they glided along trails and chatted between hard efforts. Within three years, she made the U.S. Ski Team and scored top-ten finishes at both the 2006 and the 2007 junior world championships. Then at the 2008 U23 world championships (for skiers under age twenty-three), she finished third in the 15-kilometer mass-start freestyle race. But her World Cup results were less promising. Only the previous season—2010–2011—had she begun regularly finishing in the top thirty.

Relays motivate Liz, who cares for her teammates as if they are her sisters, and she specializes in hilly races. So on each hill on the Gälli-vare relay course, she gained on Norway I. By the time she had finished her 5-kilometer leg, she had held off Sweden and Norway II *and* had pulled within 4.1 seconds of Norway I. Now it was up to Jessie Diggins, who was waiting in the tag zone alongside Norway's top skier, Marit Bjørgen, who had won four world titles the previous year, plus three Olympic gold medals the year before that, and was leading the overall World Cup standings in 2012. As they waited, Bjørgen turned to Jessie and smiled. To Jessie's young eyes, Bjørgen's smile read, "Good luck, sweetie. I'm going to crush you, but good luck."

In the gray November twilight, Jessie, a bubbly Minnesotan who at age twenty was still new to World Cup racing, forgot about Bjørgen's smile and took off after the Norwegian as if the bad guys were chasing her. She was skating with such fervor that her blonde ponytail bounced straight up over her head with every stride. She had little chance of catching Bjørgen, one of the best cross-country skiers of all time with, at that point, seven Olympic medals, three of them gold. In the Gälli-vare relay, Bjørgen was skating farther and farther into the lead. The big question was: could Jessie hold off Charlotte Kalla, the Olympic gold medalist from Sweden? She had held off the Swede the previous February in the Nové Město relay. But that was a different course. On the hills in Gällivare, Jessie soon began looking ragged, her nerves and fatigue getting the better of her. She had tried too hard on the first lap to outrun her chasers. Now, with her head down, she felt like hunchbacked Quasimodo lurching up the trail. Kalla caught the American within 2 kilometers.

This seemed to snap Jessie to attention. The Americans had trained with the Swedish women the previous summer. They could hang with them running over the Swedish tundra. Why couldn't Jessie do the same now? But it was a fine line. Jessie was on the verge of blowing up—an expression used by endurance athletes to describe the point where they can no longer go hard and must merely survive to cross the finish line. If that happened, she would quickly fade to the back of the race.

Helping motivate Jessie was teammate Ida Sargent. Standing alongside the racecourse, Ida was cheering like a wild woman. Matt Whitcomb had not named the twenty-four-year-old Vermont skier to this relay squad despite her strong contributions during the Nové Město relay the previous February. Ida knew it was a tough decision for the coaches, but it was expected. She had not been one of the top four skiers in the previous day's race. She let the disappointment wash over her. Then, rather than sit inside and stew in her own frustration, she came out to cheer on her team. Normally a smiling but quiet woman, Ida was cheering so loudly that Jessie didn't recognize her, instead thinking, "I don't know who that is, but they need me to go fast."

Jessie stayed on Kalla's tail for the first 2.5-kilometer lap. But she was spent, and Finland and Norway II were hunting her down. As the anchor-leg skiers started the second and final lap, Kalla got away. Then on one of the climbs out of the start/finish arena, Norway II's anchor skier, Marthe Kristoffersen—who had won a handful of World Cup podium finishes during her career—caught the young Minnesotan. A top-three finish for the Americans was sliding away beneath Jessie's skis.

"You've got to hang on," Jessie thought to herself. "You can lose the silver medal, but you can't lose a medal."

Out front, Bjørgen crossed the finish line in first, giving Norway yet another win. She received a polite hug from her teammates in the finish area. Kalla finished 19.4 seconds later to give the Swedes second place. She also received a polite hug from her team.

But out on the course, a battle was waging for third place. With dogged persistence and the thought that she had no choice—she would not be the one to lose the team's first World Cup relay medal—

Jessie would not let Norway II's Kristoffersen ski away with third place. With the tenacity of a terrier, she had clung to Kristoffersen for the final 2 kilometers of the relay. As the two neared the finish stretch together, Jessie used her strong finish kick to pull around Kristoffersen, and then—within feet of the finish line—pass her.

As she crossed the finish line in third, Jessie had just enough oxygen left in her lungs to howl as she fell to the snow. She had never been in so much pain in her life. Skiing out of her league for over half the race, Jessie had gone beyond her young limits. The rest of the American team—Holly, Kikkan, Liz, and Ida—ran into the finish area yelling and jumping up and down. No polite hug here. They piled on top of Jessie, screaming, crying, laughing, and hugging. For the first time ever, a U.S. team had finished on the podium in a World Cup cross-country relay race. Anyone who had missed watching the race might have thought that the Americans had won.

The Eurosport commentators called it "the shock of the day," then quickly rephrased it to "the pleasant surprise of the day"—"a new nation on the podium for the first time in a long time."

Even the other World Cup competitors were happy for the Americans, hugging them as the women rose from their happy pile. Swedish skier Hanna Falk tweeted "Congratulations USA! Fun to see and your happy faces inspire!!"

Matt Whitcomb walked around with a big smile for the rest of the day, and coaches from the other teams came up to congratulate him.

The Gällivare relay in 2012 marked a turning point for the U.S. women's cross-country ski team. In a twelve-month period, a group of women who had each had only a few good international results, but most often finished far back from the leaders, was quickly becoming a team of equals on par with their leader. Now it seemed that any one of them, not just Kikkan, was capable of finishing on the podium in a major international race.

"We've been working really hard in the United States to build a women's team," Kikkan said in a press conference in Gällivare. "When I first came to Gällivare [in November 2006], I was the only woman on the U.S. team. It was lonely. So I've been working on building a team, and now we have a team, and we train together and have lots of fun."

Two weeks after the Gällivare races, the World Cup tour came to Quebec City (in December 2012). Paired with Kikkan in the team sprint, Jessie won her first World Cup race. And in the individual sprint race in Quebec City, Kikkan won, with four other American women finishing in the top thirty. These results emphasized that the Gällivare race was not a fluke.

After that breakthrough 2012–2013 season, the U.S. women began racking up more medals, more trophies, and more titles. The Europeans began taking note. When Kikkan and her teammates took to the start line in glitter, face paint, and funny socks, their reserved European competitors no longer thought that the Americans were crazy. There's something about this American team that's working, and their sense of camaraderie rubbed off on their competition. The entire World Cup tour started to feel more like a family, where people began to realize that they could be both friends *and* competitors.

It had been a long time in the making, with many obstacles in the path. And it only began to gel after 1998, when Kikkan, a fifteen-year-old runner in Alaska, decided to find a way to stay in shape during the winter.

EARLY
CHALLENGES

WOMEN IN CROSS-COUNTRY SKIING, THE EARLY YEARS

In the United States, cross-country skiing has been a fringe sport from the very beginning, perhaps because the sport did not start here. It began in the snowy reaches of Scandinavia, Russia, and Central Asia more than 8,000 years ago, and the word *ski* or the Old Norse word *skid* for "long snowshoe" is derived from the old Indo-European language word *skhait*, for "split," as in a split of wood.

The oldest skis, found in Russia about 1,200 kilometers northwest of Moscow in Lake Sindor, were dated between 6300 and 5000 BCE, and rock carvings with depictions of skiing were found in Norway and date to 4000 BCE. Stone Age hunters in Central Asia at the end of the last ice age used skis to follow the elk and reindeer herds as the glaciers retreated, and for millennia, skis were a means of transportation for farmers, hunters, and warriors, and anyone else wishing to get around in snowy climates in the winter. A famous painting—in Nordic ski circles, at least —shows two Birkebeiner warriors on skis carrying Håkon Håkonsson, the two-year-old heir to the Norwegian throne, from enemy-held territory

I personally do not approve of the participation of women in public competitions, which is not to say that they must abstain from practicing a great number of sports, provided that they do not make a public spectacle of themselves. In the Olympic Games, as in the contests of former times, their primary role should be to crown the victors.

*

Pierre de Coubertin, founder of the modern Olympic Games

in Norway over the Dovre Mountains from Lillehammer to Østerdalen during a blizzard in 1206. Knud Larsen Bergslien painted the rescue in 1869—the Birkebeiners gliding through the woods on thin skis with elegant curls at the ski tips. (The Birkebeiner ski marathon in Norway and American Birkebeiner in Wisconsin today celebrate this journey.) Skiing was also, at times, a competitive pursuit. Old Norse sagas going back to around 900 CE tell of boastful Viking warriors competing to prove their skiing prowess.

Skiing became a more widespread sport for health and pleasure in the nineteenth century, when skis themselves began to improve, thanks to the Norwegians. They added camber, or a convex shape, which meant that skis could be thinner while still holding a skier's weight above the snow. Thinner, cambered skis floated more easily over soft snow and were easier to maneuver, wrote Morten Lund and Seth Masia in "A Short History of Skis" for the International Skiing History Association. Side cut also made skis easier to turn. In 1868, an enterprising Norwegian named Sondre Norheim demonstrated how this Telemark ski—as it was called, named after Norway's Telemark county—could turn in snow. He weighted the outside ski and trailed the inside ski behind, almost like a rudder. Up to that time, most skiers were attached to skis by simple leather-strap bindings over the toe that kept the heel free to move up and down. Norheim and his friends perfected a stiffer binding of osier (willow) roots twisted to make a stiff heel strap to keep the foot centered over the ski to make steered turns possible. Steered turns were controlled, making a run down a snowy slope less fraught with risk. Skiing with these controlled turns was actually enjoyable, making it both a means of transportation as well as a form of recreation.

Skiing was (and still is) a way of life in the Scandinavian countries. But it was not referred to as skiing. Ski is a Norwegian word for the actual device. In Norway, skiing fell under what was called Idraet, which translated to "outdoor physical exercise in which 'strength, manliness and toughness' were the goal," wrote ski historian E. John B. Allen in From Skisport to Skiing: One Hundred Years of an American Sport, 1840–1940. By the mid-nineteenth century, Idraet included even loftier goals. Outdoor exercise was meant to help a person strive "to perfect the individual soul as well as the body," wrote Allen. Ideally, it would develop "the physical and moral strength of nations." For Norwegians, it had become far more than just gliding through the woods in winter.

Skiing came to the United States with Scandinavian immigrants in the mid-1800s but did not become a nationwide philosophical movement on this continent. Geography and the sheer size of the United States meant that skiing developed in pockets, primarily in California during the Gold Rush and in the Upper Midwest, where many of the Scandinavian immigrants settled. In California in the mid-1800s, miners found that skis—or "snow shoes" as they were called because the word ski did not yet exist in the English language—were a reliable form of transportation through the snowy Sierra Nevada Range and were far better than the racquet-style snowshoes used by Native Americans because skiers could cover a good deal of terrain gliding fast downhill on the Sierras' more open slopes. Skis allowed miners to check their claims and let others living in the mining camps get around their snowbound villages during the winter months. Skis also provided recreation and amusement for mining communities, with some establishing "snow shoe clubs" that occasionally held races. According to Allen, even women skied; it was the best way to shop and visit people when the Sierra snows piled up. Women raced as well, taking care that their skirts didn't blow up into their faces. Perhaps most important to the snowbound mining camps, men on skis brought mail in the winter. In the late 1850s, a Norwegian immigrant named John A. "Snowshoe" Thompson carried the mail on skis from Carson Valley to Placerville, a distance of 90 miles over the Sierras. He was "a hero, a superman who was not subject to ordinary human frailty, but disported himself over bridges of ice and avalanches of snow and made light of Nature's stern moods," wrote Hjalmar Rued Holand, who chronicled Thompson's life.

The California miners' influence on skiing was isolated, though. The real influence came after Scandinavian immigrants, particularly Norwegians, brought the sport—or rather, Idraet—with them, mostly to the Upper Midwest. The peak years for Scandinavian immigration spanned from 1880 to 1910. They continued their traditions of hunting on skis, and they also formed clubs that held competitions. The National Ski Association (NSA) was founded in 1905 in Ishpeming,

Michigan, to regulate these clubs and their competitions. The sport was so deeply rooted in Norwegian traditions that the NSA's annual publication, *The Skisport*, carried a column titled "Fra Kristiania" ("From Christiania," as Oslo was then called). It kept the Norwegian immigrants apprised of activities in the motherland, wrote Allen. Ski clubs often had Norwegian names, and meetings were held in the native tongue. Women were rarely mentioned as skiers in the nineteenth century and served more as "decorative and useful adjuncts" in club activities, noted Allen. "Some clubs admitted women to membership to give a club a social aspect, others to swell the uniformed ranks on public display on competition day," he wrote. "There was one all-women's club, but after an initial flurry of commentary about the costumes in the local paper in 1903, nothing more was heard from the 'Nora.'"

Competition sprang up among the clubs in the Midwest. But in the American melting pot, ski jumping, not cross-country ski racing, became the popular sport. As Allen wrote, "In America those involved in early ski sport organization looked to the Idraet ideal hoping it would produce a moral person in an all-round skier. Yet America recognized the specialist achiever and measured perfection not by morality but by money." Ski jumping was more daredevil, flashier, and more fun to watch than poor souls endlessly slogging alone through the fields and woods. Cash prizes lured daring jumpers to competitions to wow the paying crowd by setting hill records and breaking ski-jumping barriers. The NSA chafed at the capitalistic display and tried to protect Idraet by abolishing cash prizes. But ski jumpers boycotted the tournaments. Instead, the NSA tried to promote the cross-country races.

The first U.S. National Cross-Country Championship was held on February 7, 1907, in Ashland, Wisconsin. A Finnish skier named Asarja Autio won the 9-mile race and then challenged anybody for one hundred dollars. There is no record whether he had any takers, probably because many Americans found the sport too physically taxing as well as socially isolating. Races were typically run as interval-start events, where competitors started a set distance apart (typically 30 seconds), and the winner was determined by the fastest time. Nationals were held again in 1912 on a course reduced to 3.5 miles. Few participated. By 1917, not one entry was received for the national championship race. "The cross-country skier's all-round ability and fitness implied were less adaptable to the American ethos, and only a few regretted cross-country's passing," wrote Allen.

Back in New England, where inhabitants had used racquet-style snowshoes to get through snow in winter, a Dartmouth College student named Fred H. Harris wanted his classmates to enjoy skiing as much as he did (or "skeeing," as he spelled it). Ever since he had made his own skis ("skees") as a sixteen-year-old at Vermont Academy, he had spent his winters exploring the snowy and hilly countryside on his new equipment. During his junior year, he wrote a letter to the college newspaper about forming a ski and snowshoe club. In the letter to the editor, he asked, "What is there to do at Dartmouth in the winter?" Harris suggested that the college form a "ski and snow-shoe club" to stimulate interest in outdoor winter sports and to host short weekly "cross-country runs," as well as one long excursion each season. That winter, Harris organized a field day with intramural snow and ice competitions on campus. The following year—on February 10–11, 1911— the Dartmouth Outing Club hosted its first winter carnival. Inspired by Montreal's winter carnival, the Dartmouth version consisted of a cross-country ski race, a ski dash, and jumping events, plus an Outing Club Ball (alpine ski racing would not start in America for another sixteen years). Dartmouth was, at the time (and until 1972), a college for men only.

When the International Olympic Committee (IOC) held the first Olympic Winter Games in Chamonix in 1924, cross-country, jumping, and Nordic combined (a combination of ski jumping and cross-country skiing) were the only skiing events on the program. It's no surprise that the U.S. ski team in Chamonix was comprised of three Norwegian immigrants, two guys from the Midwest (one whose parents were Norwegian), and a Dartmouth graduate. One of the Norwegians, Anders Haugen, who was born in Telemark province and immigrated to the United States in 1909, won an Olympic bronze medal in ski jumping —except it took fifty years before he received his medal. The four-time U.S. ski-jumping champion had been the victim of a scoring miscalculation that was only discovered decades later. In the two cross-country races, Norwegians almost swept all the medals in both the 18-kilometer and the 50-kilometer events—the only two ski races held in the first Winter Olympiad. Finnish skier Tapani Niku broke up the Norwegian podium sweep, winning the bronze medal in the 18-kilometer race. Norwegians won the rest of the Olympic medals. John Carleton, the Dartmouth grad, was the highest placed American in the 18-kilometer cross-country ski race. He finished thirtieth. No American skiers competed in the 50-kilometer event.

Women's cross-country skiing did not debut at the Winter Olympics until the 1952 Oslo Games. Although women had participated in cross-country ski races in Scandinavia in the late 1800s, Pierre de Coubertin, the founder of the modern Olympic Games and the second president of the IOC, was not in favor of women competing at all. An Olympiad with females, he said, would be "impractical, uninteresting, unaesthetic, and improper." Prevailing opinion held that it was unhealthy for women to stress themselves in athletic competition; it was also unseemly for women to sweat—or at least to be seen perspiring. Women did not compete in *any* Olympiad until the second Olympic Games in Paris in 1900, and only because de Coubertin was peripherally involved with planning that event, which was more of a months-long sporting exhibition than a true Olympiad. Of the 997 athletes competing in Paris in the 1900 Games, only 22 were women, and they were only allowed to compete in tennis and golf (except for one Swiss woman who crewed a boat in sailing that year). Although women were granted more opportunities to compete in future Olympiads, the sports in which they could participate mostly involved finesse rather than aerobic capacity: archery, canoeing, diving, and gymnastics. In the Olympic Winter Games, women could either figure skate or alpine ski—neither of which was perceived as a "sweating" sport. Women's speed skating was included as a demonstration sport at the 1932 Olympic Winter Games in Lake Placid, but the winners were not awarded medals (even though American Kit Klein's time in the women's 1500 meters was only 3.1 seconds slower than Jack Shea's gold medal performance in the men's 1500). It would be another twenty-eight years before women's speed skating made its Olympic debut as a medal sport.

For women who wanted to elevate their heart rates (and win Olympic medals), the IOC added two swimming events to the 1912 Olympic program—the 100-meter freestyle and a 4 x 100-meter relay. But no American women competed in swimming that year. In America, it was frowned upon (at best, prohibited at worst) for women to participate in activities where they showed their legs. In 1919, a talented swimmer named Ethelda Bleibtrey was arrested for "nude swimming" after she removed her stockings to swim at Manhattan Beach in California. The public outcry over her arrest loosened this suffocating social more, and women were finally allowed to swim without being encumbered by leggings. At the 1920 Olympics in Antwerp, Belgium—five days after Congress ratified the Nineteenth Amendment giving women the right to vote in the United States—Bleibtrey led an American sweep of the 100-meter freestyle race in the pool.

Eight years later, at the 1928 Games, track events for women were added to the Olympic program. Women could run short distances (100 or 200 meters), jump (over a bar or into a sand pit), or throw things (javelin, discus, shot put). The IOC also included the women's 800-meter run on the Olympic program that year—the longest distance that women were allowed to run (compared to the men, who ran distances on the track at the Olympics up to 10,000 meters). The controversy that ensued, however, set back women's endurance sports for decades.

The problem did not arise during the competition itself. By all accounts, the race was a real battle to the line. On the 400-meter track in Amsterdam's Olympic Stadium, it was an all-out race between world-record holders Karoline "Lina" Radke from Germany and Inga Gentzel of Sweden. Radke had set the world record at 2:23.8 in 1927 only to see Gentzel lower it to 2:20.4 in June 1928. A month before the Olympics began, Radke took back the world record, setting it at 2:19.6. In Amsterdam, Gentzel wanted to reclaim it. As predicted, the Olympic final of the women's 800 became a battle between Gentzel and Radke. Gentzel held the lead for the first half of the race. But in the final backstretch, Radke took over. The German held the lead into the homestretch and crossed the line first, lowering the world record again to 2:16.8 and claiming the first Olympic gold medal in the women's 800. Japan's Kinue Hitomi finished second for the silver medal, and Gentzel held on for the bronze—all three women finishing under Radke's former world record time.

Understandably, the women were tired, and they bent over at the waist after the finish to catch their breath. But many who watched—particularly male members of the press—perceived the exertion as far more than women could handle. News reports of the race described the women as collapsing at the finish. The *New York Times'* Wythe Williams claimed that six of the nine runners "were completely exhausted and fell headlong on the ground." This "plainly demonstrated that even this distance makes too great a call on feminine strength," he added. The *Times* of London called the race "dangerous" for women.

Eyewitness accounts compiled by sport historian Lynne Emery of California State Polytechnic University in 1984 dispelled the rumor that multiple women had collapsed after the race. Several women had moved to the infield to lie down after they crossed the finish line because they were winded from the effort and disappointed in their placing, wrote Emery. Men acted similarly after hard endurance efforts at the same Olympic Games, claimed the eyewitnesses. In fact, in the 5,000-meter race held the next day, the legendary Paavo Nurmi—the "Flying Finn," so named because he won twelve Olympic medals, nine of them gold, in three Olympic Games—reportedly collapsed in the infield after he lost the gold medal to teammate Ville Ritola.

After the women's 800, a furor erupted over the propriety of women engaging in difficult physical efforts, particularly in front of an audience. Count Henri de Baillet-Latour, president of the IOC at the time, favored eliminating all women's sports from the Olympics and returning to the ancient Greek program with only men competing in the Olympic Games. At an executive board meeting of the IOC, he vowed that women should only participate in "aesthetic" sports, such as gymnastics and figure skating. Swimming was considered aesthetic even though the competitors were as aerobically taxed in the pool as runners on the track. But in the pool, they would be dripping with water, not with sweat. This was apparently more acceptable.

At its annual congress in Amsterdam held after the 1928 Olympic Games, the International Amateur Athletic Federation (IAAF) voted to eliminate the women's 800 from the track program and ban women from running distances longer than 200 meters. This ban held until the mid-1950s, when the 800 was added to the program at the 1954 and 1958 European championships. In 1960, the 800 returned to the Olympic program at the Rome Games.

The International Ski Federation (FIS) was more open-minded about women exerting themselves in competition. In 1951, during its eighteenth congress, FIS voted to add women's cross-country skiing to the Olympic program the following year. The only dissenting vote came from Norway, the host country of the 1952 Olympic Winter Games. Some speculated that Norway disapproved of women competing in cross-country because skiers from Finland were the favorites; the Finns had held women's national championships for several years prior to the 1952 Games.

The only women's cross-country ski event in the 1952 Olympiad was the 10-kilometer race, and, as predicted, Finland swept the podium. Of the twenty female skiers competing, twelve were from Scandinavian countries, two from France, two from Italy, two from Yugoslavia, one from Germany, and one from Austria. None were from the United States. Four years later, the Soviet Union sent its first delegation to an Olympic Winter Games. From the 1956 Olympic Winter Games until the dissolution of the Soviet Union in 1991, the Soviets would dominate women's cross-country competition, winning over half of the fifty-four available Olympic medals, and finishing on the podium in every relay. In fact, from 1952 through the 1988 Winter Games, cross-country skiers from the Soviet Union and Eastern Bloc countries won gold medals in the 10-kilometer race in every Olympics but two. It was success brought on by well-funded institutionalized sports programs, with research into the limits of human physiology and sports medicine—as well as systematic doping. The United States would not field a women's cross-country ski team at the Winter Olympics until 1972.

* * *

Alison Owen loved sports as a kid growing up in the 1950s and 1960s in Wenatchee, Washington—known as the "Apple Capital of the World" on the east side of the Cascade Range. One of five kids, she hiked, climbed, and alpine skied with her family. And her dad even bought her a unicycle. "I was that type of young girl," she said. But in those days, there were no school sports programs or local clubs for girls. They just did what the boys did (if allowed). Or they stood on the sidelines as cheerleaders.

One day when Alison was about eleven or twelve years old, Jack Owen saw an ad in the Wenatchee World newspaper for a cross-country skiing program. Herb Thomas—who had grown up in Wenatchee, attended Middlebury College, and was in the Army's biathlon unit stationed in Alaska—had returned to help run his family's apple business. He wanted to start a ski club and teach kids how to cross-country ski. Jack signed up his five kids. The only girl in the program, Alison raced with the boys. But it did not faze her. She was used to hiking, climbing, and alpine skiing with boys.

In 1966, when she was thirteen, Alison qualified for junior nationals as part of the Pacific Northwest Ski Association boys' team and traveled to Winter Park, Colorado, for the race. Officials were unsure what to do with her at first. She was the only girl who had qualified for junior nationals. They discussed the situation in meetings and finally agreed to let her race with the boys. An ambulance stood nearby, wrote one reporter, to revive Alison should she succumb to the effort.

"They weren't sure if women were tough enough to do this," she said. "Women hadn't been doing this kind of thing, in our country anyway. So they weren't sure what would happen."

No surprise, Alison survived and became a pioneer for women's cross-country skiing in America. The following year at junior nationals, the race organizers included a girls' division. But endurance sports for women in general were still on the fringe of athletics in the United States and not popular. Even after the women's 800 was reintroduced to the track program at the Olympic Games in 1960, only one American woman competed in the event—a high school senior named Billee Patricia "Pat" Daniels—and she was disqualified after she was pushed and fell off the track. Running and endurance athletics in general was just not something that most American women did in the 1960s. And those who dared encountered any number of insults. They were prevented from entering races. And if they managed to get off the starting line, they risked being pushed off the road or assaulted by race organizers or officials. If they did find teams to join, they had no (or very poor) facilities. One woman was told to use the men's locker room; another was instructed to stay away from the boys' team lest she distract them. "It wasn't just that [women] received little encouragement," wrote Amby Burfoot in his book, First Ladies of Running. "It was far worse than that. They were widely ridiculed and routinely warned about permanent physical damage. Running might prevent healthy pregnancies, they were told. They were warned that it would surely turn them masculine, overly muscled, and unattractive."

And cross-country skiing was perceived as an even more brutish sport than running, where the women surely had to resemble mythical Amazons in order to have the strength to kick, glide, and pole for great distances over snow and through the wilds. With most races held in an interval-start format, it was also perceived as a sport for loners.

In Vermont, a math teacher and cross-country ski coach named John Caldwell thought he should do something to promote women's cross-country skiing in this country. Caldwell had competed in the 1952 Olympics in Nordic combined. Then, while teaching math and coaching skiing at the Putney School—a secondary school set on an idyllic hillside in southeastern Vermont—he authored The Cross-Country Ski Book, which helped popularize cross-country skiing in this country. Through this book, Caldwell became known as the father of cross-country skiing in the United States. He was also the U.S. Ski Team coach from 1960 to 1972 and balanced that job with his teaching and coaching responsibilities at Putney. Of the four children that he had with his wife Hester ("Hep"), one was a girl, Jennifer. And he had coached a talented young woman named Martha Rockwell at Putney. Cross-country skiing could be part of a healthy lifestyle for everyone, not just men, and Caldwell wanted to change the perception of the sport in this country.

At the 1966 world championships in Oslo, where he was coaching the U.S. men, Caldwell found an opportunity. He and the U.S. team manager Bob Tucker heard that Inga Lowdin, a Swede on the FIS cross-country committee, could help them. So they set up a meeting.

"You need some good, attractive women to come and do a tour of the U.S.," Caldwell remembered Lowdin telling him. "You don't want your girls to think that you have to be built like an Amazon and look like one as well to be a good female cross-country skier."

Lowdin said she would pick three Swedish skiers to do a promotional tour with ski clinics and races at a few places in the United States. Caldwell and Tucker then convinced Al Merrill, then the head of U.S. Nordic skiing, to include the tour and associated races in the U.S. Ski Team's 1967 budget.

"We almost locked [Merrill] in a closet and told him we wouldn't let him out until he agreed to budget something like $3,500," Caldwell said. "Tucker and I said we would get ski clubs around the United States to help with the local travel, room, and board."

In February 1967, three Swedish ski champions arrived on the East Coast: Olympic and world championship medalists Barbro Martinsson and Toini Gustafsson (Gustafsson was the only woman not from the Soviet Union to win a medal in an individual race at the 1966 world championships), and Swedish collegiate champion Aase Kaarlander served as their interpreter. Their first stop was a race in Caldwell's hometown, Putney. The night before the race, Putney School director Ben Rockwell hosted a party at his house. Ben's twenty-two-year-old daughter, Martha, was back home. A Bennington College graduate, she had been living in Greenwich Village and was struggling to find her way in life. Between jobs, she had recently returned home, started running again, and, as Caldwell put it, was "thrashing around on skis." Martha had cross-country skied while a student at Putney. But with no girls' team, she had to compete in the boys' races. In one relay, she skied the lead leg and tagged her teammate ahead of a couple of competitors. One of the boys she had beaten was later seen thrashing his skis against the side of the outdoor hockey rink.

After debating whether or not to compete against the Swedish women, Martha ended up racing. She beat all the women except the Swedes, who beat everyone, including most of the men. The Swedish women continued their three-week tour across the northern United States, including a stop in Wenatchee. Their tour ended with a race in Fairbanks, Alaska. On February 17, 1967, the *Fairbanks Daily News-Miner* made little note of the race results. Instead, the newspaper reported that the Swedish women "could have won beauty contests as easily as ski meets." The newspaper also made note of the women's heights, hair color (blonde for Gustafsson and Martinsson, dark-haired for Kaarlander), and marital status (single).

The prevailing chauvinism of the era aside, the Swedes' tour had an immediate impact on women's skiing in America. A separate girls' competition was included in the 1967 junior nationals, and by 1969, forty girls had entered the junior national championships. That spring, a handful of women were named to the U.S. cross-country ski team, and a recent college graduate named Marty Hall was appointed as the U.S. Ski Team's first women's cross-country ski coach. A physical education major from the University of New Hampshire, Hall was an outspoken coach who had been working part time helping the director of the U.S. Eastern Amateur Ski Association with Nordic competitions and Al Merrill with the U.S. Ski Team. Charged with coaching the new women's team, Hall put a "full blown program in front of them." It began with a spring training camp. Then the women met in different spots around the country for camps throughout the summer and fall—the November camp being held on snow if they could find it. That winter, the U.S. Ski Team sent its first women's team to the 1970 FIS World Championships—at the time called the FIS Championships—held behind the Iron Curtain in Czechoslovakia. Hall selected the female participants from a series of races, with combined results determining who made it, though he remembered it differently. "If they could ski 5 kilometers in under twenty minutes, they warranted our support to go to world championships," he said.

Alison Owen, then a junior in high school, made the team and was wide-eyed as she walked around Prague. Trina Hosmer, a twenty-one-year-old whose soon-to-be husband David had introduced her to cross-country skiing while she was a graduate student at the University of Vermont in 1966, also made the team. David was a captain of UVM's cross-country ski team, and Trina "got taken in" by the men on the team, who were supportive as she learned the sport. At open races (not college races), the women were allowed to ski after the men started, and Trina jumped in whenever she could. Real improvement came after she and David moved to Washington State in 1968, where Trina joined the Falcon Track Club and began running with distance-running pioneer

Doris Brown Heritage, who had just returned from running the 800 at the 1968 Olympics, and coach Ken Foreman. "When you train with the best in the world, you get good in a hurry," said Trina, who made the 1970 world championship team based on her exceptional aerobic talents.

Martha Rockwell was also on the 1970 world championship team. Since the winter of 1967, she had taken her experience racing against the Swedes and literally run with it. Born in 1944, she got her start like many kids faced with snowy New England winters: her parents put her on skis as a means of transportation. Her father built a house in Jackson, a village in New Hampshire's White Mountains, where the family spent school vacations. To access the house, the family had to hike or ski to it. Martha ski raced at Putney. But with no opportunity to ski except for recreation after college, she moved to the city and found a job. By the time she met the Swedish women in 1967, she owned a publishing business and, according to Hall, had taken up smoking. Martha quickly found her form, though. In Putney, she trained with local Olympian Bob Gray, who had competed in the 1968 Olympics (and would compete again in 1972) and owned the local West Hill Shop, which sold bicycles. Then thirty years old and married, Gray helped mentor Martha and the other women who trained in Putney. Martha, he noted, was not an especially talented skier, but when she put her head down to do anything, she just did it. And she and Gray showed others on the U.S. team that hard work would pay off. In 1969, at the first national cross-country ski championships for women, Martha won. But at the 1970 world championships, the young Americans were in over their heads. The Soviets, as usual, dominated the 5-kilometer and 10-kilometer races, as well as the relay—then a 3 x 5-kilometer race, with three women each racing 5 kilometers. Trina led off the relay for the Americans, and she remembered the skier from the Bulgarian team elbowing her off the course. "I went down this ditch, and I remember saying, 'You can't do that,'" recalled Trina. "I was so mad. She could just fling me off the course, and what could I do?" As the anchor leg of the relay, Martha skied the Americans out of last place.

After the 1970 world championships, Al Merrill retired as U.S. Nordic program director, and Jim Balfanz took his place. A ski jumper and

Nordic combined skier who had skied for Western State College from 1959 to 1964, Balfanz wanted to create a professional Nordic program with coaches who were fully dedicated to their jobs, not splitting their focus with other responsibilities, such as coaching high school or college teams (even if the organization could not afford to pay them full-time salaries). Balfanz began soliciting sponsors, creating a domestic race tour sponsored by Samsonite, developing a Nordic equipment pool so the team could pay skiers bonuses for good performances, and helping initiate a sports science program that was cutting edge for its day. He contacted a series of experts—Marvin Clein who chaired the department of sports science at Denver University; physiologist Art Dickinson; sports psychologist Dick Suinn; Charles Dillman in the field of biomechanics; and two medical doctors (Jack Murray and Fred Schoonmaker)—and Hall (whom Balfanz rehired as women's coach after initially overlooking him) learned that cross-country skiing is not just an endurance sport; it's a power endurance sport. To improve the power of the women on the U.S. team, he had them lift weights. Working with this sports science program, Hall could make a direct correlation between arm strength and their race results. "Marty had a singular focus—all we want to be is the best we can be," said Balfanz.

The American women made their Olympic debut in cross-country skiing at the 1972 Winter Games held in Sapporo, Japan. Veterans Martha—by then twenty-seven years old—Trina, and Alison, who was still a teenager, were joined by Margie Mahoney and Barbara Britch, who had both just turned twenty and skied for Anchorage's Nordic Ski Club. In Sapporo, Galina Kulakova, a twenty-nine-year-old from the Soviet Union, swept the two individual races and anchored the Soviets to the relay gold medal—finishing more than 5 minutes ahead of the Americans, who crossed the line in last place. Martha was the top American finisher at those Olympic Winter Games, coming in eighteenth in the 5-kilometer event and sixteenth in the 10-kilometer race. It would remain the best finish by an American woman for the next thirty years.

❋   ❋   ❋

From their Olympic debut in Sapporo in 1972, the U.S. women's cross-country ski team began to prove that hard work and love of a sport could pay off. Martha Rockwell—who could bench-press her body weight (130 pounds), plus 20 pounds, said Hall—almost had a breakthrough at the 1974 world championships. In sixth place for much of the 10-kilometer race, she was moving up on the Soviet skiers in the lead. She was mere seconds from finishing in the top three and winning a medal. But then on a downhill near the end, a course worker's ski pole caught Martha's ski pole basket and sent her sprawling to the snow. She ended up tenth. Although Coach Hall was livid at the time, he was proud when he looked back at what Martha had accomplished. "In four years, Martha went from being a smoker to tenth in the world," he said with a laugh.

Hall's motto was that the American cross-country skiers were going to "chase those Europeans everywhere they go." One year in the mid-1970s, Hall gave Alison Owen (by then Owen-Spencer and now Bradley) a training log with a photo of Galina Kulakova, the Soviet skier who had swept the gold medals at the 1972 Olympics and 1974 world championships. "Someday, you're going to be right there with her," Hall told her.

Alison remembered the race where Hall's prediction came true. Skiing the leadoff leg for a relay at a race in East Germany, Alison started slowly but soon gathered speed and began passing everyone ahead of her. She tagged her next teammate, and the U.S. team was in first place. "That was the first time I beat Galina Kulakova and all those women who had been my idols," she said. She does not remember how the team finished in that relay.

In December 1978, the Nordic world came to the United States, and Alison was there to show them who ruled on American snow. Tony Wise, the owner and creator of the Telemark Resort in Cable, Wisconsin, wanted to popularize cross-country skiing in this country (or at least the Midwest) so more people would come to his resort. As much a showman as a businessman, Wise had started the American Birkebeiner race in 1973, but he wanted to create an event that would bring worldwide attention to Telemark. "What cross-country needed in the United States were big events, and Wise provided them," wrote Mike Conklin in the *Chicago Tribune* at the time. In December 1976, Wise brought in foreign cross-country skiers from ten countries, including

Americans Bill Koch, Stan Dunklee, and Tim Caldwell, to compete in what he called the Gitchi Gami Games, named after the Native American word for the Great Lakes ("great waters"). William Oscar Johnson wrote in *Sports Illustrated* that FIS had sanctioned the 15-kilometer race at these Games as "an official event on the Nordic World Cup schedule for 1976–77." But the Scandinavian countries had "refused to sanction the formula, saying they would participate at Telemark only if the words 'World Cup' were never, never used." So Wise referred to the Gitchi Gami Games as the American Cup.

Two years later, Wise included a 5-kilometer women's race in the Gitchi Gami Games, and Alison won, beating her nearest rival by 14 seconds. The Russians and Finns had not made the trip to Wisconsin, but the Norwegians had, and included in the field was Berit Kvello, who would go on to win three Olympic and four world championship medals in the early 1980s. Alison remembered the race being billed as an official World Cup, and the medal she received indicated that it was the real deal. Thanks to Wise dispatching his new race PR guy, Paul Robbins, to New York with film of the event, the races were shown on NBC during halftime of college football's Liberty Bowl that year.

Alison also finished second in the Holmenkollen 10-kilometer race in Oslo, Norway. A ski recreation area created in the nineteenth century, Holmenkollen hosts an event that is Norway's Super Bowl of Nordic skiing (now a World Cup competition), and the large ski jump at the recreation area is a landmark in Oslo. A season later, in 1979, Alison was ranked seventh overall in the world. She also competed in the 1980 Olympic Winter Games.

But behind the scenes, the Nordic skiing picture in America was not rosy. The sports under the Nordic umbrella—cross-country, ski jumping, and Nordic combined—were fighting for their very existence. Unlike in the Scandinavian countries, where cross-country skiing, ski jumping, and Nordic combined are hailed as national sports, they were considered the ugly stepchildren of alpine skiing in the United States. Jim Balfanz remembered a meeting with Brad Briggs during the 1974 world championships in Falun, Sweden. Vice chairman of Ziff-Davis Publishing Company, Briggs was instrumental in forming the U.S. Ski Education Foundation, the team's funding arm, and was having good success raising money after alpine skier Barbara Ann Cochran won an Olympic gold medal in slalom at the 1972 Sapporo Games. Her older sister Marilyn had just won the World Cup giant slalom title, brother Bobby was winning alpine World Cups, and twin brothers Phil and Steve Mahre were hot new teenagers coming up through the ranks in the early 1970s.

"Briggs lit up his pipe, looked me in the eye, and said, 'If it were up to me, there wouldn't even be a Nordic program, you're draining money from the alpine program,'" remembered Balfanz.

The next year, following a dispute with Briggs over a planned cut in the Nordic team's budget, Balfanz was fired. However, the four-year program that he and Hall initiated after the 1972 Olympics paid off when Bill Koch won a silver medal at the 1976 Olympic Winter Games, giving the sport a boost, and cross-country skiing was not fully cut from the U.S. Ski Team's budget. But, except for a couple of bright spots, the sport for women in America was about to reenter the dark ages. Over the next six Winter Olympics, athletes from only six nations (the Soviet Union and then Russia, Finland, Italy, Norway, Czecho-slovakia and then the Czech Republic, and East Germany) would win Olympic medals. Hall, who could be demanding but was ahead of his time when it came to training methods that produced competitive re-sults, was let go. It would be decades before the legacy of Koch's per-formance—the youth ski league known as the Bill Koch League in New England—would begin to have an impact internationally.

❋　❋　❋

First, the good news. In the early 1980s, Bill Koch discovered some-thing that would propel him back to the podium. He brought a new technique to FIS World Cup skiing. Competing in a Swedish mara-thon ski race in 1980, Koch observed other competitors using a skating stride, similar to speed skating, along flat sections of the course. By pushing off the inside edge of the ski set at a diagonal to cross-country skiing's parallel tracks, a cross-country skier could propel him- or her-self much farther and faster down the trail (around 5 miles per hour faster) than using the traditional kick and glide technique. Over a mar-athon distance of 50 kilometers, skiers using the skate technique could finish 10 to 15 minutes ahead of those who kept their skis in the parallel tracks and kicked and glided to the finish. In 1982, using the skating technique, Koch won the overall World Cup title and a bronze medal at the world championships. That same year, Koch and Dan Simoneau finished together on a World Cup podium, the first time that two American cross-country skiers won medals in the same race. In 1986, FIS officially recognized skate skiing or freestyle as its own discipline, along with classic (traditional kick-and-glide cross-country skiing).

Skate skiing brought new excitement to cross-country skiing—skiers could glide along trails at the speed of a bicycle. But it did little to help the success of American women in the coming years. They had too many hurdles to overcome just to reach the starting line, let alone form a cohesive team, and it's a miracle that dedicated women continued to persevere in this country. Martha Rockwell retired after the 1976 Winter Olympics, and Alison Owen-Spencer retired after the 1980 Games, even though she still loved the sport. She was frustrated that she could not peak at the right times; she did not ski as well as she was capable of at the Olympics and world championships. Her best finish at the Olympics was twenty-second, in both the 5- and the 10-kilometer races at the Lake Placid Games. The dominant Soviets and Scandinavian skiers were in another league, in part due to doping that many suspected but that did not become public knowledge until the twenty-first century, but also because many of them had participated in ski racing and formal sports programs since they were very young. In this country, attracting talented women to participate in a very difficult sport that takes years of dedication was difficult. And it was also tough to keep the women who did excel.

"Society says you're going to go to grade school, you're going to go to high school, you're going to go to college," Hall said of the prevailing culture at the time. "Society says you're going to get a husband in college, and you're going to get married. You might get a job, but most likely, you're going to raise a family. There was no time for [women] to be athletes."

The women who did participate were considered oddities. Alison remembered feeling welcomed, fully supported, and "nurtured to succeed" by her coaches and teammates on the national team, including the men. But not by the press. She remembered one reporter asking if she ever felt guilty for not contributing to society. She was taken aback. In her final year racing, she made $35,000 in prize money and sponsor bonuses and felt great about her career choice.

Also working against U.S. cross-country skiers, regional development programs were not widely available, so few kids were introduced to the sport at a young age. And with few elite club teams to foster top skiers and provide them with teammates to train alongside between competitions, the nation's best skiers mostly trained on their own during the off-season, even the "Baby Blues," a team within the team that Hall created in the mid-1970s to accelerate the development of young skiers, such as fifteen-year-old Betsy Haines, a promising cross-country skier from Alaska whose older brother Chris was on the U.S. cross-country team. When the women did train and race together, they were often not a cohesive team. They were wary of each other during training and competition because it seemed like a zero-sum game. If one skier did well, it was her win and everyone else's loss. In an individual sport like cross-country skiing, they had no collective goal. Eating disorders were rampant as well. Coaches would sometimes comment on skiers' weights, which led to unhealthy eating habits. Betsy Haines remembered rebelling against the pressure and going out with the men on the team to eat hamburgers.

Women's sports were still a relatively new concept (thanks to Title IX) and some of the skiers felt as if the coaches had little understanding of how to effectively work with and support women—and there were no female coaches at the time, at least not in cross-country skiing at the elite level. Coaches at the time were accustomed to working with men, many of whom thrive on a hands-off, say-it-like-it-is approach. While the coaches were effective at developing training plans and balancing the logistics of racing for the women's team, some of the female skiers wanted more of a personal connection with the coaches. Women tend to see everything in their lives as interconnected—their friends, families, careers, and training. But their workouts could feel disconnected. Women had yet to figure out how to shake off a bad workout or race. And coaches often overlooked the fact that women can be more sensitive than men. When training and competing with the U.S. team, Betsy

Haines missed the personal connection that she had with her brother Chris when he coached her. He knew what made her happy, what made her mad, and how to motivate her to train hard. Without such a connection, Betsy found training and competing difficult. She has fond memories of her time on the team—good races and tales of traveling around the world. But it was not a system that bred widespread success.

Then there was the issue of money. Cross-country skiing is a sport that requires an investment of both time and money but promises no financial return, especially in the United States. Without Olympic or even world championship medals, U.S. cross-country skiers rarely made the mainstream news. And without media coverage, it was difficult to attract sponsors to fund athletes' training and travel. A few "factory teams" started in the late 1980s, sponsored by ski manufacturers Rossignol, Fischer, and Salomon, and even car manufacturer Subaru. These factory teams helped cover travel expenses, but only to the long 25- to 50-kilometer marathon races in the United States that were popular at the time. When women made these teams or attracted other sponsors, they often did not receive the same financial remuneration as the men.

Cami Thompson (now Thompson Graves), who made the U.S. Ski Team after she graduated from St. Lawrence University in 1984, remembered signing a meager $500 contract with a sponsor. Then she found out that one of the men on the U.S. team had also signed with the same sponsor, except he was getting paid more than the $500 that Thompson Graves was offered.

"I'm on the A team and he's on the B team, how come I can't get what he's getting?" she asked the company representative. "He said, 'It's just a fact of life, women are always paid less than men.'"

She just sat there and gulped a few times.

Ironically, while they were not treated like the men, athletic women were expected to act—and dress—like their male counterparts. Female athletes had a difficult time finding comfortable clothing to work out in—and what was available was usually designed to be pretty, not functional, and often fit poorly (too tight, too short, or cut to fit a Barbie doll figure). Athletic women had to wear men's clothing simply to stay warm and move freely. And they were also expected to have "the tough guy, hard-ass mentality," remembered Thompson Graves. At one race, she wore glitter, and coaches, officials, and other racers glared at her.

"Everyone was like, 'What is this glitter stuff?'" she said. "That's not serious. You have to be serious to race fast."

U.S. Ski Team selection criteria could also be subjective. No one knew exactly what criteria a skier had to meet in order to be named to the U.S. team for a world championship or the Olympics. The team staff might select someone who had been on their radar, not the skier who had just won a national race. Her senior year in high school, Thompson Graves remembered winning a race and qualifying for junior nationals. After the race, an official approached her and said, "So-and-so has been trying to make this team all year, so how would you feel if we took her instead of you?"

Team administration was also on shaky ground. Leadership at the U.S. Ski Team through the 1980s and early 1990s was ever changing, as were coaches. Hall was let go by the U.S. Ski Team in 1978, and Nordic ski coaches came and went over the next couple of decades. Adding to the tumult, the U.S. Ski Team merged with the U.S. Ski Association in 1988, and the new organization moved its headquarters from Colorado Springs, Colorado, to Park City, Utah. Funds were scarce, and by 1995, the organization had rung up a $2 million deficit and was teetering on the edge of bankruptcy. No money led to high turnover on the coaching staff and little consistency from year to year. The cross-country skiers went through the motions of training without much direction.

"There was no long-term outlook for us," said Luke Bodensteiner, who competed for the U.S. Ski Team in the early 1990s, including at two Olympic Games, then took a job establishing the SuperTour for the U.S. Ski Team in 1996—a job that started his long career with USSA. "It was all what was happening with this coach, this year. There was no substantial investment in personnel either. Even when I started working for USSA, the first cross-country coaches that I worked with coached in the winter, then built houses in the summer."

On the U.S. cross-country ski team at the same time, Pete Vordenberg, also a two-time Olympian in the 1990s, remembered a coach who dropped off the skiers for a workout, then left to go fishing. Without strong leadership, the skiers worked out together and became good friends. But they had no mutual goal that they were all working toward.

"There was no goal other than this vague notion of success, which I don't even know if we had defined for ourselves," Vordenberg said. "There was no method toward accomplishing anything, certainly not together."

The athletes on the U.S. Ski Team would do a couple of off-season training camps every year. But mostly, everything else was left up to the athletes, particularly the women, to figure out for themselves. One year, Nina Kemppel—a tall, lean Alaskan who had already competed in two Olympics and would make two more teams before she retired —was the only American woman racing at a high level internationally in the 1990s. The team leadership told her that she could train with the men's team. Or she could move to Norway. She moved overseas and trained with the Norwegian women for a few years.

Then in September 1996, Bill Marolt was appointed president and CEO of the U.S. Ski Association. An alpine skier on the 1964 U.S. Olympic Team, Marolt had been the U.S. alpine director in the early 1980s before taking the job as athletic director at the University of Colorado Boulder. Under his watch as alpine director, the U.S. alpine ski team had its most successful Olympic Winter Games to date in 1984, with five skiers winning medals, including three golds. No nation won more alpine medals in that Olympiad—not even Austria, the perennial alpine powerhouse. Then in his twelve years at Boulder, Marolt helped turn the Buffaloes into one of the strongest Division I collegiate sports programs in the country, winning a national football title (1990) and several NCAA ski championships. The USSA board hoped that Marolt could do the same for the U.S. Ski Team, which won no medals at the 1988 Winter Olympics. The team had rebounded significantly at the 1992 and 1994 Winter Olympics, thanks to Tommy Moe and Diann Roffe, alpine skiers who each won gold and silver medals at those Games, as well as three Americans claiming medals in the new sport of mogul skiing. But at both those Olympics, Team USA had finished fifth in the overall medal count, far behind winter powerhouse teams from Germany, Russia (or the Unified Team in 1992), Norway, and Austria. Within months of taking the helm of the USSA, Marolt came up with a vision: Best in the World.

"We defined it as winning more medals in skiing and snowboarding than any other nation," said Marolt.

To accomplish this mission, more than just alpine skiers had to finish in the top three at the Olympic Games and world championships. Alpine skiing has five events each for men and women. But freestyle skiing, the new sport of snowboarding, and the three Nordic disciplines would provide another twenty-three events in which American athletes could win medals at the upcoming 1998 Olympic Winter Games in Nagano, ten of them in cross-country ski races. Cross-country skiers would have even more opportunities to win medals at the hometown 2002 Winter Olympics in Salt Lake City, where a new cross-country ski race, the sprint—a dash around a 1.5-kilometer loop—would make its Olympic debut. The U.S. Ski Team budget was limited. But perhaps it could be re-prioritized.

As it happened, U.S. ski and snowboard athletes won six Olympic medals in Nagano in 1998, including Picabo Street's gold in super-G, and Jonny Moseley, Eric Bergoust, and Nikki Stone's gold medals in freestyle (moguls and aerials). The Nordic combined and men's cross-country teams had some promising up-and-comers as well. Their futures looked bright.

But the future of women's cross-country skiing in America looked grim, and funding to help new young skiers develop was not a priority. The Russians swept all the gold medals in women's cross-country skiing at the Nagano Olympics. The best American finish was Laura Wilson's thirty-sixth in the 30-kilometer freestyle race. In the relay, the women finished second to last.

OLYMPIC STRUGGLES

The cross-country skiers who persevered during these tumultuous decades deserve much credit. It's a testament to the passion many feel toward the sport. Gliding through the forest, particularly on skate skis, is addictive. It's one of the fastest methods of non-motorized travel over snow where gravity (or a horse) is not the driving force, and the combination of endorphins and the sense of adventure and joy of gliding along a snowy white trail surrounded by a serene forest or soaring mountains on a cold winter day can trump the physical effort. The sport brings skiers to some of the most beautiful locations in the world, and many U.S. Ski Team alumni have fond memories of training on Alaska's Eagle Glacier on sunny summer days and racing in the soaring Swiss Alps or in front of thunderous crowds in snowy Norway. The skiers who stick with it do so out of a true love of the sport.

Nina Kemppel was one of the best-known cross-country skiers through the 1990s. A graduate of West Anchorage High School and Dartmouth College, she had won eighteen national titles in the late 1980s and 1990s, and she had competed in five world championships and eighty-four World Cup races, finishing in the top thirty twenty-nine times and as high as fourteenth (the best finish since Alison Owen-Spencer won the inaugural World Cup race for women in 1978). As the calendar turned to the second millennium,

When everything seems to be going against you, remember that the airplane takes off against the wind, not with it.

＊

Henry Ford, American industrialist and founder of the Ford Motor Company

Nina was nearing the end of her long career on the U.S. Ski Team. Her fourth and final Olympic Games were on the horizon, and she saved her best for last. In her final Olympic race—the 30-kilometer classic race on American snow at the 2002 Salt Lake City Games—she finished fifteenth. It was the highest Olympic finish in history by an American woman, and one place better than Martha Rockwell had achieved at the 1972 Winter Olympics in Sapporo.

It was Beckie Scott from Canada, however, who put North American cross-country skiing in the news at the 2002 Salt Lake City Winter Olympics. The Canadian had never won a major international race. But in the pursuit, a two-part race that begins with an interval-start classic race, then skiers pursue those ahead using the freestyle technique, she finished the 5-kilometer classic portion of the race in sixth. Then in the pursuit's 10-kilometer freestyle leg, Scott made up time on three of the skiers ahead of her. At the finish, Scott lunged for the line, beating Czech skier Katerina Neumannová by a tenth of a second and winning the bronze medal, Canada's first-ever Olympic medal in cross-country skiing. Of note, Scott was the first female cross-country skier from a country other than the six that had dominated the Olympic podiums for the past twenty years (Soviet Union/Russia, Finland, Italy, Norway, the Czech Republic, and East Germany) to win an Olympic medal. Ahead of her, Russian teammates Olga Danilova and Larisa Lazutina, who had each won multiple Olympic medals in previous Games, won gold and silver, respectively. It was Lazutina's ninth Olympic medal won over a decade of competition, and she would win her tenth in the 30-kilometer race later in the 2002 Games, tying her with Soviet skier Raisa Smetanina and Italian Stefania Belmondo for the most medals won by a woman at the Winter Olympics.

But the Russians' medals won in Salt Lake City would soon be taken away. Danilova and Lazutina's blood samples taken during the Games showed the presence of darbepoetin, a synthetic form of the red-blood-cell-producing hormone erythropoietin approved by the FDA in 2001 to help kidney patients avoid anemia, and similar to recombinant human erythropoietin, or EPO, a drug also used to combat anemia but taken by some endurance athletes to increase their number of red blood cells. These oxygen-carrying blood cells can increase endurance by as much as 10 percent. EPO had been in the news throughout the late 1990s as one of the primary drugs that was propelling the pro cycling peloton—and one of the primary performance-enhancing drugs that helped cyclist Lance Armstrong win seven Tour de France titles. It was no doubt a performance-enhancing boon to cross-country skiers as well, and with EPO's patent (held by the pharmaceutical company Amgen) not extending outside the United States, the drug was available at a lower price in Europe. Darbepoetin was a new drug in the performance-enhancing category, and athletes were not yet aware that there was a test to detect it. Once it was found in their blood samples, both Lazutina and Danilova were disqualified. After their appeals failed, they were stripped of their medals from the 2002 Games and given two-year bans. Scott's bronze was upgraded to silver, then gold.

(Of note, this was the first Winter Games held after the World Anti-Doping Agency [WADA] was established in November 1999 to coordinate the fight against doping in sports. WADA was established in response to a series of doping scandals during the 1998 Tour de France, referred to as the Festina Affair [doping products were found in the Festina cycling team's car, leading to a series of searches, confessions, and arrests]. In 2003, WADA published the World Anti-Doping Code, a document that aimed to harmonize anti-doping policies, rules, and regulations among sports organizations and authorities around the world. It has since been revised but has been instrumental in cracking down on doping in sports worldwide, a battle that remains ongoing.)

While doping put cross-country skiing in the headlines at the 2002 Games (Spanish cross-country skier Johann Muehlegg was also disqualified for taking darbepoetin), the American women's results were far from the spotlight. The only other American woman to finish in the top thirty at the Salt Lake City Games was a twenty-eight-year-old named Wendy Wagner, who finished twenty-third in the 30-kilometer behind Nina. A month after the Olympics, Nina announced her retirement from the U.S. Ski Team. She wanted to attend graduate school and start a career in business.

Meanwhile, it looked as if the men in U.S. Nordic skiing were on the cusp of winning Olympic and world championship medals. At the 2002 Salt Lake City Olympics, three American men finished in the top twenty in two different races—the first time since 1992 that any American had been in the top twenty. And in the 4 x 10-kilometer relay, Kris Freeman, a diabetic who had had top results as a junior and had been on the development team in the late 1990s, teamed with John Bauer, Justin Wadsworth, and Carl Swenson. They crossed the finish line in fifth, 31 seconds from a medal.

Nordic combined—one of the sport's oldest competitive disciplines combining ski jumping and cross-country racing and only contested by men—was performing even better. Todd Lodwick and his young teammates, Johnny Spillane and Billy Demong—both junior world champions—finished fourth in the team event at the Salt Lake City Olympics, and Lodwick and Demong finished seventh and eighth in the individual sprint event, respectively. Also a former junior world champion, Lodwick had finished fifth in the individual event at the 1994 Olympic Winter Games, less than a minute from winning a medal, and since then, he had won a couple of World Cups. Perhaps the U.S. Ski Team's best bet was to prioritize funding for the men's Nordic teams, with the goal of winning an Olympic medal at the 2006 Torino Olympics or the 2010 Vancouver Games.

The following year, at the 2003 FIS World Nordic Championships in Val di Fiemme, a ski resort in northern Italy's Dolomites about three hours north of Venice, the men on the U.S. Nordic ski team again showed why they deserved team funding. In Nordic combined, Johnny Spillane won the sprint competition and became the first American ever to win an FIS Nordic world championship title. In the cross-country races, Kris Freeman finished fourth in the 15-kilometer classic race, and after falling and breaking a ski pole, Carl Swenson closed out the world championships with a fifth in the 50-kilometer freestyle race—the second and third best U.S. cross-country finishes in history, behind Bill Koch's Olympic medal.

The American women's results barely rated a sentence in *Ski Racing* magazine.

* * *

After Nina Kemppel retired, Wendy Wagner carried the flag for women's cross-country skiing in the United States. Born in Utah on Halloween 1973 to parents who loved the outdoors, her ascent in cross-country skiing began in 1994 after she transferred from St. Lawrence University in upstate New York to Western State College (now Western State Colorado University) in Gunnison, Colorado. At Western State, she joined two women who were near the top of collegiate and national standings—Amy Crawford and Gina Legueri—and the three women were named to the U.S. Ski Team in the mid-1990s. Within a few years, Amy and Gina moved on to other endeavors. But Wendy stuck with it. After competing in only a handful of World Cup races and one world championship, she finished twenty-third in the 30-kilometer classic event at the 2002 Olympics. Her best, she hoped, was yet to come.

But Wendy was essentially a one-woman team who had to find coaching and pay for racing and traveling on her own. Fortunately, she had help. After graduating from Western State, she had moved to Alaska, where she had the support of a new Nordic program at Alaska Pacific University (APU) in Anchorage. APU's cross-country ski program was one of the few clubs in the United States supporting elite skiers at the time. She could live on the APU campus and receive coaching. To help her pay for travel and other costs, the community hosted occasional fundraisers, and local sponsors also helped her defray costs. If she did receive any funding from the U.S. Ski Team, she considered it "icing on the cake," but she knew she couldn't count on it. Aelin Peterson, also from Alaska, occasionally competed and traveled with Wendy. They would rent a car together, share motel rooms, and eat ramen noodles and spinach for dinner to keep the food bill down. In the first part of most winter seasons, they stayed in North America, racing in the United States and Canada, where Wendy was hard to beat. Then later in the winter, Wendy traveled to Europe to compete in an occasional World Cup, sometimes hitching a ride with the American men if there was room in the van.

Even with the support from the community or traveling with the men, Wendy was lonely. Competing in Europe, she often finished far off the leaders, and she had no teammates to make the experience more fun. "That was the hard part," she said. "I didn't feel like I had any partners in crime."

Cell phones were not ubiquitous, and Internet access was via dial-up modem. Wendy talked to her family maybe once a week when she was racing in Europe. She traveled with a computer, but she mostly used it to watch movies—DVDs that she carried in her luggage. "I remember spending hours just trying to get an email to my boyfriend at the time," she said.

❄   ❄   ❄

Then in 2003, another promising female skier emerged—or rather, reemerged—on the national cross-country ski scene. In the annual season-opening SuperTour races in West Yellowstone, Montana, Rebecca Dussault beat Wendy in a sprint race. Rebecca (then named Quinn), who had just turned twenty-three, had been a promising junior racer who competed in three junior world championships (1998 to 2000) and one senior world championship (1999) before marrying childhood sweetheart Sharbel Dussault and stepping back from ski racing. She is a devout Catholic and felt as if she were compromising her faith and morals to be on the team. She also wanted to start a family. Son Tabor was born November 21, 2001.

Just over fourteen months after Tabor's birth, in February 2003, the Rocky Mountain Intercollegiate Championships came to Crested Butte, Colorado, Rebecca's hometown, and the race was open to anyone who wanted to enter (not just NCAA Division I skiers). She had been skiing with Tabor in a front pack, then in a backpack, but hadn't seriously trained since her junior racer days. But ever the competitor, she could not pass up entering a race in her hometown. On the start list was University of Utah recruit Katrin Smigun, an Estonian who had won a world junior title in 1998. Smigun had also competed in two Olympic Winter Games (1998 and 2002) and was undefeated in NCAA collegiate racing. Without much training, Rebecca had no clue how she would do competing against someone of this caliber. She was game to find out.

Rebecca finished well in the classic race—fifth or something, she remembered. Then the next day in the 10-kilometer freestyle mass-start race, Rebecca and Katrin broke away from the pack, then exchanged the lead over the 32-minute race. The two finished so close that it was difficult to tell who won. Rebecca joked that a tie goes to the local. After the race, Sharbel said to his wife, "You have a gift, you have a talent that we've put away. It needs to be used well, and it needs to be used now." But Rebecca had never considered returning to ski racing. It was a phase of life that she assumed was behind her. After much thought and more discussion, Rebecca realized that she could handle the ski-racing life again if she had what she called her "domestic church" on the road with her—"people to pray with me and play with me," she said. "Whether I raced well or poorly, it didn't really matter because I had all my pillars of life with me on the road."

Rebecca started the 2003–2004 season with a bang, dominating the domestic races. In nine races, she beat Wendy Wagner in all but two. Then at the 2004 national championships in early January, Rebecca won three national titles, only missing the sprint win. At the end of the season, Rebecca ran away with the SuperTour title, winning ten races and earning an invitation to compete in a handful of end-of-season World Cup races in Europe. She finished twenty-eighth in a 15-kilometer free-style race, earning precious World Cup points (given to those finishing in the top thirty), and was named *Ski Racing* magazine's U.S. Nordic Skier of the Year.

Not far behind Rebecca was a twenty-one-year-old Alaskan named Kikkan Randall. One of the youngest Americans on the 2002 U.S. Olympic cross-country team, Kikkan was becoming a force in North American cross-country ski races. She had finished in the points at her first World Cup race in 2001. Then, as a nineteen-year-old, she had won the freestyle sprint race at the 2002 U.S. nationals in early January, her first national title (a win that helped her qualify for the 2002 U.S. Olympic team). The following winter, she won the SuperTour sprint race at the West Yellowstone season opener in November 2002, her first major win, and qualified for her second world championship team in 2003. The following year, Kikkan won her second national sprint title and finished second to Rebecca in SuperTour standings. Kikkan's results were good enough to land her first major sponsor: Matanuska Maid, a dairy in Alaska.

For the 2004–2005 season, two women were named to the U.S. Ski Team: Wendy Wagner and Rebecca Dussault. Kikkan, who had often shared the podium with Wendy and Rebecca the previous winter, was on the development team, a designation given to promising young junior skiers whom U.S. Ski Team coaches hope will develop into elite skiers through training camps and other programs. Mostly she stayed in Alaska and trained with her APU coach and teammates. As the 2006 Olympics neared, these women were building momentum. But trouble was brewing for this growing team.

❋   ❋   ❋

The word *team* implies that a group of people is working together toward a common goal. Wendy, Rebecca, and Kikkan were trying to do well in cross-country ski races—a common goal. But they did not often train as a team. Mostly, they trained individually. The U.S. coaches encouraged them to move to Park City, where the coaches lived and the men were training. Kikkan, however, was happy with her training program at APU in Anchorage, and Rebecca lived at home in Crested Butte with Sharbel and Tabor and trained on her own. She wished that she lived closer to her teammates, whom she saw at training camps. But at the same time, her life felt more balanced when she was at home. And when the American women did come together for training camps or races, the team culture did not feel inclusive. "I still felt like I was sitting at the dinner table with my rivals instead of my best friends and best teammates," said Rebecca.

Wendy started the pre-Olympic season (2004–2005) as the only American woman racing on the World Cup tour, where she finished near the bottom in almost every race except a sprint in mid-December. Rebecca and Kikkan remained Stateside, where Rebecca won almost every race that she entered. But she was frustrated by the lack of coaching and the general attitude toward the women. With limited resources, the U.S. coaching staff was stretched thin, and Rebecca did not feel there was a coach solely devoted to the women or individual programs tailored to each skier's needs. When Rebecca underwent physical testing at the U.S. team's sports science department, her results showed that she was an anomaly, and the coaches often did not know what to do with her scores. Growing up above 9,000 feet in the Colorado mountains, she had always skied hard and fast, but not for long stretches. The coaching she received wasn't structured to her specific physiological makeup. When she spoke up, she felt as if her feelings were pooh-poohed, and she was labeled a whiny woman.

Kikkan was also struggling. She only won one race in the early season—a smaller competition in Anchorage. She was typically the top American skier in a sprint race, but not at 2005 nationals. Lindsay Williams, a student at Northern Michigan University, beat her in the sprint. Since graduating from high school in 2001, Kikkan had committed her entire life to skiing, foregoing college to chisel her way up the steep face of elite cross-country ski racing. But when she was not the top American in a race, she questioned her choice. "It was hard to be patient and to continue believing that I would get to the top," she said.

Despite her struggles, Kikkan joined Wendy and Rebecca in Pragelato, Italy, for her second World Cup race. It was preparation for the upcoming world championships, and Kikkan did her best to crank up the team spirit, packing a box with what Rebecca called "crazy paraphernalia" to celebrate while they were in Europe. She also dyed the tips of her blonde hair pink. She had seen a photo of an alpine skier in Ski Racing magazine with pink tips in her hair and thought it looked cool. She thought that it might counter the image that cross-country skiers are conservative and boring.

"She brought this notion of, 'Hey, we're a team, we're going to have so much fun traveling the world as a team, and we're going to do this as a team, and we have no reason not to believe in ourselves,'" said Rebecca.

In the Pragelato World Cup race, Kikkan paired with Wendy in a team sprint, and they finished twelfth. But in her next World Cup—a 10-kilometer freestyle—Kikkan finished dead last. She wasn't having fun anymore, and she wanted to go home, back to Anchorage and her APU teammates. She started sleeping sixteen hours each night. Rebecca did not fare much better.

Their results did not improve at the 2005 world championships in Oberstdorf, Germany. In her first race—the 10-kilometer freestyle—Kikkan finished sixty-fifth (or eighth from last). And Rebecca came down with a respiratory infection; a doctor put her on a three-week course of antibiotics. Her best finish was forty-first in the classic sprint. Sarah Konrad, a thirty-seven-year-old with a PhD in geology who had left cross-country skiing to try biathlon (a sport that combines cross-country skiing and shooting), gave the U.S. women's team one of few bright spots; she finished twenty-third in the 10-kilometer freestyle. Wendy gave the U.S. another twenty-third place in the classic sprint.

The ultimate blow came in the 4 x 5-kilometer relay. Wendy skied the leadoff leg but struggled mightily and tagged Rebecca in last place, 3 minutes behind the leaders. Rebecca tried to gain on those ahead of her but couldn't, her illness slowing her pace. By the time Sarah Konrad took over, the leaders were about to lap her. Officials pulled the Americans from the race, and Kikkan was not able to even start the anchor leg. She managed one top-thirty finish at worlds that year—a twenty-ninth in the sprint qualifier. But it was not good enough to put her into the quarterfinals (prior to 2006, only the top sixteen qualified for the sprint quarterfinals, not the top thirty).

While the Americans struggled, the Canadian women were making headlines. Canadian Sara Renner finished third to become the first North American cross-country skier to ever win a world championship medal. Her teammate, Beckie Scott—the pursuit gold medalist from the 2002 Olympics—finished fourth in the pursuit. On the eve of the 2006 Olympic Winter Games, the Canadian women were the ones to watch.

Then the U.S. Ski Team dealt a severe blow to women's cross-country skiing—and to Kikkan and everyone else's Olympic dreams. No women were named to the team for the 2005–2006 Olympic year. The belief was that all the funding should go to the men's team because they had the best chance of winning medals at the 2006 Torino Games.

"The message that sent to women's skiing in the U.S. was near fatal," said Rebecca.

Up in Alaska, training with her APU teammates, Kikkan hit rock bottom. Her goal was to become the first American woman to win an Olympic medal in cross-country skiing. But how would she accomplish it when there was no women's national team? She didn't even know whether she would make another Olympic team.

TORINO

If the pre-Olympic World Cup races were any indication, the Canadian women's cross-country
ski team was going to have a stellar 2006 Olympic Winter Games. Suddenly, it wasn't just 2002
Olympic gold medalist Beckie Scott representing Canada on the World Cup podium. Sara Renner and Chandra Crawford had moved to the top
of the results sheet as well. In eight World Cup
races before the 2006 Torino Games, Beckie,
Sara, and Chandra finished in the top three in
seven of them.

It's important to note that Sara and Chandra's
podium performances did not come out of thin
air. Over a decade, the two women had inched
toward the front of the World Cup pack. Renner, twenty-nine years old at the time of the 2006
Olympics, made her World Cup debut in 1996,
scored her first World Cup points in 2001 (by finishing in the top thirty), and was consistently in
the top ten by 2004. Chandra's ascent was more
rapid. Within a year of making her World Cup
debut in 2005, the twenty-two-year-old scored
her first World Cup top-ten finish, then made the
jump to the podium a month later. The Canadian
team's podium assault was a bellwether performance that was not lost on the Americans.

After the early season World Cup races, U.S.
coach Trond Nystad presciently told *Ski Racing*
what he might have also told the women on the
U.S. team. The Canadian women "have been

Champions keep playing
until they get it right.

❋

Billie Jean King,
twelve-time Grand Slam
tennis champion

on a long road to get where they are," he said. "Beckie and Sara have [placed] in the fifties and sixties, too, but they've been willing to put in the effort and the time to be among the best in the world. It takes a long time. I've said it takes ten years to really develop. We've got women with promise and several men who could be fighting in there too. If they have the commitment, the guts, and the heart, what Beckie and Sara are doing can happen for them too."

Although no U.S. women's team was named for the 2005–2006 season, the coaches would still select women to compete in the 2006 Olympic Games—with travel costs funded by the U.S. Olympic Committee. Olympic selection would come down to the early season Super-Tour races in Fairbanks, Alaska, and West Yellowstone, Montana; four Canadian World Cup races in December; and the 2006 U.S. nationals in early January.

Kikkan was, by now, one of the top American cross-country ski racers—and the top sprinter. Even though she lacked much international experience, she was consistently on the podium in North American races. At the 2006 nationals, the twenty-three-year-old with pink hair highlights won the sprint and the 10-kilometer classic, and tied a recent high school grad named Liz Stephen for the win in the 5-kilometer freestyle. Then eighteen years old, Liz had never finished a big race in the top three before, and as she climbed up to collect her gold medal with Kikkan, she accidentally dropped her skis on Kikkan's head. Liz was mortified. But fortunately, cross-country skis do not weigh much.

"I came into the week hoping for two wins, so three is pretty incredible," Kikkan told Ski Racing reporter Paul Robbins. Perhaps pink hair was a good luck charm.

Rebecca Dussault, still battling sinusitis and the effects of too many antibiotics that she took during the 2005 world championships the previous February, won the only other event at nationals, the 15-kilometer freestyle. But it was not easy. Racing had become physically painful; she felt as if her lungs were ripped out of her body after every hard effort. She limped into nationals wondering whether she would make it to Torino—and hoping that one day soon, she would feel better.

The rest of the podium spots at nationals foretold the future for U.S. women's cross-country skiing. Two junior skiers also made the podium

—Liz Stephen and nineteen-year-old Morgan Arritola from Sun Valley, Idaho. Both had only started cross-country skiing recently. A promising soccer player, Morgan had taken up cross-country skiing after her family moved to Sun Valley when she was sixteen. The soccer program in Sun Valley was not as good as she had hoped, so as a junior in high school, she put her considerable athletic talents toward mastering cross-country skiing. She worked very hard—because she hates "being bad at things"—and two years later, in 2005, she won a junior national title. Then at senior nationals in 2006, she finished second in two races.

From East Montpelier, Vermont, Liz had also won a national title within three years of switching from alpine to cross-country skiing while a student at Burke Mountain Academy, a ski-racing academy in northern Vermont. She had finished second at Junior Olympics—just over two years after taking up cross-country. Two years later, at the 2006 senior nationals, she tied Kikkan for the gold medal in the 5-kilometer freestyle race, then finished third in the 10-kilometer classic race, right behind Kikkan and Morgan. And she finished fourth in the 15-kilometer freestyle race.

"If we can band together and push each other and train well, I think it's a really bright future [for the U.S. women]," Kikkan told Robbins. "I think this is where the Canadian team was five or six years ago with a young group that's committed, so I'm kind of excited about it. I've got some solid experience that, hopefully, I can share with them."

Wendy and Kikkan made their second Olympic teams, along with Olympic first-timers Rebecca Dussault and Abigail Larson, a Northern Michigan University graduate. Sarah Konrad would join them in the Olympic relay. Lindsay Williams and Lindsey Weier would miss classes at Northern Michigan University to attend the Torino Games.

Liz and Morgan just missed making their first Olympic team. The U.S. coaches and team administrators thought it was important that young skiers not skip to the highest levels of competition too quickly. Morgan was upset. But Liz considered the 2006 Olympics "a far-distant goal," she said. If she made the team, great. If not, "I'm young and there will be other opportunities."

*　*　*

On the eve of the Torino Olympics, the American team was hit with two health snafus. Carl Swenson caught a cold. And the day before the Opening Ceremony, FIS issued Kikkan a "start prohibition" for five days. The reason? High hemoglobin values.

Hemoglobin is a protein molecule in red blood cells that carries oxygen from the heart to the rest of the body and returns carbon dioxide to the lungs. In adult women, normal values range from 12 to 16 grams per deciliter. At the time, doping regulations mandated a start prohibition when a female athlete's hemoglobin value exceeded 16 grams per deciliter (17 for men). High hemoglobin values cause blood to be more viscous, increasing the chances of blood clots and impairing circulation. For health reasons, FIS requires athletes with high hemoglobin values to rest until their levels drop.

Kikkan was not alone. Seven other Nordic skiers from other countries also received start prohibitions. The next day, three more were added to the list. Olympic officials emphasized that these athletes had failed health tests, not doping tests. In fact, the tests were issued by FIS, not the IOC. High hemoglobin values can be caused by dehydration or athletes adjusting to high altitude. And they can occur naturally. But they can also be a sign of doping. Drugs like EPO and darbepoetin stimulate production of oxygen-carrying red blood cells. Athletes with naturally occurring high levels must submit documentation to FIS before the start of each season. Documentation must show high hemoglobin values from "an early age in life," read the FIS rule. During the 2006 season, FIS granted six athletes dispensation, and six more were granted dispensation during the Torino Games. Although Kikkan does in fact have naturally occurring high hemoglobin, she did not know it before Torino (she also has Factor V Leiden, a genetic blood-clotting disorder that was discovered after she developed life-threatening blood clots in April 2008). In Torino, she was not one of the athletes granted an exemption. Kikkan was suddenly making national news in the U.S. —and not for the reason she wanted. Newspapers across the country cast suspicion upon the skiers. The *Wall Street Journal* called hemoglobin the hobgoblin of the Games.

Although pestered by the press, Kikkan was unconcerned. She knew she was clean. "I knew I was dehydrated," she told the *New York Daily*

News. "I didn't expect the negative media blowout." She was tested five days later, and after rehydrating, her level had dropped to within the acceptable range. The hemoglobin hubbub died down, and cross-country skiing dropped out of the headlines in the U.S. media.

For all their hopes leading up to the 2006 Olympic Games, the men's team mostly floundered. Kris Freeman, who had finished so tantalizingly close to the podium at the 2003 world championships, was sidelined for the first week of the Games with exhaustion. He would rally to finish twenty-second in his best race—the 15-kilometer classic. But it was far from expectations. And in the first race, the 30-kilometer pursuit, Swenson was the highest placed finisher for the American men —in thirty-ninth place. In the relay, where they had come so close to the Olympic podium four years earlier, they finished twelfth (of fifteen teams), almost 5 minutes off the leaders. Only two American men finished the 50-kilometer freestyle race on the final day of the Olympics. Andrew Johnson crossed the line in thirty-fourth. Freeman finished third from last. Carl Swenson, so close to a medal at the 2005 world championships, was listed as a DNF (for did not finish).

The U.S. women did not do much better in their distance races or in the relay in Torino. Sarah Konrad's thirty-second place in the 30-kilometer freestyle race was the best finish for the Americans in the longer races (pursuit, 10-kilometer classic, and 30-kilometer freestyle). And they finished fourteenth in the relay, with Rebecca skiing the tenth fastest anchor leg. For Rebecca, the entire Olympic Games had been a stressful slog. Traveling with her family, she was unable to stay in the Olympic Village and so had to rent a house. The house was right across from the cross-country ski venue's finish area. But her husband and son were not allowed entry there. They had to take a bus into town, then walk forty-five minutes back up to the race venue and enter with the spectators.

"Those things stressed me out," she said. "They were not recognizing that anyone could deviate from the norm. For me to make ski racing work was just about heroic."

But fortunes improved for the Americans in the sprint races. A cross-country sprint is a race held on a 1-kilometer (or so) course. It can be a classic sprint, where skiers race using the kick-and-glide technique, or a freestyle sprint, where they use the faster skating technique. And the technique varies in each Olympics. In Torino, it was a freestyle sprint. Racers qualify for the heats in a time trial held early in the day. At the 2006 Olympics, the fastest sixteen qualified for the quarterfinal heats. From the quarterfinals, the top eight moved on to the semifinals. Then the top four competed in a final (called the "A Final"), with the others competing in a "B Final" (the format has since changed, with six skiers moving on to the final; the B Final is no longer contested).

In Torino, American fortunes looked great when Andy Newell, a twenty-two-year-old Vermonter who was recruited onto the U.S. development team in 2002 while he was still a high school student at the Stratton Mountain School, qualified in second place in the men's freestyle sprint. He had finished in the top ten in the sprint at three world junior championships in the early 2000s and scored points in the sprint almost immediately after starting his first World Cup races in 2004. Then, a couple of weeks before the 2006 Olympic Games, Newell had finished fourth in a World Cup sprint in Germany, making him an outside favorite to win an Olympic medal in Torino. But luck was not with him in the Olympic quarterfinals. In his heat, he got pinched by other skiers going through a corner on the course and crashed, thereby ending his medal hopes in Torino.

In the women's team sprint—an event featuring two skiers who take three turns each racing around the sprint course—Kikkan put the hemoglobin debacle behind her and paired with Wendy. The two women finished tenth, the best finish yet in a team event at the Olympics by American women. Ahead of them, Canadians Beckie Scott and Sara Renner claimed silver behind the gold-medal-winning Swedes.

A week later, Kikkan claimed another best-ever-American finish for a woman in an Olympic cross-country ski race. In the freestyle sprint, she qualified tenth, right behind her Canadian friends, Sara and Chandra, and Beckie Scott, who qualified first. It was only the second time that Kikkan had qualified for the quarterfinals in a major international sprint race. In her quarterfinal heat, Kikkan faced five other women, including Beckie Scott and Aino-Kaisa Saarinen from Finland, who had won the Olympic bronze medal in the team sprint a week earlier. Kikkan beat everyone except Beckie and advanced to the semifinals. From the semis, she did not advance to the finals, putting her in ninth place in the sprint. Her goal was to finish the sprint in the top twenty. She had more than hit her benchmark and was on track to be a medal contender at the Vancouver Olympic Games in four years. Better still, her friend Chandra stunned everyone when she won the sprint and claimed Canada's second Olympic gold medal in cross-country skiing—and the Canadian cross-country team's second medal at the Torino Games.

After Torino, Kikkan decided to stay in Europe for a few World Cup races—on her own euro.

※　※　※

Two weeks after the Olympics ended, on March 7, 2006, Kikkan made skiing history again. Skiing under the lights on a horse-racing track in Borlänge, Sweden, she qualified for both the quarter- and the semifinals in a World Cup sprint and ended up racing in the B Final (the top four raced in the A Final). She won the B Final, placing her fifth overall in the race. It was the best World Cup finish for an American woman since Alison Owen-Spencer's win at the Telemark World Cup in 1978. After seven years of hard work, Kikkan finally felt like she could compete with the best in the world. As Robbins wrote in Ski Racing, "Americans finally have a horse in the race."

A week later, Andy Newell scored America's first World Cup podium in over two decades when he finished third in a sprint in Changchun, China.

As Kikkan began gearing up for another Olympic quad—the four years that separate Olympic Games—she knew there had to be a better path than the one she had followed leading to Torino. If she was going to win an Olympic medal at the 2010 Vancouver Olympics, she needed both funding and teammates—to train with, to push her, and to make the whole endeavor more fun. She thought back to her high school years in Anchorage when she was on close-knit cross-country running, skiing, and track teams.

"I enjoyed that experience," she said. "I was motivated by my teammates, I was motivated by our team goals of finishing high in the standings. I was used to having teammates around me, and I had that at APU. But on the national team, I felt . . ." She trailed off.

She thought about the Canadian women. They had built on Beckie Scott's 2002 Olympic success and between 2002 and 2006 had become a world-class team.

"There were multiple Canadian women doing well at the same time," said Kikkan. "I envied that."

To anyone who would listen, she mentioned the Canadians and said, "Look what they're doing with their team, they're pushing each other. We need that in the United States."

On her way home from the Torino Olympics and the end-of-season World Cup races in Europe, she stopped in Presque Isle, Maine, to compete in a series of spring races. Out bowling one night between races, she met Jeff Ellis, a Canadian skier and runner. He was wearing a Brooks running shoe T-shirt, and Kikkan, who had been working at a running store in Anchorage when she was home in the off-season, struck up a conversation.

"I threw out some smart-ass comment about running shoe technology, and he chimed right in," said Kikkan.

As a former runner with her eye on the NCAA, she was impressed with Jeff's track background. A sprinter, middle-distance runner, and hurdler, he had graduated from the University of North Carolina, where he had earned a track and field scholarship and had broken the school record in the 800 meters (indoors). He had also competed in the 400-meter hurdles in the 1999 IAAF World Championships in Spain but had missed making the 2000 Canadian Olympic Team. And his athletic accomplishments did not stop there. In high school, he had been an Ontario provincial cross-country ski champion eight times. And he had been an all-star on his school's volleyball team, which he captained three times. His school had named him Athlete of the Year four years running.

After Kikkan returned home to Alaska, she waited to hear from the U.S. Ski Team about plans for the 2006–2007 season. Would they fund a women's team? Would she be named to the team? Would she have teammates? Wendy had retired, and Rebecca was taking another break.

Talking to Jeff one day on the phone, Kikkan had an idea.

"It was our fifth phone call," she remembered. "I said, 'Do you mind if we get married? I'd like to join the Canadian team.'"

THE TEAM'S BEGINNING

TEAM LEADER

Kikkan Randall did not have to wait to see whether Jeff Ellis would accept her marriage proposal to find herself a team—although within two years, she would marry Ellis anyway, but for love, not his Canadian citizenship. Shortly after the snow melted in spring 2006, she was named to the U.S. Ski Team's A team, and a handful of young women were named to the U.S. development team, along with several men. Older and more experienced than this group—and with better results—Kikkan could have remained aloof, doing her own training. But she was not raised that way. Kikkan learned very early the value of being part of a good team.

Kikkan was born into a large family, and the instigator of family adventure was her grandfather, Lewis Haines. He had grown up in Connecticut and, in the early 1940s, attended Middlebury College in Vermont, where he participated in the gentlemen's sports of fencing and tennis. He also skied, which back then meant cross-country as well as alpine skiing, with the same skis often used for both. He also ran on the college's cross-country team and from accounts in the college newspaper, was fiercely competitive. He graduated in 1943, fought in World War II in the U.S. Army Air Corps, then returned home and married Verna Tones in 1948. He called her Tone. They moved out west, and in the postwar baby boom, Tone and Lew had their first of seven

A leader isn't someone who forces others to make him stronger; a leader is someone willing to give his strength to others so that they may have the strength to stand on their own.

❋

Beth Revis, author of
Across the Universe

kids while he was studying for his PhD in educational administration at Washington State University in Pullman, in eastern Washington near the Idaho border. In the winter months, the family skied. In the summer, Lew hiked, played tennis, and ran marathons—in his corduroy trousers and tennis shoes. His kids often joined him.

Always up for adventure, Lew took a job as the director of student affairs at the University of Alaska in 1964, and Lew and Tone moved their brood to Fairbanks. President Eisenhower had granted Alaska statehood only five years earlier, and an Atlantic Richfield drilling crew had yet to discover oil on Alaska's North Slope. A few months before the Haineses moved to Fairbanks, the Great Alaska earthquake had leveled much of Anchorage. A city with a population of around 13,000, Fairbanks was still very much a frontier when the Haineses arrived. The long winters in Fairbanks made for lots of time on skis, and it paid off for the eldest son, Chris. Within two years of moving to Fairbanks, he was the Alaska state cross-country ski champion while a student at Lathrop High School and was on his way to the U.S. national team.

Once the snow melted, Lew got his kids out running. Betsy Haines —Lew and Tone's second youngest daughter—remembered running the Equinox Marathon in Fairbanks when she was in sixth or seventh grade. In 1966, Deborah, a middle daughter, won the women's division. She was twelve years old at the time, and to this day remains the youngest winner of the race.

In 1969, the family moved 360 miles south to Anchorage after Lew was named provost of what was then called the South Central Regional Center, which administered a consortium of community colleges in the area, as well as military education and a handful of graduate programs. The city was in the midst of the oil-discovery boom, and the city's population increased by more than 50 percent from 1960 to 1970. Lew's job was to help the consortium grow into a full-fledged accredited university, now known as the University of Alaska-Anchorage.

The Haines's multisport lifestyle continued in this booming town. Built on an alluvial plain at the foot of the Chugach Mountains—which soar from sea level to 3,000 feet right from the edge of the city—and on the shores of the Cook Inlet, Anchorage lends itself to the outdoor life. In the 1960s, members of the Nordic Skiing Association of Anchorage laced the city with trails for both skiing and hiking. And Chugach State Park, 495,000 acres of alpine meadows and snowy peaks, is criss-crossed with almost 300 more miles of trails. The park sits mostly within Anchorage's municipal limits, and the Glen Alps Trailhead, with access to 3,510-foot-tall Flattop Mountain—the most climbed peak in Alaska—is only a thirty-minute drive from downtown Anchorage.

"My mother was not into sports at all when she met my dad," said Deborah, "but my dad got her to take up everything: golf, tennis, run-ning, skiing, biking. The whole family did everything together. No-body got a pass. We'd go on a family hike, and the kids would call it FFF—forced family fun. But once we got out there, it really was fun."

For Lew's seventy-fifth birthday, the whole family—including Kik-kan, then age thirteen, and a dozen or so of her Haines cousins—hiked 17 miles over 3,500-foot-high Crow Pass in the Chugach National Forest, from the Eagle River Nature Center south to Girdwood. Most people do the hike in two days. The Haineses did it in one, finishing around midnight.

Two of Lew and Tone's kids became particularly good at cross-country skiing. Chris tried out for the 1972 Olympic cross-country ski team but missed it, then made it four years later. At the 1976 Olympic Winter Games in Innsbruck, he competed in the 30-kilometer race and finished fifty-second. It was the same race in which Bill Koch won a sil-ver medal, the first and so far only Olympic medal for the United States in cross-country skiing.

Chris's younger sister Betsy would be the next Haines Olympian. Nine and a half years younger than Chris, she looked up to her older brother as a hero. She hung out with him during the summers while he taught tennis, and she even trained with him, sometimes running the same loop in the opposite direction.

"He would say, 'I'll go this way, you go that way, when I see you, turn around,'" said Betsy. "This was just normal for me to go do this stuff."

By the time she started cross-country ski racing in sixth or seventh grade, Betsy was beating most of the girls her age. She particularly ex-celled at running. In her four years competing at East Anchorage High School, she was undefeated in cross-country running and track and field. In 1977, she set the mile record on the track at 4:55.3—a record that stood until 2015, when Allison Ostrander, a budding NCAA cross-country running and track star, broke it. Betsy was also very good at tennis. But cross-country skiing was her primary sport, and in high school, brother Chris, who had returned to Anchorage to teach, was her coach.

After winning junior national titles, Betsy was named at age fifteen to the U.S. Ski Team's development group called the Baby Blues. A year after she graduated high school, Betsy made the 1980 Olympic team competing in Lake Placid. She finished thirty-seventh in the 5-kilometer race—a disappointing result, but it was all she could do. She had peaked a month earlier while trying to make the 1980 U.S. Olympic team.

Betsy's older sister Deborah preferred cheerleading to endurance sports. When the family moved from Fairbanks to Anchorage, Deborah—an outgoing, fun-loving teen—tried out for cheerleading but didn't make it. So she tried gymnastics but "was dreadful." With few other sports options for girls in the late 1960s and early 1970s, she turned to cross-country skiing. With snow falling as early as September in Anchorage, and as late as May, cross-country skiing is as much a lifestyle in the Alaskan city as a sport. At least on the cross-country ski team, she would have teammates to cheer on. With the Haines genes, she was also a good endurance athlete. In addition to her Equinox Marathon win at age twelve, she also won the infamous Mount Marathon race, a grueling 3.1-mile run straight up the 3,022-foot mountain that looms over Seward, Alaska. One of the oldest footraces in America, it started in 1908 after a barroom discussion about whether the mountain could be climbed (and descended) in under an hour. Legend has it that Seward grocer Gus Borgen put one hundred dollars on the table and said it couldn't be done. Al Taylor, a young clerk at Brown & Hawkins, a local general store, offered to give it a try. Taylor finished the run in one hour, twenty minutes, and Borgen kept his money. But word spread, and others tried to break the hour barrier. In 1915, Mount Marathon became an official race, run annually on July 4. Seward local James Walters won that year in 1:02:02. The hour barrier was broken the following year when Alec Bolan climbed and descended Mount Marathon in 55:12. Since then, the race has attracted renowned endurance athletes. A separate women's race began in 1985. But that did not keep women from entering in previous years. The first woman entered the race in 1963. Eleven years later, in 1974, Deborah entered and was the fourth woman across the line in 1:11:30. She entered two more times, in 1976 and 1981, finishing as high as second place. Sister Betsy won three consecutive times, from 1979 to 1981.

Deborah left Alaska in the late 1970s to attend the University of Utah, where she cross-country skied and helped the Ute women's ski team win at least one AIAW National Championship title (AIAW is the Association of Intercollegiate Athletics for Women, the equivalent of the NCAA for women from 1971 until women's sports fell under the NCAA umbrella in the early 1980s). After college, she moved to Kirkwood, California, 30 miles south of Lake Tahoe, to teach skiing at a touring center. There, she met Ronn Randall, a Midwesterner whose love of alpine skiing drew him to California's Sierra Nevada. The two eventually married and moved to Salt Lake City, where Deborah attended law school.

On New Year's Eve 1982—between law school semesters—their first child, a baby daughter, was born. Ronn wanted to name her Kiki, after Kiki Cutter, the first American skier to win an alpine World Cup race—a slalom in Oslo, Norway, on February 25, 1968, when Kiki was eighteen. Deborah preferred Meghan. They settled on Kikkan.

* * *

Before she even learned to walk, Kikkan was going places, with or without anyone's approval. Both Ronn and Deborah remember the day that they visited a park in Salt Lake City, set their squirming daughter down on the grass, then watched her crawl with intent toward a playground that she had spied. The playground was about a quarter mile away.

"She never did look back, she just kept going," said Ronn. "Most kids will go a little way, then stop and look back at their parents. Not Kikkan. She was just born that way."

For her first birthday, Kikkan received a pair of alpine ski boots from her dad. Ronn buckled them onto his young daughter's feet (they came up to her knees). He then built a hill from snow in their front yard in Salt Lake City, tied a rope around her waist, and pulled her to the top of the mound. Down the hill she slid, smiling all the way.

In 1985, after Deborah received her law degree from the University of Utah, the Randalls moved to Anchorage. Deborah wanted to return home to be closer to family. And Kikkan soon had siblings—and many cousins. Tanner, a brother, was born three years later, and sister Kalli three years after Tanner. All three grew to like different activities (fashion for Tanner, theater for Kalli). But Kikkan was driven by adventure. And competition.

As she grew up, Kikkan tried just about every sport available in Anchorage. She ran, hiked, biked, and played soccer—sometimes with her friends, sometimes with cousins. Her parents emphasized having fun, being a good sport, and making friends. Once, when Kikkan was in grade school, she traveled to California to play in a soccer tournament. Ronn told her to take several postcards of Alaska, write her name and address on the back, and hand them out to girls she met from other teams. He thought that she might make a few pen pals from other parts of the country.

At age six, Kikkan started cross-country skiing just because that's what many people do in Anchorage in the winter. Over 100 miles of cross-country ski trails loop around Anchorage, with about two-thirds of these trails in Kincaid Park, a large wooded section of Anchorage that noses out into the waters of the Cook Inlet and Turnagain Arm. About 10 miles of Kincaid's trails are lighted in winter, and once a week, several dozen skiers gather in the park to participate in the Tuesday night races. On one Tuesday night, kids were paired with adults in the races, and Kikkan, then six or seven years old, was paired with local skiing phenom Nina Kemppel. Then a teenager and student at West Anchorage High School, Kemppel was just starting her legendary cross-country ski career. Kikkan, though, was unimpressed. She wasn't that wild about cross-country skiing. She liked chasing her cousins around on the trails. But she "didn't love it," she admitted. "I liked it for the hot chocolate and the games."

What she did love was alpine skiing—the faster, the better. Ronn often took her to Alpenglow (now Arctic Valley), a small ski area about thirty minutes from their home in Anchorage. In the base lodge, Kikkan saw a flyer on the wall advertising the Alpenglow Ski Club Racing Team, or ASCRT (pronounced "assert").

"Can I do that?" she asked her dad. She was seven.

Working as a lifeguard, Ronn was short on funds but promised to consider it for the following season. He hoped that she would forget. She didn't, and the following year, she was an alpine ski racer competing for ASCRT. Going fast on alpine skis seemed way cooler than cross-country skiing, where the customary outfit at the time was knickers and a wool sweater. It was also a sport where skiers competed mostly on their own against the clock, skiing kilometer after kilometer through the woods alone. Kikkan wanted to be the next Picabo Street, America's fastest downhill ski racer in the 1990s. Street won her first Olympic medal at the 1994 Winter Games—a silver in the downhill.

Kikkan soon learned how to do more than ski fast on ASCRT. The coach, Eric Heil—a school teacher and commercial salmon fisherman from Anchorage and winner of the Arctic Man competition, a crazy Alaskan ski race involving snowmobiles—taught the ASCRT kids what it meant to be part of a team. "He got them to cheer for their fellow skiers and care for the other skiers," said Ronn. "It wasn't just all about you."

In 1997, Kikkan had her first major ski victory. On a course at Alpenglow, she set the Alaska state speed skiing record for women at 74.14 miles per hour. In a deep tuck, she looked fearless heading straight down the trail. She was fourteen. Ronn told her to look at the trophy and remember this victory, that others would likely follow. "You'll get bigger ones, and this won't mean anything," he said. "But you have to remember that these were once important to you, and you wouldn't get those without getting these."

Only 5-foot-5 with muscular legs, Kikkan is built like an alpine skier. But she had inherited the Haines genes—and their determination. She might have been fast on alpine skis, but she was also a fast runner. She ran her first race inadvertently at age four when Ronn took her to a charity 5-kilometer run and couldn't find anyone to watch his young daughter while he ran. She trotted along with him, climbing on his shoulders when she grew tired. Through the years, Kikkan continued to join him at weekend races—soon running the races from start to finish without hitching a ride on anyone's shoulders.

In sixth grade, Kikkan's physical education teacher decided to turn the mile run into an annual event on the last day of school. At age eleven, Kikkan ran a 6:06 minute mile and set the middle school record. Soon, she was hooked on running. As a freshman at East Anchorage High School, she won the state title in the 800-meter run. It was the first of ten state titles in cross-country running and track that she would win for East Anchorage High. Her goal was to attend college on a track scholarship and compete for a NCAA Division I school. She also wanted to beat Aunt Betsy's mile record of 4:55.3. (She never did. Kikkan's fastest mile in high school was 5:00.2.)

But more than state titles and records, Kikkan enjoyed her teammates. The girls' cross-country running team called themselves the East High Distance Babes, and they made sports bras with that moniker emblazoned across the front, then wore them all season. They did everything together, and before big meets, the coach, Harry Johnson, would host a spaghetti feast for the team.

This camaraderie carried over to the cross-country ski and track teams—both teams also coached by Johnson. He emphasized the importance of working as a team and made sure that his East Anchorage High athletes wore good-looking uniforms, with their collars zipped up. Everyone also had to attend awards, even those who had finished near the back of every race. Even on their day off (Sunday), the girls met and ran together. And every season, they would gather and make a piece of team gear, such as headbands or lucky underwear or socks in team colors. One year, they made crowns and wore them in a relay. When she got braces on her teeth, Kikkan asked the orthodontist to fit her with red, white, and blue brackets—East Anchorage's school colors.

When winter came, Kikkan wanted to continue alpine ski racing for ASCRT. But she also wanted to cross-country ski race for the huge high school team (East Anchorage did not have an alpine ski team). The alpine and cross-country ski race schedules conflicted, and the equipment for all the ski disciplines was prohibitively expensive. She would need a different pair of alpine skis for slalom, giant slalom, and super-G. She also needed a helmet and speed suit. For cross-country, she needed classic and freestyle skis, for the two different disciplines, plus two sets of boots. Ronn agreed to buy the equipment using his share of Alaska's permanent fund dividend (the oil money given out annually to permanent residents) but told his daughter, "You're really going to have to start making some decisions because I can't keep this afloat." He figured that she would see how her freshman year played out, then pick the ski team that she enjoyed the most. But Kikkan made her decision immediately: cross-country. She wanted to stick with her high school team.

"I was having way more fun with the cross-country people," Kikkan said. "In my mind, I was going places in running, so cross-country skiing was going to be the best thing to contribute to that. So I gave up on the alpine and focused on cross-country."

It was 1998.

Helping her make the decision was her new best friend, Tara Hamilton. The girls met at a running race when they were in seventh grade and hit it off right away. They soon had sleepovers at each other's houses and ran together whenever they could. Kikkan loved the pop song "Barbie Girl" (by the band Aqua), and she and Tara would blast the music before races and jump around to the fast beat to get amped up ("I'm a Barbie Girl, in a Barbie world . . . ;" looking back, "people must have thought we were ding dongs," said Tara). But when it came to high school, Tara attended rival Service High School. If Kikkan competed on East's cross-country ski team, they would regularly see each other at races. Running, though, was still Kikkan's primary focus.

But after freshman year at East Anchorage, Kikkan's running career hit some hurdles. The summer before her sophomore year, her knee started bothering her. While attending a Death Camp, a weeklong training camp in nearby Girdwood where coach Johnson kept the kids hiking, biking, and doing, in Tara's words, "an insane amount" of other activities, Kikkan had to back off the regular camp activities. Instead, she worked out in a nearby pool every day where she could exercise without stressing her knee. Tara had stress fractures in her legs that summer, so she joined her friend rehabbing in the pool. One day while riding their bikes to the pool, Kikkan hit a bump in the road and flew off her bike. She landed on her shoulder and broke her collarbone. After spending the day in the hospital, she was back at Death Camp that night, ready to run and hike the next day. She started the school year wearing a shoulder brace, and although she still trained with the cross-country running team, the injury slowed her down.

Then that spring, Kikkan crashed while skiing in a fun downhill race and compressed four vertebrae in her back. Most people probably would have skipped the upcoming track season. Not Kikkan. She has a high tolerance for pain, so she put on a back brace and continued to run. Her teammates dubbed her Kikkanimal.

That summer, she learned that the coach who had managed the summer running programs that she had participated in since seventh grade was moving. About that time, Deborah heard about another coach who was moving to town and was starting a summer training program for juniors—but in cross-country skiing, not running. His name was Jim Galanes, and he was a three-time Olympian who had moved to Anchorage to help start a cross-country ski program called Gold 2002 at Alaska Pacific University. Galanes and APU junior coach Frode Lillefjell looked at Kikkan's training logs and told her that she had potential in cross-country skiing. "OK," thought Kikkan, "I'll join the program for the winter to train for running."

Within weeks of discovering cross-country ski training, she changed her goals. Cross-country skiing, she found out, had everything that she loved about running, plus speed and power. "Running," she said, "was just a little bit more boring." And she was intrigued by the fact that no American woman had won an Olympic medal.

"I'm going to switch to try to make world juniors in skiing instead of trying to make Foot Locker in running," she announced to her coaches and parents, referring to the running shoe retail chain that sponsors the cross-country running national championships.

Better still, she had a knack for cross-country skiing. Aunt Betsy remembered a Tuesday night ski race in Anchorage where the race organizer set the course through a frozen bog. Kikkan was fourteen at the time and caught her aunt on the trail (even though they had started at intervals, with Betsy heading out first).

"I'm slogging along, and she came up behind me, and she's talking the whole time," said Betsy. "Pretty soon, she's two steps ahead, then three, four, five. She left me in the dust, and I thought at that moment, 'Well, here we go. I'll never see her again.'"

The Team's Beginning

A similar situation happened during summer training on Eagle Glacier outside Anchorage. Kikkan saw Nina Kemppel skiing the groomed loop on the glacier and jumped in behind her. Already a three-time Olympian, Kemppel couldn't shake Kikkan.

"I was thinking, who is this girl?" said Kemppel. "She stayed with me every day until she just couldn't do it anymore. Then she'd get back out there and try it again the next day. I thought, 'This girl's got some spirit.'"

Others were soon referring to Kikkan as "Little Nina."

Despite poor ski technique (she wanted to run on her skis, not let them glide), Kikkan was soon racking up high school wins and junior national titles in the sport. Luke Bodensteiner, the two-time Olympian who started working for the U.S. Ski & Snowboard Association in 1996, watched Kikkan at junior nationals in Ishpeming in Michigan's Upper Peninsula. The wind was howling across a golf course where the event was held. "It was miserable outside, and here was this kid with a huge smile on her face just destroying people," said Bodensteiner. He thought, "Here we go, we've got something here."

At those same junior nationals, Ronn noticed something else. Tara was also competing in Ishpeming, and out on the course, the two girls raced elbow to elbow, fiercely trying to beat each other. They crossed the finish line and would not look at each other for a few minutes. Once they caught their breath, they hugged each other, then skied off together to warm down. Ronn was impressed.

In Alaska, her rivalry with Tara became legendary. At the state cross-country ski meets, she and Tara vied for the skimeister title, given to the skier with the lowest time in both the classic and the freestyle races. Tara won a record four years in a row. "It was amazing how we could tear each other up on the racecourse and then just have so much fun immediately after," Kikkan said.

"If someone else who you respect and you know works just as hard as you do goes out there and wallops you, well, you've got to be happy for them," said Tara. "You see them out there every day training. You know that they're just as dedicated to the sport. If they go out there and they have a better day, that's awesome. That's what it's about. It's not about just winning."

In the team relay one year, both Kikkan and Tara were competing as the anchor legs for their respective high school ski teams. Their teammates tagged them about the same time, so the two girls skied much of their anchor legs together, trading the lead so they could take turns drafting off each other. About 300 meters from the finish, the course turned a corner and climbed a hill that was lined with cheering spectators.

"We poured on the gas," said Tara.

As they charged up the hill, Kikkan pulled around Tara and began to pass her. Suddenly, as the two girls began to climb up the hill, Tara's right ski tip crossed Kikkan's left. Both girls fell. Kikkan stood up first, but her skis were underneath Tara's. So she fell again. Tara clamored up and made a dash for the finish. Kikkan got up right behind her and began chasing her friend. She came close but was unable to catch her. The Service High School team won the relay, and Kikkan hugged Tara. To this day, the two women still laugh when they think about the race.

At another meet—the 1999 Alaska regional championships—Service High and East Anchorage High were battling for the team title. It would come down to the final relay, with both Kikkan and Tara skiing their usual anchor legs for their teams. By the final leg, Service High was ahead of East, and as the Service skier came into the transition zone, Tara knew her friend would be hunting her down. She took off "balls to the wall" and managed to hold off Kikkan, giving the Service Cougars the regional win—until an official disqualified Service because Tara had taken off before she was officially tagged by her teammate. East Anchorage was declared the winner of the girls' relay, which gave them the regional title. After the East Anchorage team members accepted their relay medals and the big team trophy at the awards ceremony, Kikkan asked the Service girls to join them on the podium. Then each of East's four relay skiers handed over her medal to one of the four Service relay skiers. Kikkan gave her relay medal to Tara, as well as the team trophy.

"We knew they deserved it," Kikkan said at the time. "They won fair and square. If they were first across the finish line, they deserve it."

Her final two years of high school, Kikkan balanced international competition with high school meets. She was named to the U.S. team competing at the FIS Junior World Ski Championships three years in a row (2000 to 2002). After her first world juniors, she was named to the U.S. development team. The next year, she finished sixth in the freestyle sprint at world juniors.

Like Tara, who was headed to Denver University, Kikkan applied to college. She considered the strong NCAA Division I ski programs at the University of Utah, her mom's alma mater, and Northern Michigan University, where Sten Fjeldheim coaches a cross-country ski team that has produced six NCAA champions, including two-time Olympian Pete Vordenberg. Her plan was to apply to these universities, then defer for a year while she tried to make the 2002 U.S. Olympic team competing in Salt Lake City.

Kikkan graduated from East Anchorage High School in 2001 and her mom threw a party called "It Takes a Village to Raise a Kikkan" in part to thank everyone who had so far helped her daughter reach the heights that she had in skiing. So many people around Anchorage had contributed to Kikkan's success, from her coaches and her family to Ronn's former boss, who once gave Kikkan a chronographic sports watch for her birthday.

Not long after graduation, Aunt Betsy talked to Kikkan about her post–high school plans. When she was racing in the late 1970s, Betsy's plan had been to make the Olympics, then go to college (she attended the University of Vermont after the 1980 Winter Olympics). Kikkan told her aunt that she had a ten-year plan to win an Olympic medal, and she laid out her interim goals. Betsy was taken aback.

"I thought, 'Wow, this gal, she's got it organized, she'll make it happen,'" said Betsy.

With high school behind her, Kikkan began training full time with Jim Galanes at APU. On January 5, 2002, in Bozeman, Montana, with the Olympic Games just over a month away, Kikkan won her first national sprint title. Standing on the podium, she had to decide whether or not to accept the prize money. If she accepted it, she would no longer be eligible to compete in NCAA Division I skiing for either Utah or NMU (the NCAA forbids collegiate athletes from accepting sponsorship or prize money if the monies exceed the cost of competing in that specific competition).

"I just had this feeling, like, you know what, I'm really getting comfortable in this full-time ski racing thing," she realized. "That's where I set my sights. I see being successful. I think I'm going to make that decision for myself right now."

She took the money.

It was the start of her career as a professional athlete. Over the next four years, she would begin ticking off milestones that she wanted to achieve on her path to winning an Olympic medal—national championship titles, the start of World Cup racing, a top-ten finish at the Olympic Games. Nurturing a team was not in her ten-year plan. But as it would turn out, Kikkan would be the right person with the right personality for the job, someone with a go-get-'em, it's-impossible-but-I-can-do-it attitude. A respected trailblazer full of optimism, enthusiasm, and encouragement, she would lead and inspire a team that, even if she fell short of her goal, might be able to achieve it anyway. It would just take a few more years.

THE COACH

Elite ski coaches lead a vagabond life. Often, they are good skiers in their youth, then segue to coaching after they retire from competition. Although no longer leading the monastic life required for elite training and competition, they still live half their lives out of a duffle bag, traveling to races in the winter with the skiers they coach and running training camps around the world in the spring, summer, and fall. And some of the camps are literally halfway around the world. It takes its toll, especially for those wanting to put down roots and start a family. Or be with the family that they already have.

So it was no surprise when the U.S. cross-country team's first sprint coach, Vidar Loefshus, stepped down after the Torino Olympics, along with Trond Nystad, who had been head coach for four years and had recently married German skier and Olympic medalist Claudia Kuenzel. Coach turnover after an Olympic quadrennial is common. In Nystad's place, Pete Vordenberg, a two-time Olympian who had worked as an assistant coach since 2002, was promoted to head coach.

One of the nation's top cross-country skiers in the 1990s, Vordenberg had grown up in Boulder, Colorado, where his parents dragged him into the mountains every winter weekend to cross-country ski through the thick pine forests. He hated it. Then in sixth grade, he joined the Lake Eldora Racing Team and became a very good

A servant-leader focuses primarily on the growth and well-being of people and the communities to which they belong. While traditional leadership generally involves the accumulation and exercise of power by one at the 'top of the pyramid,' servant leadership is different. The servant-leader shares power, puts the needs of others first, and helps people develop and perform as highly as possible.

✳

Robert Greenleaf, author of *The Servant as Leader*

cross-country ski racer. In 1990, after high school graduation, he left Boulder to train in Sweden for a year. The following fall, he was lured back to the States to attend Northern Michigan University in Michigan's Upper Peninsula, or U.P.

"College-aged ski racers from all over the United States migrated to NMU to race for the university ski team over the boundless snow of the U.P., under the tutelage of Coach Sten Fjeldheim," wrote Vordenberg in his book, Momentum: Chasing the Olympic Dream. "We dreamed of winning Olympic medals, Sten dreamed of coaching an Olympic champion, and we all imagined that the copious U.P. snow furthered our dream."

From 1992 through 1994, Vordenberg competed in two Olympic Winter Games and, as a college student at UNM, won an NCAA title in 1993, one of few Americans to have beaten the European skiers who are recruited by Division I schools such as the Universities of Colorado, Utah, and Vermont to help them win championship titles in skiing (Trond Nystad from Norway won an NCAA title for the Vermont Catamounts in 1992 and helped UVM win two national titles as a team). Vordenberg made his first Olympic team at age twenty in 1992 and thought it was a good sign of things to come. He finished fifty-first in the 30-kilometer and fifty-seventh in the 50-kilometer races at the Albertville Games, then set his sights on the 1994 Winter Olympics in Lillehammer. Training with friends and teammates such as 1992 Olympian Ben Husaby and soon-to-be three-time Olympian Justin Wadsworth, Vordenberg was propelled by dreams of winning an Olympic medal. In his book, Vordenberg recounted doing a 35-mile run through the Michigan woods, a grueling workout that their coach had suggested they do as a team, with one teammate riding a bike for a portion of the distance, then switching off with the running teammate so that each only ran a portion of the 35 miles. Vordenberg and his friends ran the entire distance. He would also do self-directed killer workouts, such as one-legged hops and other plyometric exercises on the mountain trails around Boulder. He got strong, but after a while, his confidence flagged when competing against the top Europeans who crossed the finish line minutes ahead of him. In retrospect, he realized that he had not been on the right path to achieve his goal.

"What we had were good friends, but that's not a good team," he said years after he retired from ski racing. "There was not a team goal that we all bought in to. There was no goal other than this vague notion of success, which I don't even know if we had defined for ourselves. There was no method toward accomplishing anything, certainly not together."

Vordenberg started coaching the U.S. skiers after he retired from competition in 2002. His focus had changed since the early 1990s, and he helped his soon-to-be wife, Barb Jones, make the 2002 U.S. Olympic team. He was impressed by what coaches such as Chris Grover were doing with the American athletes. Quiet, thoughtful, and with a dry sense of humor, Grover never wanted to coach skiing. Until he tried it. An English literature major at Dartmouth, he thought he wanted to be an attorney. But he had cross-country skied at Dartmouth and after graduation in 1993, was offered a job teaching and coaching at the Stratton Mountain School, a ski-racing academy in southern Vermont. There, he realized that he gravitated toward coaching. After a year at SMS, he took a job coaching in Sun Valley, Idaho, so he could move out west again (he grew up in Anchorage, Alaska). The nomadic coaching life then took him to Bend, Oregon, until the U.S. Ski Team hired him in 1999 to start a development team based in Park City, with talented guys like Andy Newell and Kris Freeman. It was a position that Grover held until 2004, when he went back to Sun Valley to coach a sprint program there. The United States hadn't really had a cross-country development team since Marty Hall's "Baby Blues," and it gave Vordenberg a glimmer of hope. It was a change in the team's structure, and it seemed to be having a positive impact on the skiers' development.

From 2002 through the 2006 season, the U.S. men's cross-country ski team looked like it was on the edge of a breakthrough. Freeman had finished fourth in the 15-kilometer classic at the 2003 world championships, with Carl Swenson taking fifth in the 50-kilometer race. Young Andy Newell had finished twelfth in the classic sprint at the 2005 world championships, and Kikkan Randall was clearly on her way up. But the team needed more money to continue improving. Even before the organization pulled funding away from the women's team in 2005, the skiers did not have enough money to compete in every World Cup, so they had to pick and choose which races they would enter. They would usually stay in North America in November and December and race SuperTours and NorAms, then nationals in early January. Then they would head to Europe for the last half of the winter to race with the world's best.

"When Kikkan and I started to get our first podiums, we were still at the point where we couldn't fund an entire World Cup season, even with just four athletes on the team," said Andy Newell.

Rather than be dragged down by the situation, Vordenberg felt energized. If the Americans were going to challenge the Scandinavian countries and Russia as "Best in the World," they needed more money.

In the spring of 2006, Vordenberg was the newly appointed head cross-country ski coach, and he approached USSA CEO Bill Marolt with an ultimatum: Give the cross-country team a $1 million budget or the coaches would walk. Although Nystad and Loefshus, both Norwegians, ended up moving on anyway, Marolt agreed to the budget increase. At the Torino Olympics, Kikkan's performance in the sprint had "turned on a light" for Marolt. He saw talent and potential. Her future in ski racing was worth funding. So was Andy Newell's.

But Luke Bodensteiner, who at that time was USSA's Nordic director, did not want to continue funding the veteran skiers whose best years were likely in the past—a tough decision because some of them had been his teammates in the 1990s. "We just couldn't see the pathway to becoming a team that would win medals by just doing the same thing with the older athletes," he said.

Vordenberg and Bodensteiner wanted to create another development team—and a new team culture. They hired Chris Grover back from Sun Valley and appointed him World Cup sprint coach. For development coaches, they hired Pat Casey, an NCAA All-American who graduated from the University of Utah in 2002, then had coached in Sun Valley and at Bogus Basin near Boise, Idaho. Vordenberg was impressed by Casey's rapport with the kids and with his charismatic leadership. Vordenberg also brought Matt Whitcomb on board. A 2001 Middlebury College graduate who had been coaching at Burke Mountain Academy, Whitcomb had caught Vordenberg's attention while coaching the Burke team at a junior race in Fairbanks, Alaska, that year. He had a good vibe with the kids, and the Burke cross-country ski-ers looked like they were loving the sport. Of all the cross-country ski teams that Vordenberg had seen across the United States, he was also struck by the Burkies' camaraderie.

"They were having fun, but not just fun," said Vordenberg. "They were having both kinds of fun, yee-ha fun but also the fun of working on their skiing, the harder earned fun."

❊   ❊   ❊

Matt Whitcomb never thought he would be a ski coach. Nor did he even want to cross-country ski. He took up the sport as a bargain with his mom. If he cross-country skied with her at Hickory Hill, a small ski area near their home in Worthington, Massachusetts, then she would take him to see snowmobiles. A quiet, inquisitive kid, Matt was fascinated by snow machines and the two-foot-wide revolving tracks that propel them. "I couldn't believe things could move over snow like that," he said. Mrs. Whitcomb did not have to take young Matt far, though. Lo-cated in western Massachusetts, Worthington is interlaced with miles of snowmobile trails in the winter, and the machines often flew through the meadows near Hickory Hill. Matt would stop, point, say "snow-mobile," and only resume skiing when all the snowmobiles had dis-appeared down the trail. As he grew older, Matt started skiing up to Hickory Hill from his house along a snowmobile trail. But he rarely got to ride on a snow machine. His family was into fitness, not motor sports.

Around 1985, when Matt was seven years old, a mom named Mary Hamel from nearby Westhampton started a Bill Koch League, a youth cross-country ski program named after the United States' only cross-country Olympic medalist, at Hickory Hill. The Whitcombs became in-volved, and Matt, the eldest of three, soon convinced his parents that he had to ski every weekend. One day, his parents told him that a ski race was coming to town. Without even thinking about it, young Matt and his siblings wanted to do it. They ended up being fast little skiers, so they just kept signing up for races.

But the BKL program at Hickory Hill was about more than ski rac-ing. Ed Hamel, Mary's husband, had become the coach—by default, he said, after other volunteers who actually knew how to ski did not show up. Ed had never participated in an endurance sport. He played football, basketball, and baseball at the high school in Holyoke, Massachusetts, and he had to learn ski technique. Mostly, he relied on the coaching philosophy learned from some of his better high school coaches. Hamel emphasized getting the best out of athletes through fun and adventure.

"Your practice is successful as long as they want to come back the next day," said Ed. "You have to make your practice enjoyable enough and good enough that they can't wait to come back again."

The kids would meet every Saturday, even in the off-season, and would go off on some adventure. They never knew what Ed had in store for them, they only knew where to meet in the morning. On an adventure one summer, Ed hiked with the kids along the Holyoke and Mount Tom ranges—a trek that required figuring out how to ford the Connecticut River (they "hitchhiked" on a boat). Matt and his friends wore Nike ACG high-top hiking boots—the sleek hiking shoe of the day—and they treated their faithful footwear well.

"To a fourteen- and fifteen-year-old, those Nikes were like our first car," said Matt. "They were like our babies. We cleaned them when we got home."

The hard work disguised as fun continued on the trails in the winter. They would do some of their hardest workouts the day before races, then push beyond their limits in the races. But the kids never minded the toughness. "We had this great sense of togetherness," said Matt Molyneux, Matt Whitcomb's best friend.

One year, after the annual BKL Festival in Jackson, New Hampshire, Ed took the kids on the chairlift up nearby Wildcat Mountain, an alpine ski area on a 4,000+-foot ridge that sits across Pinkham Notch from Mount Washington, New Hampshire's highest peak. It had snowed heavily the previous night, and two feet of fluffy snow covered the mountains. From the summit of Wildcat, the group spent the day descending the 16-kilometer-long Wildcat Trail on their skinny race skis. A backcountry ski trail, it winds through tight pine forests on the back of Wildcat Mountain, dips into gullies and over steep embankments, and plunges over the occasional ledge before ending up on the groomed trails of the Jackson Ski Touring Center.

"There were moments where you would hit a jump, and you didn't care what happened because there was so much soft snow to land in," remembered Matt Molyneux. "It was the end of the season, the big races were over, so it was just about the joy of it."

But Ed was not a coach who sent the kids off on their own. He led from the front. If he told the group that they were going to scramble down a cliff, he would be the first to try the route. The same went for finding a way up a cliff. "There was always this other level that you could hit, pushing yourself beyond the literal boundaries," said Molyneux. "It became an instinct for all of us. You come to a cliff, [you think] how are we going to get up it?"

Ed's coaching philosophy also focused on the group, not individual stars. In one training session on a hot summer day, he took the kids to the Connecticut River to cool off. They reached an island in the middle of the river, then walked across it to reach a beach. In the middle of the path stood a patch of stinging nettles. The kids could have diverted around the nettles. But once one of them had waded through the nettles and was scratching at itching, stinging skin, they all had to do it. It became a bonding exercise. Another time, they were on a long hike in the woods when someone declared "no bridges," meaning that for every stream or river they encountered on the trail, they had to figure out how to cross it without using a bridge.

"We'd be running down a path and Ed would say, 'See that hillside right there?'" recalled Matt Whitcomb. "It would be replete with pricker bushes and thorns and downed trees and crag. We'd have to run to the top as fast as we could. Then halfway down, he'd say stop wherever you are and do fifty sit-ups. You might be climbing over a log. So you'd see people doing sit-ups on a log or in a pricker bush, just developing this level of toughness and belief and confidence that was really special as a kid. Nothing ever could touch us."

Matt carried this confidence to school on Mondays. Lacking in confidence socially as a kid, he could identify as a hard-working skier and after any awkward encounter at school, always knew that he had a group in which he felt comfortable.

"He was little, we were both young for our grades," said Molyneux, who was a year ahead of him in school. "We have late May and June birthdays. We were used to always being the little, mousy, effeminate guys in our classes. I think it gave Matt a tremendous amount of empathy more than anything."

In addition to toughness, Ed encouraged teamwork. One time, the entire ski group was running along the Chesterfield River in western Massachusetts. To keep it interesting, Ed occasionally diverted the kids off the trail to overcome obstacles, such as climbing up on a ledge or over a large rock. On one rock in particular, the two Matts (Whitcomb and Molyneux) easily climbed the rock, then immediately lowered themselves onto their stomachs and began extending their arms down to the younger kids who needed a hand. The older kids also lent moral support to the younger ones on the team. At the annual Bill Koch League Festival in 1989, Ed remembered that his daughter, Carina— then about five years old—had not done as well as her older teammates. She was crying with disappointment when Matt Whitcomb picked her up, put her on his lap, and consoled her. He was only eleven years old.

"Matt never made a big deal of it," said Ed. "Everyone looked up to him because he was a natural leader. He led by example. He was never the bossy type. He would set a tone that people would automatically follow."

Matt also developed what his best friend called a strong moral compass. When the two boys were in high school, Molyneux acquired a couple of beers from a neighbor's refrigerator. He convinced Matt to join him in the woods for a little private party. Matt joined him but wanted nothing to do with the illicit beer and made his older friend drink both bottles. "That was our first beer together," said Molyneux with a laugh. "He always did what was right."

By high school, Matt Whitcomb was one of the best skiers in western Massachusetts. After his sophomore year, he transferred to Wahconah Regional High School where his dad taught. It was about a half hour west of Worthington, but unlike his local high school, Wahconah had a cross-country ski team. Matt was state champion his senior year, and Ed encouraged Matt to pursue ski racing. He was accepted at the Stratton Mountain School, a ski-racing academy in Vermont with a strong cross-country ski program, for a post-graduate year. Then he went to Middlebury College in 1997 and skied for the Panthers for four years, captaining the team his senior year. In his thirty-one years coaching the Middlebury Nordic Ski Team, Coach Terry Aldrich called Matt the best captain he had ever had. Even if they had just endured a five-hour van ride home from a race, and the temperature was below zero outside, Matt was the first skier on top of the van unloading skis and carrying equipment into the building, even before he touched his own bag. When everything was inside, Matt would ask if there was anything more the team could do before everyone departed for the night.

We are our own worst critics, and Matt has a different memory of his year as captain. Although he was friends with his teammates, Matt thought he was a lousy captain because he wasn't a deliberate leader at the time. "Maybe there's something to be said for being easy to be around," is the only concession he gives himself. Of his ski career, he will say this: "I've just always had coaches that loved skiing and really cared about me."

After college, he moved out to Whitefish, Montana, to be a ski bum and a fly fisherman, a sport that he picked up at Middlebury and one that suits his calm, unflappable demeanor. He had lost the desire to ski race, and a strained abdominal muscle made training painful anyway. One day, he ran into a woman who commented that Matt—6-foot-3 and lean—looked like a cross-country skier. She asked if he would help coach a junior cross-country ski program that winter because the head coach, Pete Phillips, had recently had ankle surgery and couldn't ski. Matt agreed, and that winter, he made a meager $750 every two weeks and learned the ropes of ski coaching from Phillips.

"Pete has a rare ability to combine his vast intelligence with an artist's creativity and could work any athlete out of a ski-technique puzzle with an on-the-spot analogy," said Matt.

At the end of that winter, two kids whom Matt coached qualified for the Junior Olympics (JOs, now called junior nationals), the annual national championship for racers age nineteen and younger. At JOs, Whitcomb ran into a friend who coached at Burke Mountain Academy, a ski-racing prep school in Vermont's remote Northeast Kingdom with a small cross-country team. The friend was leaving Burke. Would Matt like a coaching job?

Matt moved back east in the fall of 2002 and jumped into coaching at Burke before the snow even fell. A petite young alpine ski racer named Liz Stephen, who had lost interest in racing gates but who loved to run, was debating whether or not to return to Burke that winter for her sophomore year. She didn't feel as if she fit into the alpine ski-racing world, where she struggled against her more successful teammates. Should she switch to cross-country skiing, as her coaches and the Burke headmaster were suggesting? Or should she give up competitive skiing altogether and return to Union-32, the name of her public high school in Montpelier, Vermont? Matt wanted to help her decide. So he drove two hours across the state to Williston, Vermont, where Liz was racing in a cross-country running meet for U-32 (she was only attending Burke in the winter and spring, so she could run competitively with her local high school team in the fall). After the running race, Matt introduced himself as the new cross-country ski coach at Burke and said how much he would like to have her on his team—even though Liz had never even strapped on a pair of cross-country skis. He then returned to Liz's home in East Montpelier to introduce himself to her parents and tell them about the program that he envisioned at Burke.

"He just made me want to be a part of it," said Liz. "I didn't even know what I was getting into, but I didn't care. This guy was someone who I wanted to be around. He was so adventurous and fun and just wanted to include people. It was such a difference from how I'd felt at the end of my alpine career, where I just really felt left out."

At Burke, Matt wanted to start a program similar to what Ed Hamel had done with the western Massachusetts BLK group—training through fun and adventure. One such adventure involved circumnavigating Burke Mountain. It sounds simple enough, except for the fact that Burke is located in one of the most remote areas of Vermont. Running Around the Mountain, as it became known, is a 20-mile (or so) trail run and bushwhack through the towns of Victory (population sixty-two) and Granby (population eighty-eight). The skiers and their coach had to claw their way through pricker bushes and wade into mud pits, sometimes up to their knees, sometimes up to their waists. The first year, just the cross-country ski team made the trek. But it would soon become a school event. Matt built himself a cabin on a dirt road that winds around the side of Burke Mountain. It's not too far from one of the biggest mud pits.

In the fall of 2004, he helped start a girls' cross-country running team at Burke (so Liz would not have to spend the fall at U-32). Liz won the state championship race that year, with Burke taking third in the team standings. One of the mottos at Burke was "all leaders, no leaders," and Matt's experience played into this. Teams did not have a captain. As he had experienced with Ed Hamel, everyone was expected to be a leader.

"I really feel like that's a critical component of a team," said Matt. "Many teams have people that are just along for the ride."

One spring, Matt started something he called "60 Days of Toughness," an initiative to keep the cross-country skiers active and focused in the off-season. The skiers were supposed to challenge themselves mentally or physically every day to make themselves tougher. They might swim in frigid snowmelt in a stream after a run. Or do a couple hundred sit-ups on a log. Or even challenge themselves in their classwork.

Beyond a string of tough workouts, Matt built relationships at Burke. The kid who had been socially awkward and shy had always had an easy rapport with adults in the ski community, and Matt Molyneux noticed that this characteristic blossomed at Burke.

"He was the kind of guy who couldn't make it across campus because everyone would want to stop and talk," said Molyneux, who started teaching and coaching after he also graduated from Middlebury. "Everybody always loved him. And he valued the people he met. So many people build relationships for networking reasons. Matt doesn't do that. There's so much authenticity to the guy."

As a coach, Matt became a buoyant trailside cheerleader, enthusiastically urging on his skiers when they were doing well and sympathetically encouraging them when they were struggling. Or he was calm and patient when everyone else was nerved up for a race—channeling the fly fisherman in him. His faith in his skiers showed in their performances.

The team that Matt built at Burke attracted more young skiers. One was Ida Sargent, who had grown up chasing her older sister and brother around the trails at nearby Craftsbury, Vermont, and was keeping up with skiers twice her age.

"It just seemed like the Burke kids were having a lot of fun and also working hard and skiing fast," said Ida. "They were a close-knit group. I wanted to be part of it."

It was a group bonded by the kind of adventure that most people considered crazy, the kind of adventures that make lifelong stories, like the run around the mountain. Now the run is a school tradition that everyone does on graduation morning in June, including the school's alpine skiers. The student body then shows up for graduation, the girls wearing nice dresses with pricker-bush scars and a little mud still on their legs. By the time Matt left Burke, he had built the cross-country ski program from four to ten skiers.

Matt wanted to bring this kind of adventure and team building to the U.S. Ski Team—and he had certainly had success with Liz Stephen, who scored her first national title just a few years after picking up the sport (tying with Kikkan in the 5-kilometer freestyle in 2006). The team would be based in Park City, with the athletes traveling to the Utah ski town for regular training camps. The model seemed to be working for the men's team. Andy Newell, who was named to the development team right out of high school in 2002, was flourishing, as was Kris Freeman, who was just a few seconds off the podium in several races. If all went well, another group of young skiers might, if nurtured properly, start putting the Stars and Stripes near the front of cross-country ski races. But the model would need refining and tweaking. And not every skier would flourish.

THE DEVELOPMENT TEAM AND GROWING PAINS

The 2006–2007 season began on a bright note. The $1 million that Pete Vordenberg had secured from USSA meant that the team now had enough money to fund a men's and a women's team, or about $100,000 per person. About a third of the budget would cover travel: a season's worth of World Cup racing in Europe, plus four camps each year in places like Bend, Oregon; Anchorage and the Eagle Glacier in Alaska; New Zealand; and Park City, Utah. Beyond the cross-country team's budget, USSA would cover overhead for infrastructure used by and personnel administering all snowsport disciplines governed by the organization (Nordic, alpine, freestyle, snowboarding, and freeskiing). For example, USSA's Center of Excellence, its headquarters and training facility in Park City that opened on May 1, 2009, is used by athletes in all the snowsport disciplines, and its overhead is not included in every sport's budget.

But the cross-country skiers would still be competing against far better funded teams. Norway, for example, spends about fourteen times as much on its cross-country ski team, although it's difficult to compare because Norway includes its domestic skiers, not just its elite World Cup

Failures, repeated failures, are finger posts on the road to achievement. One fails forward toward success.

✻

Charles F. Kettering, American inventor, engineer, and businessman, in *The Reader's Digest*, "Education Begins at Home," February 1944 skiers, in its budget. The cost of funding a domestic program in the United States, or what is considered the development pipeline, is now covered partly by Nordic clubs around the country, such as APU, Stratton Mountain School, CXC, and the Craftsbury Outdoor Center, and mostly by parents who sign up their kids for the Bill Koch League teams in New England and youth programs in the Midwest, West Coast, and Alaska. Although most junior programs try to provide every child who wants to take part with ski equipment, parents pay for most of their kids' ski clothing and equipment—which can cost into the thousands for teens who need different skis, boots, and poles for classic and skate skiing, plus wax. This means that the sport is limited not just geographically (to regions where snow falls) but by financial means as well. Although cross-country skiing costs far less than alpine skiing, it can still take a chunk from the family budget. (When Olympic gold medalist Ted Ligety first made the U.S. alpine ski team, he wrote "Mom & Dad" on a white sticker and adhered it on the front of his helmet, the advertising space usually used by skiers' primary sponsors.) Parents are also responsible for driving their kids to races often held many miles away, not just at the school across town. With weekends consumed by training and racing, the best junior racers often come from families who have literally bought into the sport and are willing to spend every weekend outside on the ski trails.

In countries like Norway, most kids start skiing around the time they can walk, then continue through grade school. Cross-country skiing is a national sport in Norway, and kids join local ski clubs, which are ubiquitous. The Norwegian ski federation is comprised of sixteen regional groups that include more than 1,100 clubs (of the eight women named to the Norwegian national team for the 2016–2017 season, each came from a different ski club). Once promising skiers make the national team, their expenses are covered, and many of them become national celebrities—six of the top-ten most recognized sports heroes in Norway are cross-country skiers or biathletes. Part of the Norwegian ski federation's funding is derived from the government, which considers its elite cross-country skiers ambassadors in the countries where they race, and at the world championships and Olympic Games. In fact, every team against which the U.S. cross-country skiers compete derives at least some of its funding from the government. By comparison, USSA receives no government monies. The organization raises about 40 percent of its budget from corporate sponsors, such as VISA and L.L. Bean, 40 percent from private donations, and 12 to 13 percent from the U.S. Olympic Committee. The rest is derived from membership fees and merchandise sales.

The U.S. cross-country ski team's $1 million budget covers all training, travel, and racing costs for athletes named to the A team. Those named to the B, C, and development teams must contribute about $25,000 per year. This money covers the cost of travel and waxing their skis. But the B, C, and development team skiers are not billed for coaching, training, or medical support while they are with the team. And all the skiers, even those on the A team, must raise additional money to help pay for the cost of living (rent payments or mortgages, food and utility bills, car payments, student loans, credit card bills, etc.). Many skiers rely on generous sponsors from their hometowns or states to help fund their careers; in turn, the athletes often appear in ads for their sponsors and wear their sponsors' names on their hats and headbands. Others apply for grants, and many benefit from hometown fundraisers. Prize winnings from SuperTour, NorAm, national championship, and World Cup races, as well as other competitions, also contribute to their bottom lines. It's a lot to expect of world-class athletes to handle the business side of a sport in addition to the high volume of training. But it's the price that American athletes are willing to pay when they have become passionate about—and good at—a fringe sport.

Luke Bodensteiner, who became the executive vice president of athletics for USSA in 2008, knows what it is like to fund a ski career. When he was competing, he had to raise $40,000 just to make it through 1994 (the year he made the U.S. Olympic team competing in Lillehammer, Norway), and he met his fundraising goal thanks to his hometown community in Wisconsin. But he noted that the U.S. team had different budget priorities back then. The U.S. Ski Team paid for hotels and plane tickets. But the skiers lacked consistent coaching, decent training facilities, and good medical support. In 2006, the budget not only increased but also the focus shifted. USSA began investing in coaching, cutting-edge sport science and training facilities, and medical teams to support the athletes and help them improve. To offset this budget shift, athletes outside the various snowsport A teams would have to cover their travel costs.

"The idea was to provide the things that only we can provide—excellent coaching and really good sports science—with the idea that anyone else can pay for an athlete's plane ticket," said Bodensteiner. "If we're paying for something that they can probably get from their community, sponsors, or families, then we're never going to get there."

Raising money can be difficult for athletes who have little time or energy between training and racing, and many lack experience writing sponsorship and grant proposals. Some go the college route, where athletic scholarships pay for their tuition, room, and board. But college often will not launch them to the next level of elite cross-country skiing —and in many cases, has distracted talented athletes who have found other interests and pursuits while in college. In a sport that takes years to develop, promising but not-quite-there-yet skiers must raise about $30,000 each year—the equivalent of a year's salary had they pursued a more traditional career. It can and has driven some talented skiers from the sport. But Bodensteiner believed that this funding strategy is what the U.S. cross-country skiers needed to improve performances going toward the Vancouver Olympics.

"It's not a perfect way to do it," he said. "But given that we're financial underdogs compared to virtually everybody we compete against, it's a choice we made."

For many skiers with an Olympic dream, the investment is worth it. They don't want to look back and regret passing up opportunities because money stood in their way.

❊   ❊   ❊

Even with the financial considerations, it was not difficult to find talented skiers for the development team after the Torino Olympics. Although still considered the poor cousin to alpine, cross-country skiing had become far cooler than it once was. Endurance sports had become more mainstream in the late twentieth century and early 2000s; sprint racing, with its head-to-head competition on a short loop, was added to the World Cup tour in 1996 and Olympic program in 2002, which made cross-country skiing more exciting for both spectators and participants. Bill Koch League and other junior programs began to flourish in the late 1990s and 2000s, with parents wanting to keep their kids active in winter. Talented teens who wanted to pursue the sport enrolled in ski academies, like the Stratton Mountain School or Burke Mountain Academy, or joined the Sun Valley Ski Education Foundation, Craftsbury Green Racing Project, CXC team in the Midwest, or APU, to name the primary ones. The only limit to the sport is snow—and a demographic that understands and encourages endurance sports and can afford it.

The women named to the U.S. development team in the spring of 2006 represented a wide geographic region in the United States. Torino Olympians Lindsay Williams and Lindsey Weier were the most experienced skiers on the new development team. High school friends and rivals from Minneapolis, they both studied and trained at Northern Michigan University. Liz Stephen from Vermont, who had tied Kikkan for the 5-kilometer freestyle national championship title right before the Torino Olympics, then finished seventh in pursuit at the 2006 world junior championships, was also named, along with Morgan Arritola, who had learned to cross-country ski as a high school student in Sun Valley and had scored two second-place finishes at the 2006 nationals and just missed making the Torino Olympic team; Tazlina Mannix, a promising skier from Alaska who had chosen to attend APU over Middlebury College; and Morgan Smyth, who, like Lindsay Williams and Lindsey Weier, was a student at Northern Michigan University. Liz, Tazlina, and the two Morgans had competed at the 2005 and 2006 junior world championships. These development team skiers would be based with their regional teams, then would gather for training camps in Park City or Alaska during the off-season. Park City's altitude (around 7,000 feet above sea level) would serve as a training tool, and with the coaches based in Park City, it was a relatively inexpensive place to hold the camps. Then during the winter, the skiers on the development team would race in the domestic SuperTour races and NorAms in Canada, and before or after world junior and U23 championships, they would compete in Alpin Cup races, the equivalent of the SuperTour in central Europe. Kikkan would head to Europe in November and spend her first full season racing on the World Cup tour.

But this new group—one of the largest development teams ever named—would face growing pains. For starters, the six women were spread across three different programs. Lindsay Williams, Lindsey Weier, and Morgan Smyth attended Northern Michigan University, where Sten Fjeldheim was their coach, and their priority was their coursework and college races, particularly the NCAA Championships. Morgan Arritola and Liz had both forgone college to live in Park City and train with the U.S. Ski Team coaches. And Tazlina remained in Alaska training at APU. They would work with their home coaches when they were not at training camps or races. But it was a new system that required communication between the coaches, and the home team coaches sometimes had different training philosophies or plans than the national team coaches. Like any relationship, it would take time and effort to figure out how to best work together. It also cost money for these skiers to travel to training camps. Initially, they were given a stipend to cover travel costs. But one skier noted that the money started to dry up when the economy began to teeter.

Meanwhile, APU was going through changes, too. APU Nordic program founder Jim Galanes stepped down, and assistant coach Erik Flora took over. Tazlina, who was nineteen years old at the time, remembered it as a positive change, but a change just the same. And when athletes are training as hard as cross-country skiers and pushed to the limits of fatigue, any change can throw them off. When she attended U.S. Ski Team training camps, Tazlina would stick with Flora's training plan, and it did not necessarily mesh with what everyone else was doing—because they too would come to the camp with their own coaches' plans. Whose plans were they supposed to follow?

"We were kind of like guinea pigs," said Taz. "There were bumps in the road when we were on the team."

When winter came, the women were competing all over the map, too. Many of them traveled to the SuperTour and NorAm events in the early season. But after the holiday break, Lindsay Williams, Lindsey Weier, and Morgan Smyth focused on collegiate races and the NCAA Championships (at the 2007 NCAA Championships, the three NMU skiers swept the podium in both the 5-kilometer freestyle and the 15-kilometer classic races). Lindsey Weier also qualified for the 2007 world championship team. Tazlina and Morgan Arritola competed in the season-opener SuperTour races, followed by U.S. nationals in early January. Then they traveled to Tarvisio, Italy, near the border of Austria and Slovenia, for the U23 world championships (for skiers under age twenty-three). Meanwhile, Liz spent most of her first season on the development team racing in Europe.

On their way to the junior and U23 world championships in Italy that February, Liz, Morgan Arritola, and Tazlina joined Kikkan in a World Cup relay in Davos, Switzerland—the first World Cup for Morgan and Tazlina, and for coach Matt Whitcomb. Liz had competed in her first World Cup race the previous day, finishing forty-eighth in a 10-kilometer freestyle race—three places ahead of Kikkan, who reached her physical limit in the middle of the race (referred to as "blowing up" in ski racer parlance) and came in last. Morgan and Taz did not yet have low enough FIS points to qualify for an individual World Cup race. But FIS rules allowed them to compete as part of a World Cup relay team. Skiing the anchor leg, Tazlina pulled the team from dead last into eleventh place.

Matt was shocked when neither Kikkan nor Liz finished near the top thirty in the 10-kilometer race, and then the relay team was basically slaughtered. "It was definitely a high going to the World Cup," he said. "But it was a distinctly humbling moment. It allowed us to see really quickly how long the road actually is."

But there were a few glimpses of what the skiers could become. From that relay, Liz went to the 2007 world junior championships, where she finished seventh in the 5-kilometer freestyle race. At the U23 world championships, Taz finished ninth in the 15-kilometer pursuit —a superb result that made up for a slow start to the season after she had had an appendectomy. Considering that American women had for decades finished far down in results, these high placings were good cause to cheer.

The following winter, Liz stood on her first international podium. At the 2008 U23 world championships, she was skiing in the lead pack in the 15-kilometer freestyle mass-start race. Also in the front group were Taz and Morgan Arritola. As they dropped down the final hill into the stadium, two of them had a good chance of finishing on the podium, and worst case, three in the top eight. The American women had never finished that well at a world championship—junior or senior. With just a few hundred meters to the go, three women got tangled in the pack and went flying off the trail into the woods. Among the three were Taz and Morgan. Liz escaped the carnage and finished third in the race for the bronze medal.

That spring, two more women were added to the development team: Rosie Brennan and Alexa Turzian, who had become the youngest national champion when, at age eighteen, she won the 10-kilometer freestyle race at the 2007 nationals, beating Kikkan. Brennan had taken up cross-country skiing when she was in eighth grade—only four years earlier—but had quickly shot up the junior ranks, winning a Junior Olympic title in 2006. Both were headed to college in the fall—Rosie to Dartmouth, Alexa to Middlebury. Their training and race plans would fit in with the three women enrolled at NMU.

At the same time, a few other women not yet on the development team had results that foreshadowed their future in elite cross-country ski racing. Sadie Bjornsen, an eighteen-year-old who had grown up beating the boys on her home trails in Winthrop, Washington, qualified for the 2007 world junior team, along with Rosie and Alexa. The following year, two Vermonters joined Sadie, Rosie, and Alexa at the 2008 world juniors: Dartmouth freshman Ida Sargent, and a high school senior from Stratton Mountain School named Sophie Caldwell —John Caldwell's granddaughter and Tim Caldwell's niece (Tim had competed in four Olympics from 1972 to 1984 in cross-country skiing). It was Sophie's second international trip. Two years before, shortly after her fifteenth birthday, she had competed in spring races in Sweden. And in one of those races, she had beaten Swedish darling Charlotte Kalla, who had an Olympic gold medal in her future.

*　*　*

Although the women named to the post-Torino development team were starting to dip their ski tips into the international racing scene, Kikkan continued to be the only woman named to the U.S. Ski Team's A team. This meant that, yet again, she was on her own in Europe, almost always racing without teammates. "It was me and four guys," she said.

"She had drive and internal belief even though there was nothing but a hole for her to fall through," said Pete Vordenberg, who was impressed with her perseverance. "She just kept going."

She did not wallow in loneliness, though. On the World Cup tour at the time, the teams from other countries mostly kept to themselves. But there was no rule barring them from socializing between races. And if Kikkan couldn't be named to the Canadian women's cross-country team, there was nothing saying that she couldn't hang out with them when time allowed. With natural talents in sprinting, Chandra Crawford and Kikkan became friends.

Whether it was her new friends or the fact that she was building experience at the front of the pack or just her dogged determination, Kikkan began to find her groove. On January 21, 2007, in Rybinsk, Russia, about 300 kilometers north of Moscow on the Volga River, Randall made U.S. skiing history again. On a course created from blocks of ice and ice cubes (because no snow had fallen in northern Russia that winter), Randall qualified ninth in the freestyle sprint. She progressed through the quarter- and semifinals. Then in her first World Cup sprint final, she dashed toward the finish with Arianna Follis from Italy and Olympic silver medalist Claudia Kuenzel-Nystad from Germany. Follis crossed the finish line first. Behind her, Kikkan and Kuenzel-Nystad lunged for the line. The photo finish went to the German, with Kikkan taking third, her first World Cup podium finish.

"It was wild," Kikkan said after the final.

It was her first time standing on the World Cup podium—and the second time an American woman had reached a World Cup podium (and the first time in twenty-eight years). Kikkan's strongest memory from the day is how excited the U.S. Ski Team staff was, especially Pete Vordenberg and the team's new wax technician, Peter Johansson.

Eleven months later, on December 16, 2007, Kikkan headed back to Rybinsk for another World Cup sprint. It was the final World Cup before she would head back to Alaska for the holidays, and Kikkan was ready to be home. The season had not started as well as she had hoped, and she was tired. It had also been a long trip to reach Rybinsk—a three-hour flight from Switzerland to Moscow, then almost a five-hour drive north to the dreary Russian city. By race morning, Kikkan did not even want to get out of bed. She finally rallied and finished second in the sprint qualifier.

"OK, not bad," she thought to herself.

As she progressed through the quarterfinals and semis, she felt better and better. By the final, she had a plan. She was going to stay with reigning sprint world champion Astrid Jacobsen from Norway for as long as she could.

"I'm just going to hang with her," said Kikkan. "I don't care if I have to roll my eyes back into my head. I'm just going to follow her and see what that feels like."

The final started, and Kikkan stayed glued to Jacobsen. But when they reached the steepest hill on the course, Kikkan realized that the Norwegian was not climbing as quickly as she expected. So she jumped around Jacobsen and charged to the top of the hill. Now it was just a downhill, then the finish stretch. But had she made a mistake? Would Jacobsen draft off her down the hill, then jump around her before the finish line?

Kikkan crouched into a tuck on the descent and watched for Jacobsen's shadow to come around her. But as she raced toward the line, Kikkan felt as if her legs were springs. With each diagonal skate stride, she propelled herself forward. She was too fast for Jacobsen or any of the other four women in the final. Kikkan had won her first World Cup race.

"Last year, I was too tentative to make a move on the uphill," she told Ski Racing. "This year I figured no guts, no glory, and I was ready to make the move."

The Olympics were just over two years away. And winning a World Cup race was a major stepping-stone on her path to the Olympic podium. But then the path almost ended abruptly.

*   *   *

In early February 2008, Kikkan started feeling a faint pain deep in her abdomen above her left hip. It wasn't painful enough to mention to anyone. But it was noticeable. She told herself that she would get it checked out after the racing season ended. By late March, the pain had worsened and spread to her back. Burned out from a long season of mostly frustrating races (and one race win), she returned home from the World Cup a week early. Then she flew south to Vancouver to compete at the Canadian nationals on what would become the 2010 Olympic courses. It was the first time that she had seen Jeff since the season began, and their wedding was coming up in May. The two slept on a pullout couch in a friend's condo, which Kikkan thought might be contributing to her continued back pain. Despite how she felt, Kikkan ended the 2008 season on a good note, winning the Canadian national 5-kilometer classic race as well as the sprint title—beating her friends Sara Renner and Chandra Crawford, who won silver and bronze medals, respectively, in the sprint. Then the morning after Canadian nationals ended, she woke up with a very tight and tense back. Maybe it was from a hard crash she had taken while skiing the day before? Or from sleeping on a thin, lumpy mattress?

She flew home to Anchorage, spent the night, and then drove six hours to Fairbanks for more spring races. By this time, she felt as if she were coming down with the flu. She skipped the first race, then saw a physical therapist who thought that her spine and hips were out of alignment. After an adjustment, Kikkan felt better. The next day, she tried to ski a pre-race warm-up. But her left leg felt incredibly tired —and weird. It was also red and swollen. Listening to her symptoms, coach Erik Flora was alarmed. He had had a friend develop a blood clot in his leg, and the symptoms were similar. He insisted that Kikkan head to the emergency room to get it checked out. At an ER in Fairbanks, doctors did an ultrasound on her hip and found the clot. Called deep vein thrombosis, the clot was located where the common iliac vein and artery split, with branches heading into each leg. The clot extended from her left hip down below her knee.

"They called people in to see the clot on the ultrasound because it was the biggest one they had ever seen," said Kikkan.

Doctors determined that Kikkan's blood clot was caused by a "perfect storm" of factors. First, she has Factor V Leiden, the inherited genetic mutation that increases the chance of clots forming. Second, she learned that she has another disorder called May-Thurner syndrome, a rare condition where the left iliac vein is compressed by the overlying iliac artery. It can lead to blood clots. Compounding these two risk factors, Randall had started using a NuvaRing birth control device the previous November. The number one side effect of this device is blood clots. Doctors in Fairbanks prescribed blood thinners, kept her overnight, and said that the clot would likely dissolve over time but advised her to stay on blood thinners.

The next morning, Kikkan flew home to Anchorage and sought a second opinion. A vascular surgeon at the Providence Alaska Medical Center recommended actively removing the clot because of Kikkan's ski career. On April 3, 2008, she had surgery. It involved the surgeon inserting a catheter behind her left knee, then spraying a clot-busting drug through the catheter. He also used angioplasty balloons to try to stretch the narrow section of the pinched vein. After a night in the cardiac intensive care unit, Kikkan went home. Her leg was still swollen, and walking hurt. But the leg improved each day. As it improved, Kikkan tried to dive back into training. Every time, however, simple exercise caused her leg to tire and swell again. This went on for ten days.

On April 14, she went to a scheduled appointment with a hematologist to discuss her blood work. Even though she has Factor V Leiden, the hematologist was not concerned and told Kikkan that she did not have to take blood thinners for life, only six months. But before she left the office, he suggested that they do a follow-up ultrasound to see how the vein was doing. The news was not good. The clot was back and bigger than the first one. She would have to have the catheter inserted again, this time with the clot-busting drug inserted slowly over three days.

Kikkan was readmitted to the hospital the following day, and the vascular surgeon reinserted the catheter. She lay in bed connected to tubes. The clot-busting drug seeped through the catheter behind her knee and began slowly breaking up the clot. Blood-thinning drugs dripped into her arm from an IV bag. And every day, the doctor performed angioplasty again and again on the narrowed vein. Other than rolling around in bed, she wasn't allowed to move. Six days later, she was released.

"I was so happy to get up and walk around," Kikkan said.

The nurses wanted to wheel her out. But she insisted on walking. She limped to the elevator and as she waited for it to arrive, she suddenly felt as if her sock were wet. She looked down and her rubber Croc shoe was full of blood the color and consistency of a pink-ish zinfandel. Her thinned blood was pouring out from the wound where the catheter had been inserted. She limped back to the nurse's station, and they quickly put compression on the wound until it clotted and stopped bleeding. Hours later, Kikkan was finally cleared to go home.

Within a few days, she felt normal again and slowly began walking. Six weeks later, doctors recommended that she have a stent inserted into the narrowed vein. That invasive surgery would have set her back months, so she convinced them to hold off on the procedure. If the clot reformed, she would reconsider it then. For now, she wanted to get back to training. Two weeks later, she was skiing again. But she had missed several weeks of training. It would take a while to catch up. And with every ache, she wondered if more clots were forming. For some, it would have halted their athletic careers. But Kikkan did not consider quitting. With stubborn optimism, she considered it a bump in the road, a condition that could be managed.

On May 16, under an arch made of cross-country skis, Kikkan and Jeff Ellis were married in Anchorage. From there, they flew to Jeff's hometown in Ontario for a Canadian reception, then to Moab, Utah, for their honeymoon. Doctors had advised Kikkan to limit risk while she was on blood thinners; any open gashes could lead to rapid blood loss that would not easily clot. But the skier did not temper her activities too much. She and Jeff mountain biked all over the red rocks of Moab, including a rocky 15-mile descent down the Porcupine Rim Trail that ends in a single track along a cliff face above the Colorado River.

That fall, Kikkan asked Chandra if she could join her in Canmore, Alberta, for a friendly training camp. Randall liked her APU teammates. But she knew that she needed to train with an established world-class competitor who would push her. They dubbed their camp the North American Women's Training Alliance (or NAWTA). It was the beginning of an annual international camp. Kikkan was motivated to regain fitness, especially with the 2009 world championships coming up that season. This time, worlds would feature a skate sprint—her specialty. And she wanted to win a medal. Coach Flora appreciated her enthusiasm but tried to be realistic.

"He was encouraging me," said Kikkan. "But at the same time, he was like, 'This is going to be a hell of a thing to pull off.'"

❊   ❊   ❊

The season before the Olympic Winter Games can be as rife with competition as the Olympics themselves. Skiers want to move up in rankings, show that they deserve to be Olympians, and mostly gain confidence. The pre-Olympic season always features the FIS world championships, and usually a World Cup held at the upcoming Olympic venue. This World Cup serves as a test event for the venue.

The 2008–2009 season for the U.S. women's cross-country ski team was just such a season. Kikkan was still the only woman on the A team. But below her, the ranks were booming. Those who had been on the development team were promoted to the B team, and the roster had exploded to nine women: Morgan Arritola, Lindsey Weier (now Dehlin), Lindsay Williams, Tazlina Mannix, Morgan Smyth, Liz Stephen, Alexa Turzian, Rosie Brennan, and newcomer Laura Valaas. A Whitman College graduate, Valaas, twenty-four years old at the time, had a breakout year in 2007–2008, finishing as runner-up to Kikkan in the national sprint championship and taking second overall in the Super-Tour standings. She also had several World Cup races on her racing resume. It looked like these ten women would be competing for the half dozen or so spots on the 2010 U.S. Olympic team that would compete in Vancouver the following year. They spent the early season competing in NorAm and SuperTour races in North America, then went to 2009 nationals in Anchorage, where Kikkan won the sprint title and Caitlin Compton, who had graduated from Northern Michigan University five years earlier, won the 5-kilometer title.

In January 2009, the World Cup moved to western Canada to test the 2010 Olympic Nordic venue—a network of trails in the Callaghan Valley about 16 miles west of Whistler, British Columbia. Still trying to regain her form after the blood clots the previous spring, Kikkan finished fourteenth in the classic sprint. But then in the team sprint, Kikkan teamed with Liz. The young B team skier was fresh off a third-place finish in the 15-kilometer freestyle mass-start race the previous year at

U23 worlds, as well as three national titles, one of which she shared with Kikkan (the 5-kilometer freestyle title in 2006).

In the World Cup test event that January, Kikkan and Liz took turns each racing three times around the 1.3-kilometer course in the team sprint. They came in fourth, a little over one second out of the medals. They each earned 1,500 Swiss francs, a big payday for skiers used to earning nothing (or very little) on the World Cup tour. It was Liz's fourth World Cup race and the best result ever for the women in a team event.

The banner season for this young team continued. Liz finished seventh in the 10-kilometer freestyle at U23 worlds, right ahead of Morgan Arritola in eighth. Then in the 15-kilometer pursuit at U23 worlds, Liz and Morgan showed the team's growing depth, finishing fourth and fifth, respectively. It boded well for these two young women going to world championships in Liberec, Czech Republic, in February.

❊   ❊   ❊

Traveling to Liberec, Kikkan did not know what to expect. She had not finished in the top three of a World Cup individual sprint since her win in Rybinsk two years earlier. And after surgery in April 2008 to remove the blood clots, she had had a slow start to the 2008–2009 season. "It was not easy to come back from surgery," she admitted in a media call during the championships.

She was also tired. During the off-season, Flora had emphasized intensity during APU workouts—shorter, very hard efforts done repeatedly to increase strength and pain tolerance. Kikkan felt fried before the season even started. And when her season did start, good results didn't come like she had hoped. She didn't qualify for the sprint heats in any of the early season World Cup races. After the New Year, she won the sprint race at U.S. nationals (her seventh national title), but by the end of January she had not finished higher than fifteenth in a World Cup sprint. In the last World Cup before the world championships, she made a sprint final but finished last (sixth). In the lead-up to the 2009 worlds, Kikkan wasn't even listed as one of the favorites. That honor went to skiers like Slovenia's Petra Majdic, who had won the sprint

World Cup title the previous season, and Italy's Arianna Follis, who had won the World Cup sprints during the 2009 Tour de Ski, a multiday race modeled on cycling's Tour de France. The Tour began in 2007 and is held annually in early January.

As world championships approached, Kikkan was freaking out—although it was difficult to tell. With a combination of New England reserve and Alaskan pluck, she maintains a calm, sunny demeanor on the inside no matter what life throws at her. Despite the intense training, she didn't feel in shape. She did, however, have experience on her side. This would be her fifth world championships—held every other year on odd years—but the first time since 2003 that her best event, the sprint freestyle, would be held. The 2005 and 2007 world championships had featured sprints in the classic technique.

But she was more ready than she knew. In the eleven days between the final World Cup sprint held before worlds and the world championship sprint, Kikkan was able to recover. By February 24, 2009—the day of the world championship sprint—she had found her gears, a term she uses to describe the level of effort needed to win a World Cup race. It's a level of effort that's only reached through a series of hard race efforts, a level equivalent to a race car reaching its fastest speed and the driver shifting into high gear for the final lap to the finish. She also realized that she had nothing to lose—a thought that alleviated most of the pressure that she felt at world championships. She had almost lost everything the previous April with the blood clot. Yet here she was, competing at another world championship. Why not just go for it and see what happens?

In the sprint qualification—a time trial on the morning of the sprint heats that places the top thirty skiers into the quarterfinal heats—Kikkan kept her effort pinned just under 100 percent and qualified a solid seventh. She was almost 5 seconds behind Natalie Matveeva. The Russian would soon be disqualified from worlds after a positive drug test for EPO.

Racing in the second quarterfinal, Kikkan knew her toughest competition would come from Charlotte Kalla, Sweden's former junior world champion who had won the grueling multi-race Tour de Ski the previous winter and had qualified third in the world championship sprint, four places ahead of Kikkan. The top two in each quarterfinal heat would move on to the semifinals, and Kikkan and Kalla had no problem securing those two spots. Then in the semis, Kikkan made the final. But Kalla did not, instead qualifying for the consolation B Final. (Majdic, a pre-race favorite, did not even make it to the semis.)

Even without Kalla and Majdic, Kikkan had impressive company on the starting line at the world championship sprint final. The five other women in the final hailed from countries where skiing is practically a national sport. To her left was Arianna Follis from Italy, who had already finished on the World Cup podium seven times that season. Also on the start line was Olympic gold medalist Anna Olsson from Sweden; U23 world championship silver medalist Ida Ingemarsdotter, also from Sweden; world championship silver medalist Pirjo Muranen from Finland; and Matveeva from Russia. Randall realized that if she had any hope of medaling, she had to race like the hero of her running days, Steve Prefontaine (a poster of "Pre" hangs in her workout room at home in Anchorage). The legendary distance runner won races on the track in the early 1970s by running as fast as he could from start to finish. He did not worry about pacesetters or drafting. He simply pinned it from the start, took the lead, and hung on until the end. If other runners were going to beat him, Pre once said, "they are going to have to bleed to do it." Like Pre, Kikkan wanted to control the race from the front. And now, eleven years into her ski career, she was strong enough to pull it off.

On a foggy afternoon in Liberec, Follis was the one who shot out to an early lead in the sprint final. But within 30 seconds, Kikkan took over.

"Oh my God, I'm leading world championships!" she thought, then quickly chastised herself. "Don't think that! Go go go!"

Kikkan held the lead until the final hill coming into the homestretch. Using a higher tempo, Follis came around Kikkan and gained almost a second by the finish. She crossed the line first for the gold medal. Behind her, Kikkan was still charging to the finish, but Muranen from Finland was gaining. Kikkan lunged at the line, holding off Muranen by a boot-length. After a season of frustration and a blood clot that could have ended her career, Kikkan had won a world championship silver medal. It was the first world championship medal won by a U.S. cross-country skier since the days of Bill Koch—and the first for an American woman. Standing on the podium, Kikkan didn't even know how to pop the cork from the Champagne bottle.

Kikkan's silver was not the only medal for the U.S. at the 2009 FIS Nordic World Ski Championships. The entire championship became a watershed event for the U.S. Ski Team. In snowy Liberec, American Nordic skiers won six medals: four gold, one silver, and a bronze. Even at its best world championship—and best Olympics—the U.S. alpine team had never done better. Across the five Nordic disciplines—men's and women's cross-country skiing, men's and women's ski jumping, and Nordic combined (only men)—the U.S. Ski Team finished fourth in the medal count behind perennial winners Norway, Germany, and Finland. Nordic combined skiers Todd Lodwick and Billy Demong won four of the U.S.'s six medals (and three of the gold medals). And in the world championship debut for women's ski jumping, Lindsey Van won a gold medal—a step in her quest to get women's ski jumping on the Olympic program. Kikkan credited her Nordic teammates for inspiring her. Van, Lodwick, and Demong all won gold medals before the women contested the freestyle sprint. Whenever an American skier won a medal in Liberec, the entire team attended the awards ceremony.

"I want to be up there someday," thought Kikkan.

In U.S. ski circles, the Nordic world championship medal haul in the Czech Republic was such a big deal that *Ski Racing* magazine put photos of Kikkan, Lindsey Van, Todd Lodwick, and Billy Demong on its cover, relegating alpine superstar Lindsey Vonn and her second overall World Cup downhill title to small font above the header. The title of the issue read "Stimulus Czech."

Elsewhere in results at the 2009 Liberec world championships, three other American cross-country skiers scored top-thirty finishes. Kris Freeman finished fourth yet again in the 15-kilometer classic race, a heartbreaking 1.3 seconds out of the medals—and his second fourth place at a world championship. Andy Newell qualified second in the men's freestyle sprint, then finished twelfth—or sixth in the consolation B final. And in her first senior world championship, Liz Stephen finished fifteenth in the pursuit, less than 2 minutes behind winner Justyna Kowalczyk from Poland.

"The more we race over here, the more normal it becomes, and it's fun to know we can mix it up with the best," Liz told reporters.

Then in the 30-kilometer race, Liz finished seventeenth and Morgan Arritola came in twenty-first. Liz was twenty-one years old, Morgan twenty-two.

"To have two in the top twenty-five in a distance race, I don't know if we've ever done it," said coach Pete Vordenberg. "It's unbelievable; this is their first real taste, their first world championships. The future is really exciting."

Except cross-country skiing is a brutal sport. And a big, strong development team does not seamlessly become an elite team without some casualties.

✳ ✳ ✳

To understand attrition in any sport, it is necessary to look at the forces that athletes face daily, and how those forces affect their bodies. And cross-country skiing, while not difficult to learn, is known as one of the most physically taxing of all sports. Skiers use almost every muscle from their shoulders to their toes to propel themselves across the snow, poling with their arms and shoulders, using their strong stomach and back muscles to augment poling, and driving themselves forward across the snow with their legs and hips. Races vary in length from 1-kilometer sprints to 50-kilometer marathons. At the Olympic and World Cup level, women never race farther than 30 kilometers. But even that distance keeps skiers on the trail for up to an hour and a half, depending on snow conditions, the difficulty of the racecourse, and the technique (classic technique is slower than skating). For example, at the 2006 Olympics, Katerina Neumannová from the Czech Republic won the 30-kilometer freestyle race in 1:22.25.4—giving her an average speed of 13.5 miles per hour, or the speed of a recreational bicycle ride. Skiing this hard can burn up to 1,000 calories each hour—the equivalent of two McDonald's Big Macs. Add that extra half hour in a 30-kilometer race, and skiers can have fries with that. Or rather, a huge bowl of pasta, with grilled chicken on the side.

Sprints are no easier. Although they are shorter than distance races, they require more intensity. Races start with an all-out time trial around the 1-kilometer (or so) courses that lasts 3 to 4 minutes per skier, with racers skiing about 20 miles per hour (at the 2009 world championships, Kikkan skied the 1.3-kilometer course at an average speed of 17 miles per hour, up hills and down). This time trial serves as a qualifier, with the top thirty finishers moving on to the sprint heats. The heats —quarterfinals, semifinals, and a final—run back to back and are all-out efforts, each again lasting 3 to 4 minutes. The top two in each quarterfinal heat move on to the semis, plus two "lucky losers" (skiers with the next fastest times in the quarterfinal heats). Then the top two from semis move on to the finals, along with two more lucky losers. By the time sprinters have finished the day—assuming they make it all the way through the finals—they have raced at or beyond their aerobic thresholds four times in one day, for a total of 12 to 16 minutes. And to keep their legs loose, they never stop skiing between heats—unless they are vomiting, which is not uncommon. The event requires both endurance and power.

"Cross-country skiing places a higher demand on the cardiovascular system than any other sport, bar none," wrote Pete Vordenberg in his book, *Momentum: Chasing the Olympic Dream.* "Humans are bipedal creatures—we use only our two legs for locomotion. Our internal energy systems expect to supply energy to the legs for moving and the arms for working, but not both the arms, legs, and whole trunk for hauling you across the snow at great speed. Cross-country skiing uses the whole body all at once, hard, for a long time. . . . Our quadrupedal mode of transportation doubles the load on the cardiovascular system and so the investment of time required in years and hours to develop the physiology to be strong enough to support high-level racing is long."

So what attracts people to this brutal sport? And what keeps them in it? For starters, it's exhilarating and calming at the same time. Skiers can fly along trails, achieving automobile speeds on the downhills. Yet gliding through the forest, quiet and still with winter's cold, is serene. The movement of cross-country skiing, with its alternate poling and gliding over the snow, is both energizing and meditative, almost yoga-like in flow. For the best cross-country skiers, there's a sense of accomplishment from being able to travel along the trail faster than anyone else, and a sense of satisfaction from mastering a difficult sport. As Jessie Diggins would say after the seven-stage Tour de Ski in 2017, "It's the challenge of doing something so hard that most people in the world can't or won't do it. When you're standing at the top, you feel this huge sense of hard-earned accomplishment and say, 'Hey, I did that.'"

Most Olympic medalists in the sport are in their late twenties. They started cross-country skiing when they were very young and then began training seriously in their teens. Norway's Marit Bjørgen, for example, did not win her first individual Olympic medal until she was twenty-six years old, and she didn't win any of her six Olympic gold medals until she was almost thirty in 2010. And Canadian Beckie Scott was twenty-eight years old when she won her first Olympic medal in 2002.

This level of success is only achieved if a cross-country skier's physiology can handle the load of high-level training and racing. By the time cross-country skiers on the elite path are in their late teens, they are training 550 to 700 hours per year. The best cross-country skiers in the world train upwards of 750 to 900 hours per year, with a few notable exceptions. One of Norway's top female racers logs over 900 hours each year, while a male teammate trains over 1,100 hours annually. Considering that a 40-hour workweek is a total of 1,040 hours worked per year, this means that these two Norwegians are training about seven hours per day, six days a week (or eight hours, five days a week). It's an astonishing amount of work.

So why doesn't everyone who wishes to compete with the best in the world train this much? Because in order to make gains from training, athletes' bodies must absorb the workload. And many break down from high volumes of training. Muscles get micro-tears that don't heal, tendons become inflamed, any slight skeletal misalignment leads to strained muscles and tendonitis, and many people become so fatigued that they cannot recover. They train themselves into the ground. In other words, more does not always equal better when it comes to training volumes. The athletes who can handle huge training volumes have a rare gift.

"What we see in cross-country is that somewhere between 500 to

550 to 600 hours is a breaking point for a lot of human beings, physically," said head coach Chris Grover. "You can absorb training up to that point. But you are a very talented special piece of physiology if you can go beyond that and really absorb training and thrive from it. At some point, increased training tends to break people down. There's a reason that most athletes on the World Cup train somewhere between the 750- to 850-hour level. That seems to be the threshold of where the best people in the world tend to thrive, where it builds them up to where, if provided with adequate recovery and rest, they can actually ski fast. Beyond that, it seems to be where people's bodies start falling apart. They have chronic injuries, chronic fatigue syndrome, constant illness. The human body at some point is not benefitting from added training."

The chronic injuries and illness are what often sideline promising careers. Overuse injuries such as tendinitis, stress fractures from running, and a very painful condition called compartment syndrome, where fluid pressure builds up in muscle fascia in the lower leg and cuts off the blood supply to the muscle, can derail cross-country ski careers for weeks, months, and sometimes years. Some chronic injuries develop because athletes are not making the required movements correctly, or their skeletons are slightly misaligned, or they have muscle imbalances, and the repetitive motions of training for many hours over many years can gradually lead to injuries. For example, cross-country skiers might develop overuse injuries in their shoulders or backs because their core muscles are weak, which overworks other shoulder and back muscles. Or they might develop knee issues because tight muscles in their hips or thighs cause imbalances in their legs and tracking problems with their knees. As APU coach Erik Flora said, "A lot of [cross-country skiers] come from backgrounds where they learn to move in a certain way that doesn't have a long-term health benefit. It works great until you're about twenty-one, twenty-two, or twenty-three years old. Then everything starts to break down." Many of these imbalances can be corrected. But it takes time, patience, commitment, an adequate support system (coach, physical therapist, chiropractor, masseuse, etc.), and belief.

Athletes also adapt differently to altitude training, where they are asking their bodies to train at a high level, but with less oxygen to fuel the effort. At sea level, the air contains about 20.9 percent effective oxygen. But at 7,000 feet, there is 25 percent less oxygen in the air. Hard, fast efforts during training are more difficult at altitude; longer, slower training sessions are easier to handle.

"It takes very careful training and more of an anomalous engine to really benefit from and sustain high-altitude training for long periods of time," said Matt Whitcomb. "It takes periodization, or blocks of high- and low-altitude training, and we were spending too much time up high. For some athletes, it was too much. This was a mistake I made."

Illness can have an equally devastating effect on any athlete's career. With their bodies pushed to extremes and struggling to recover from repeated hard efforts, cross-country skiers' immune systems have a difficult time fending off viruses and infections that are rampant in winter—and on airplanes. And when they do become ill, athletes often don't rest adequately before returning to training and racing. They don't want to lose the fitness that they worked so hard to build, and fitness quickly falls off over a week's time. Or an obsession with maintaining fitness can prevent them from getting adequate rest. A simple cold can progress to a sinus infection. A cough can become bronchitis. Sometimes, viruses such as mononucleosis can linger for months, leaving skiers feeling too rundown to train or even get off the couch. Unable to do much other than rest, athletes can't participate in the sport that they love—that has defined them since their youth. Morale can quickly tank.

The demands of life can also derail athletes. For athletes who have not yet made the A team, the demands of raising money—filling out grant applications, preparing proposals, organizing fundraisers, and asking benefactors for money—can be exhausting and distracting. Cross-country ski racing also requires an almost monastic lifestyle, with strict adherence to time-consuming training schedules, diet, and rest, which leaves little time or energy for outside pursuits, such as jobs, relationships, or a social life. Athletes often feel pressure to earn money or get out of debt, or they want to start a family. Or they find other satisfying interests, especially if they are in college. It takes complete commitment and belief in oneself to stay focused on an elite cross-country ski career. It also takes a degree of luck. Only a few stay committed and are able to successfully navigate the pitfalls over the years. Attrition from illness, injury, and the demands of life can take its toll.

This attrition was apparent when the U.S. Ski Team announced its roster for the 2010 season. Only six skiers met the objective criteria that had been laid out to make the U.S. Ski Team. The objective criteria stated that athletes would be selected to the 2010 U.S. Cross-Country Ski Team if they attained a top-fifty ranking in the 2009 final World Cup overall or FIS distance points list; or attained a top-thirty ranking in the 2009 final World Cup sprint ranking list, FIS sprint points list, or 2009 final World Cup distance ranking. Four skiers qualified using these criteria, three men and one woman: Andy Newell, Kris Freeman, Torin Koos, and Kikkan Randall. Two others—Liz Stephen and Morgan Arritola—were added to the team by coaches' discretion.

The good news was that Liz and Morgan were promoted to the A team and would join Kikkan. It was the first time in almost a decade that more than one woman had been named to the A team. The bad news: the selection criteria also included several stipulations concerning team status. One of those stipulations stated that athletes who had been on the team for three years without measurable and appropriate performance improvement would not be chosen without approval. Many factors worked against their improvement, including—ironically—too much training. Tazlina Mannix started out well on the team and was ranked second in the U.S. by the end of 2007—and first in distance points. Skiing was an emotional outlet for her, and by the end of 2009, her results began to slip. She had overtrained, pushing her body farther than it wanted to go. The result: She was ill much of the time. She would take time off, feel better and start training again, just to slide back into exhaustion and illness. By the Olympic season, she struggled to finish in the top ten at SuperTour races. She did not make the 2010 Olympic team and, once dropped from the ski team, it was hard to even consider the training required to get renamed.

"It makes you not believe in yourself when the U.S. Ski Team doesn't believe in you," said Taz.

Illness and injury also took a toll. Lindsay Williams had undergone surgery for compartment syndrome in both legs in the spring of 2008 just to have the symptoms return in 2009. This time, doctors found the real cause of her leg pain: popliteal artery entrapment syndrome. Her muscles were strangling the arteries running down her legs. She had surgery again in 2009. After moving to Park City that summer to train full time with the team, she hoped that she would make the 2010 Olympic team. She knew it was her last straw. "I'll do whatever they say until it fails," she said.

Living on the edge of poverty also grew old. At the time, sponsorships in cross-country skiing were rare, and many of the women had little idea how to identify or approach a potential sponsor. After she moved to Park City to train full time, Lindsay Williams could not find a job; between training camps and races, she simply was not in town for long enough stretches to hold down employment.

"I was dirt poor, living out of my car or in people's basements, and I had all these injuries," she said. "I was pretty low in my mental state at that point."

"I don't need to be rich," she added. "But having to worry about money that much and paying for plane tickets to Alaska at $1,500 each time, it's draining on you."

After 2010 nationals in Alaska, when it was apparent that she would not make the team competing in Vancouver, Lindsay changed her airline ticket and flew home to Minnesota rather than back to Utah. Her car was still in Park City, but she needed a break, and she needed to take care of her body. Her legs still hurt badly.

"I was over it," she said.

After she returned to Minnesota, she had four more surgeries in a span of five months. In the spring, her father flew to Utah on business and drove home with her car. Shortly after that, Lindsay entered culinary school.

In retrospect, Matt Whitcomb realized that he should have worked with this group of developing athletes differently. These skiers were some of the most talented athletes he had ever coached, and he acknowledged that he failed them, calling the coaching knowledge that he had between 2006 and 2010 "bush league." They were taking athletes with different physiologies and training them the same way. People handle training stressors, such as high altitude, differently, and back then, the prevailing coaching wisdom was that what was good for one athlete was good for everyone.

"There was a lack of training knowledge, a lack of how to handle altitude, a lack of our ability to utilize all of USSA's resources like sports science and nutrition," he said.

Looking at the skiers' results since they were named to the team three seasons prior, the U.S. coaches began to realize that the model they had chosen was only partially working. At the time, Pete Vordenberg told Fasterskier.com, "By a process of examining who on our team was making the most progress and who wasn't, we began adjusting the team and program structure to match the pathway most of our athletes are taking."

The team started encouraging elite skiers with their eye on international success to train full time for two years after high school graduation, then decide whether to attend college. Liz and Morgan Arritola had chosen not to attend college—as had Kikkan. They trained full time, and their results had improved dramatically over the three-year period. The athletes who had gone the college route had not shown similar improvement on an international stage. Classes competed for their time, as did the lure of training with college teammates. After she was named to the team in 2007, Rosie Brennan had felt pulled in three different directions—by the U.S. coaches, her college coaches, and her home club coach. She missed the fall and winter U.S. team camps and ended up focusing mostly on collegiate racing and junior world championships. But losing the support of the U.S. Ski Team was a big blow. When she was dropped by the U.S. Ski Team at the end of her sophomore year at Dartmouth, she was devastated. In that moment, her dream of competing at the highest level, of going to the Olympics, seemed to dissolve before her eyes. She wanted to quit skiing, but her college coaches and teammates convinced her to continue. She might not be valuable to the U.S. Ski Team, but she was a valued teammate on her college squad.

With the 2010 Olympic Winter Games approaching, it looked like the U.S. women's team would have limited numbers. But being a member of the U.S. Ski Team was not a requirement to qualify for the 2010 U.S. Olympic Team. Skiers with a top-fifty overall ranking or top thirty in either distance races or sprints on the World Cup would receive an automatic nomination to the team competing in Vancouver, no matter their status as national team members. The Olympic women's cross-country ski team could be as large as twelve skiers per gender, with additional spots filled through coaches' discretion and use of USSA's national ranking list. In other words, the early season SuperTour races and 2010 U.S. nationals would serve as de facto Olympic Trials.

Kikkan took off for Europe to race in early season World Cups, where she scored several top-thirty finishes, qualifying her for her third Olympic team. Liz and Morgan, whose specialties were distance races, joined her. Although they were less successful in scoring top-thirty finishes, they were still gaining international experience that would serve them well at an Olympic Games. The coaches would likely select them to compete in Vancouver.

Back home, battle was waging in the SuperTour races. And a new name emerged at the top of the standings, but she was not a young junior skier. Holly Brooks, a twenty-seven-year-old ski coach, won four of seven early season SuperTour and NorAm races. In the other three races, she finished second twice and fourth in the classic sprint in West Yellowstone, Montana. One of the women whom she beat was Daria Gaiazova, a World Cup competitor from Canada. Holly's story is literally the Olympic dream.

Sophie Caldwell

Jessie Diggins

Rosie Brennan

Ida Sargent

Holly Brooks

Sadie Bjornsen

Kikkan Randall

Liz Stephen

U.S. Ski Team women pose with their podium flowers and in their relay socks after a historic first-ever World Cup relay podium in Gällivare, Sweden, November 2012. Left to right: Jessie Diggins, Holly Brooks, Kikkan Randall, and Liz Stephen.

The illustration that German cartoonist Thomas Zipfel created after the U.S. women's cross-country ski team finished on the podium in the Gällivare relay.

Kikkan Randall, holding her first World Cup sprint globe, and Matt Whitcomb after the 2012 FIS Cross Country World Cup finals in Falun, Sweden.

Holly Brooks, front, reaches the turnaround point with Kikkan Randall close behind on July 4, 2011, during the Mount Marathon race in Seward, Alaska. Holly was first to the top, but Kikkan emerged a first-time winner after pulling away from Holly in the final few hundred yards of the 3½-mile run up and down the 3,022-foot peak.

Kikkan Randall crossing the finish line first in the team sprint at the 2013 FIS Nordic World Ski Championships.

Kikkan Randall and Jessie Diggins celebrate after winning the team sprint at the 2013 FIS Nordic World Ski Championships.

Kikkan Randall and Jessie Diggins celebrate with their gold medals after winning the team sprint at the 2013 FIS Nordic World Ski Championships.

Holly Brooks and Liz Stephen at the 2013 FIS Nordic World Ski Championships.

North American Women's Training Alliance (NAWTA) camp in Alaska, summer 2013. Left to right: Liz Stephen, Ida Sargent, Holly Brooks, Kikkan Randall, Sadie Bjornsen, Jessie Diggins, and Matt Whitcomb.

Jessie Diggins kisses Sophie Caldwell at the 2013 world championships.

U.S. Cross Country coaches Matt Whitcomb (left), Chris Grover (right), and APU coach Erik Flora celebrate after Jessie Diggins and Kikkan Randall win gold in the team sprint at the 2013 FIS Nordic World Ski Championships.

U.S. women's cross-country ski team at the 2014 Sochi Olympic Winter Games. Left to right: Kikkan Randall, Sadie Björnsen, Sophie Caldwell, Ida Sargent, Liz Stephen, and Jessie Diggins.

Kikkan Randall

A team cheer during the 2014 Sochi Olympic Winter Games. Left to right: Liz Stephen, Holly Brooks, Sadie Bjornsen, Sophie Caldwell, Ida Sargent, Jessie Diggins, and Kikkan Randall.

Kikkan Randall

Sophie Caldwell, Sadie Bjornsen, and Ida Sargent dressed to cheer on their teammates at the 2014 Sochi Olympic Winter Games.

Matt Whitcomb/U.S. Ski & Snowboard

Kikkan Randall leads Liz Stephen in hill bounding during the 2014 cross-country summer training camp in Alaska.

Sarah Brunson/U.S. Ski & Snowboard

Sophie Caldwell competing in the quarterfinals of the freestyle sprint at the 2014 Sochi Olympic Winter Games.

Jessie Diggins lunges at the finish to take third in the opening sprint of the Ski Tour Canada stage race in March 2016.

Kikkan Randall (front) and Liz Stephen training on the Eagle Glacier during the U.S. Cross-Country Ski Team Alaska Camp in July 2016.

Jessie Diggins and Kikkan Randall lead up a hill during a roller ski workout during a U.S. Cross-Country Ski Team October training camp at Soldier Hollow near Park City, Utah.

Coaches Chris Grover (left) and Jason Cork on Eagle Glacier during the 2016 U.S. Cross-Country Ski Team Alaska Camp.

Jessie Diggins (right) and Kikkan Randall, holding son Breck, celebrate their sprint silver and bronze medals at the 2017 FIS Nordic World Ski Championships.

Sadie Bjornsen skis out of the exchange zone during the team sprint at the 2017 FIS Nordic World Ski Championships.

Jessie Diggins outsprints Sweden's Stina Nilsson in the final meters of the team sprint at the 2017 FIS Nordic World Ski Championships.

Sadie Bjornsen kneels to hug Jessie Diggins after the pair won the bronze medal in the team sprint at the 2017 FIS Nordic World Ski Championships.

Matt Whitcomb encourages Jessie Diggins during the 4 x 5k relay at the 2017 FIS Nordic World Ski Championships in Lahti, Finland.

USA women's 4 x 5k relay team at the 2017 FIS Nordic World Ski Championships: Coach Chris Grover, Jessie Diggins, Sadie Bjornsen, Liz Stephen, Kikkan Randall, and Coach Matt Whitcomb (left to right).

Jessie Diggins and Sadie Bjornsen leap onto the podium after finishing third in the team sprint at the 2017 FIS Nordic World Ski Championships.

Kikkan Randall competes in the first leg of the 4 x 5k relay at the 2017 FIS Nordic World Championships.

USA women's 4 x 5k relay team at the 2017 FIS Nordic World Ski Championships: Jessie Diggins, Sadie Bjornsen, Liz Stephen, and Kikkan Randall (left to right).

Left to right: Liz Stephen, Ida Sargent, Sadie Bjornsen, Holly Brooks, Kikkan Randall, Rosie Brennan, Sophie Caldwell, and Jessie Diggins.

BUILDING
THE TEAM

BELIEF

World-class cross-country skiers are all very fit. They train for years and, if tested, would likely show similar physiological traits (strength, oxygen uptake, etc.). What often separates the good from the great is confidence. In sports, confidence is defined as an unshakable belief in one's own ability to win or achieve goals (such as a top-ten finish if an athlete is still working toward a win). Athletes with what sports psychologist Dr. Jim Taylor (a former alpine ski racer) describes as prime confidence—a deep, long-lasting, and resilient belief in their abilities—will stay positive, motivated, intense, focused, and emotionally in control. When training or competition becomes difficult, they are not negative. They seek out tough workouts, the stiffest competition, and other difficult challenges and see them as a route to improvement.

It's easy to feel confident when performing well. But it's also easy for confidence to flag when results falter or don't meet expectations. "What separates the best from the rest is that the best athletes are able to maintain their confidence when they're not at the top of their games," wrote Taylor in a blog post on his website titled "Confidence Matters." "By staying confident, they continue to work hard rather than give up because they know that, in time, their performance will come around."

Confidence is a skill that can be learned, said

Keep your dreams alive. Understand to achieve anything requires faith and belief in yourself, vision, hard work, determination, and dedication. Remember all things are possible for those who believe.

❋

Gail Devers, American track and field sprinter and three-time Olympic gold medalist

Taylor. But some athletes, like Kikkan, seem to have been born with it. More likely, though, they were born into families that instilled them with confidence at an early age. Even when Kikkan wasn't the best, she carried herself like the best, said her APU coach Erik Flora. She was realistic and knew that it would take years to achieve world-class success, and she maintained her belief even during the times when her results fell off or when she was injured. Only outside forces (the U.S. Ski Team not naming a women's team for the 2006 season, for instance) shook her belief. Then when the opportunity to win presented itself—when she made the sprint final at a World Cup or world championship—she had the belief that she belonged, that, like her competitors, she too was one of the best cross-country skiers in the world. She did not defer to the more decorated competitors in the race. She seized the opportunity and, like her hero Steve Prefontaine, raced aggressively at the front. Kikkan's natural optimism also helped her view disappointing performances as learning experiences, not negative reflections of her ability.

Holly Brooks is also an outgoing, naturally optimistic person who smiles easily. But by her own admission, she was a mediocre ski racer in her youth. And she would not learn true belief until she was in her twenties. In fact, she was twenty-seven years old when she realized that the 2010 Vancouver Olympics were a viable goal. And then she had less than six months to prepare.

※　※　※

Holly was born on April 17, 1982, in Seattle into a family of cross-country skiers. The family owned a remote cabin on Snoqualmie Pass, about an hour east of Seattle. The only way to reach the cabin in winter was via cross-country skis. So every winter weekend, Holly's parents would load up the car, and Holly and her younger triplet siblings would drive an hour east to the pass, then ski about 3 kilometers into the cabin. Her grandparents and uncles were also part of the party. Everyone in the family was a ski instructor—and Holly also became an instructor when she was nine years old. Every Saturday morning, they would ski out from the cabin to teach skiing at the ski area on Snoqualmie Pass, then ski back to the cabin that night, then repeat the trip on Sunday. It was the highlight of Holly's childhood.

Back at school in Seattle, she was afraid to show her uncool Nordic roots. Many of her friends were not familiar with cross-country skiing, and those who were associated it with quiet loners wearing woolen knickers. Soccer was the big sport in Seattle, and Holly played that too. But on winter weekends, as a member of the Snoqualmie Nordic Club —with her dad as her coach and her three siblings as teammates—she would travel to races in the Pacific Northwest. In 1997, when she was a freshman in high school, she qualified for Junior Olympics. She didn't know anyone else at JOS, because no one else on her small team qualified, so she had to room with a coach. She soon met other skiers in the Pacific Northwest, so her trips to JOS became less lonely. But she never did very well, usually the fortieth or fiftieth skier across the line. In the summers, she joined other teams in the Pacific Northwest for training camps but was the odd one out.

Her junior year in high school, she let her friends have a glimpse of her Nordic side. For a social studies assignment called "claim your voice," she donned her one-piece spandex race suit and roller skied down the hall. It was a bold move for a seventeen-year-old girl.

In 2000, she went to Whitman College in Walla Walla, Washington. A small liberal arts college in the eastern part of the state, Whitman had a ski team that participated in the U.S. Collegiate Ski Association nationals. USCSA is to NCAA skiing what minor league is to baseball, and Holly did well. She dominated USCSA competition, usually sweeping the sprint, classic, and freestyle races. But it was a case of a big fish in a small pond. When Whitman did participate in regular-season NCAA races in the western region—a rare occurrence given the Whitman team's limited budget and the high cost of travel to collegiate races in locations stretching from Colorado to Alaska—Holly was middle of the pack against the NCAA's European recruits. Her best race was her sophomore year. She finished eleventh in the 10-kilometer classic race at the western regionals in Alaska. Her coach, Ethan Townsend, said she was one of the most dedicated, focused athletes he had coached.

But Whitman itself is not exactly in a snow belt, and training was inconsistent. School came first, skiing second. Junior year, Holly—a sociology and environmental studies major—took part in Whitman's first "Semester in the West" program, where she met with a variety of leaders in conservation, ecology, environmental writing, and social justice, and she spent the fall camping around the western United States.

"I'd wake up at 5 or 5:30 a.m. in my sleeping bag in Dinosaur National Monument and go roller skiing before everyone else would get up," she recalled. "It wasn't ideal training."

Then senior year, she got sick. At western regionals hosted by Denver University that year, she finished near the back of the pack in one race, then dropped out of another. It was time to move on.

Holly graduated from Whitman in May 2004 and moved to Alaska that summer. She had fond memories from her one good NCAA race in Anchorage, and she was fascinated by the idea of living in a place with snow, not a city where she had to drive an hour every weekend to find snow. She had two job offers in Anchorage: outdoor program director at Alaska Pacific University, where she would lead outdoor trips for college students, or cross-country ski coach at West Anchorage High School, a seasonal part-time job that paid $3,000 total. She chose the coaching job, supplementing the meager income with a job in a ski shop.

"In everyone's lives, there are decisions you make that are so formative," she said. "What if that had never happened?"

When she interviewed for the job, she was told that the West Anchorage ski team was small. But when she started the job, over one hundred kids showed up. Rather than feeling overwhelmed, Holly was excited. She came from a town where cross-country skiing was considered weird and where people would yell and swear at her for roller skiing down the street. Now she was in a city where cross-country skiing was embraced. The West Anchorage ski team had everyone from junior national champions to foreign exchange students who had never skied. With this group, her goal was to create a really tight team. She started by having the kids hold spaghetti feeds every Friday night, and every dinner would have a theme. One time the theme was "identity theft," where kids had to dress up as someone else on the team. Another time, it was a twin theme. Each member was paired with a secret buddy whom they had to help and cheer for at the upcoming races. Then during workouts, she skied with the kids, a young, energetic, effervescent woman who worked as hard as they did and smiled as she did it. It became uncool to complain and slack off, and the team got stronger and faster. By the 2005 state championship, West Anchorage skiers finished on the podium four times, with one state champion. And the boys finished second in the relay. The previous year, West skiers had not finished anywhere near the front at the state championships.

Where did the self-proclaimed mediocre junior racer learn to coach like this? Holly doesn't really know, but noted that she was the bossy older sister of triplet siblings. "I would put them through school," she said.

She had only planned to stay in Alaska for one year. So after the snow melted in Anchorage that spring, she traveled to South America for vacation. While there, she realized that she was dreaming about some of the kids on the West Anchorage High ski team. She took it as a sign; she needed to return to Alaska.

Back at West again for another season, she had to find a second job to supplement her part-time income. This time, an environmental consulting firm hired her. She had a couple of job offers but admitted that she took the one that required the fewest hours while still providing benefits. But the job ended up providing more than money; it was interesting. She traveled to New Orleans after Hurricane Katrina to assist with cleanup and was also the lead on a project to clean up unexploded ordnance in Alaska.

In March 2007, she took a few of her high school skiers to Junior Olympics held on the Soldier Hollow trails outside Park City, Utah. There, she met Erik Flora through her boyfriend Rob Whitney, a former national team cross-country skier. Flora was coaching at APU and needed help. After a coaching shake-up at APU the previous season, Flora was the new head coach with no assistants and few skiers. Would Holly join him as an APU coach?

She promptly quit the consulting job and joined APU as the masters (adult) and junior coach. Her days began with office work at APU. At noon, she would head outside to coach masters until 2 p.m., then head over to West to coach the high school kids. Then in the evening, she ran ski-training sessions for junior skiers. Not the type of coach who stands beside the trail and watches skiers, Holly skied along with whomever she was coaching, doing intervals when they did intervals, and doing distance when they skied distance. Or, if she had a night off, she would ski with her friends on Anchorage's many lighted trails. She was almost constantly on skis. But she was also having fun, thrilled to have friends who skied, then went out for a few beers and a bite to eat afterward.

The following winter, Rob convinced her to try racing again. But Holly would say no, insisting that she was a horrible ski racer. "You're better than you think," he kept insisting.

In March 2008, she finally entered the Tour of Anchorage's 50-kilometer freestyle race. A long-held point-to-point race, it starts at Service High School, winds along trails in the hills outside Anchorage, passes through APU's campus, and then travels out to the coast, where it finishes in Kincaid Park. Holly won, beating top NCAA skier Kasandra Rice. She thought it was a fluke.

Then that summer, Holly entered Mount Marathon, the suffer-fest dubbed Alaska's most famous footrace. It's a rite of passage for fit, young Alaskans (Nina Kemppel has won it nine times). Holly finished second, climbing and descending the 3,022-foot mountain in 55:29— over a minute and a half faster than Kikkan had ever finished the race. Again, she thought it a fluke. In February 2009, Holly entered the American Birkebeiner, the granddaddy of marathon cross-country skiing in the United States. She finished second in a photo finish to Rebecca Dussault, who was making another comeback after the birth of her second child and helping her husband recover from a life-threatening autoimmune disease that he developed in 2007. Again, Holly thought her performance was a fluke. At the end of the 2009 season, she entered spring nationals races, held in Anchorage that year. She finished fourth in the pursuit, 9.8 seconds behind Kikkan. A fluke again, she insisted. It was the end of the season and all the real competition was tired.

On July 4, 2009, Holly again entered Mount Marathon. On a hot day, she took the lead on the scramble up the 3,022-foot peak and held a 51-second lead at the summit and a 1-minute, 36-second lead over Kikkan, who was third to the summit. Holly was still leading as she descended into Seward. But then running along the streets of Seward toward the finish line, she passed out and collapsed onto the pavement.

Holly woke up in the emergency room. She was diagnosed with exertional rhabdomyolysis, an uncommon condition where the cell membranes in the muscles break down from extreme exertion. The result: her legs stopped working. She had literally run herself to exhaustion.

Lying in the ER, hooked up to an IV, Holly had a thought. "This sounds really corny, but I had this vision that I was going to try to make the Olympics," she said. "I had come close to doing really well in the biggest race in Alaska. That lit my competitive drive and got the athletic fire started over again."

First, though, she had to finish Mount Marathon. Only finishers can enter the race the following year, and Holly wanted to compete again. So she checked herself out of the hospital, hobbled across the finish line, and then checked back into the hospital.

Also on Holly's agenda that summer: a wedding. She and Rob married a week later, on July 11, 2009.

After Mount Marathon, she took off eight weeks to recover. Then she sat down with her boss, Erik Flora, at a picnic table in Anchorage's Kincaid Park and told him her plans.

"Erik, I think I want to try ski racing," she sheepishly admitted. Then she whispered the next part: "I kind of want to make a run for the Olympics."

Rather than laughing, Flora nodded and said okay. He had had a similar athletic past, making a comeback in cross-country skiing in 2005 with his eye on the 2006 Olympics.

When Holly stated her goal to her husband, Rob's first thought was, "Finally!"

"I wouldn't have nagged her for that long if I didn't strongly believe she could do it," he said. "I was so frustrated with the fact that I didn't make [an Olympic team]. When you see someone who has the potential to make it, you're like, 'You've got to do it, man.'"

On August 24, 2009, Holly began training with APU's Elite team when it fit into her work schedule, which was not often. Three months later, she entered the SuperTour races in West Yellowstone, winning the 10-kilometer freestyle race and finishing second in the 5-kilometer classic.

"There I was at age twenty-seven, never having won a race in my life really . . . ," she said, trailing off. "That was the first race that I truly believed. I won and that was legitimate. That was a pretty huge moment."

Over the next month, Holly won two more SuperTour races and finished on the podium in three NorAms (including one win) in every event from sprints to 10-kilometer classic races.

Then came the 2010 U.S. Cross-country Ski Championships. Top results would likely lead to an Olympic berth. Working to Holly's advantage, Anchorage was hosting the championships that year. Everyone whom she had coached came out to cheer, and someone made a "GO HOLLY!" sign and erected it on the big hill in Kincaid Park.

"There was a ton of pressure," said Holly, "but I had nothing to lose."

* * *

The 2010 nationals were also a home event for Kikkan, and she stormed through the championship, winning all four races. But her silver medal at the 2009 world championships the previous season, combined with good results on the early season World Cups, meant that Kikkan had already made the 2010 Olympic team. Liz and Morgan Arritola were also likely candidates, given their international experience, with a few top-thirty World Cup results. Vying for the other spots were Holly, who finished second to Kikkan in the 20-kilometer classic race at nationals, Laura Valaas (also a Whitman College grad); Rebecca Dussault, who was back after the birth of her second child; and Caitlin Compton, who had competed for the U.S. twice at Nordic world championships and once at biathlon worlds but whose age (twenty-nine at the time) had kept her from being named to the U.S. Ski Team. Compton was the runner-up to Kikkan in the 10-kilometer freestyle race at 2010 nationals and was third behind Kikkan and Holly in the 20-kilometer classic race. But Olympic selection no longer came down to one-race Olympic Trials. Instead, the team would be chosen based on points earned in races over the previous year. And after 2010 nationals, Kikkan and Liz were ranked first and second. Caitlin had moved from fifth to third, with Morgan fourth and Holly fifth.

On January 19, 2010, eight athletes were named to the 2010 U.S. Olympic cross-country ski team, four men and four women: Kikkan, Liz, Morgan Arritola, and Caitlin. The team was smaller than at previous Olympic Games because of quotas mandated by the IOC. But the coaches were optimistic that more spots would become available as the Olympics approached and other countries tightened their rosters.

A week later, Holly's phone rang. After nationals, she had returned to Anchorage to continue her coaching duties at APU. She was standing in her house when Pete Vordenberg called to tell her that she had been nominated to the 2010 Olympic team. She hung up the phone and drove to work, where she was scheduled to coach a noon masters group —a group of about twenty moms. Everyone was hugging her and crying. Reporters from local TV stations and newspapers showed up.

"I think I'm one of the few Olympians with a full-time job," Holly told the *Anchorage Daily News* reporter.

The next day, she flew to Canada for her first World Cup races in Canmore, Alberta. These races would serve as a warm-up for the Olympics—a way for skiers to adjust to the time change (if they were coming from Europe) and to get their legs going before the Olympic races. For Holly, it was her first international race.

"I liken it to going to the Super Bowl and playing your first NFL game the week before," she said. "It was crazy."

❄   ❄   ❄

In a perfect world, Kikkan Randall would have been a medal favorite at the Vancouver 2010 Olympic Winter Games. She was twenty-seven years old and was nine years into her ten-year plan set in motion back in high school. According to that plan, she would one day win an Olympic medal. There was just one problem. The sprint at the Vancouver Games was a classic sprint. So far, Kikkan had only won medals in freestyle sprints, the technique that best suited her powerful build and aggressive style. The closest that she had come to the podium in a World Cup classic sprint was seventh, and she had only finished that high in results once. Chances were better that Andy Newell would win an Olympic medal in Vancouver. He had been on the U.S. Ski Team for eight years and had collected a couple handfuls of top-ten finishes in World Cup classic sprints. But Kikkan could not change the Olympic program. So she set realistic goals for her third Olympic Games. She would consider the Games a success if she finished top twelve in the classic sprint and top six in the team sprint, which was slated as a freestyle race. A top-twelve finish would mean that she made the semi-finals in the classic sprint; a top-six finish in the team sprint would mean that she and her teammate would qualify for the final.

Although nationals in Anchorage had gone well for Kikkan in early January, the Canmore World Cup races, held in a stunning mountain valley west of Calgary at the beginning of February as a warm-up for the Vancouver Olympics, were "less than ideal," she wrote on a blog for SkiTrax magazine. In the 10-kilometer freestyle race, she finished forty-fourth and was the fifth American across the finish line behind Caitlin, Morgan, Holly, and Liz. The classic sprint the next day went better for Kikkan but was far from encouraging. She qualified twenty-second (right behind Holly and almost 16 seconds out of the lead). It was good enough to qualify her for the quarterfinal heats. Then she made the semifinals but did not advance to the finals, finishing tenth.

"It took a lot of mental strength and confidence to ignore the results and feelings from Canmore, and stay positive that everything would come together in Whistler," she wrote for SkiTrax.

From Canmore, the team flew to Vancouver. Olympic Nordic competition started in earnest for the Americans on Valentine's Day with Nordic combined. In the normal hill ski-jumping portion of Nordic combined, Todd Lodwick jumped 101.5 meters and landed in second place. At 100.5 meters, Johnny Spillane sat in fourth. Lodwick would start the 10-kilometer ski race that afternoon 34 seconds behind Janne Ryynänen from Finland, and Spillane would start another 10 seconds later. The two Americans quickly found themselves in a four-man pack at the front of the race, with Lodwick at the front pushing the pace. People who did not even know what Nordic combined was stopped to watch TV. As the four men raced toward the finish line, the American Nordic community held its breath. Jason Lamy-Chappuis from France claimed the gold medal with Spillane lunging across the line 0.4 second behind him. His silver medal would be the first ever won by an American skier in Nordic combined. Lodwick finished fourth and missed out on an Olympic medal by 0.6 second. Italy's Alessandro Pittin won the bronze. And Billy Demong came in sixth for his best Olympic finish to date.

The Olympic cross-country competition started a day later with the women's 10-kilometer and men's 15-kilometer freestyle races. Kikkan decided to sit out this race to rest for the sprint. While Sweden's Charlotte Kalla won her first Olympic gold medal, Caitlin Compton was the top finisher for the American women, coming in thirtieth.

On a sunny Wednesday on the trails at the Whistler Olympic Park, the sprint day started well for the U.S. cross-country team. Before the sprint qualifier, Kikkan did not feel great. But once she was on course, she felt "more fresh and strong" than she had all season. Kikkan qualified tenth, giving her a spot in a quarterfinal heat. But in the men's sprint qualifier, American medal hopes were dashed when Andy Newell, who had finished fifth in the classic sprint at the world championships a year before, crashed on a downhill corner during his qualifier. He got up and finished but not quickly enough. He was 5 seconds from qualifying for the quarterfinals, ending his day in forty-fifth place.

"It was really heartbreaking," said Pete Vordenberg. "He was super ready. We had a legitimate hope we could have something really good happen, but it wasn't enough."

The only American male to make it to the quarterfinals was recent Middlebury College graduate Simi Hamilton, who qualified twenty-ninth. It was Simi's first Olympics, and he did not advance beyond his quarterfinal heat.

At 12:30 p.m., the sprint quarterfinals began. For most of Kikkan's heat, her medal hopes did not look good. Marit Bjørgen, who had qualified first, kept the pace fast, with those in her quarterfinal heat scrambling to keep up. The six women in the heat were strung out, with Kikkan sitting in fourth. Only the top two would advance. If she finished any lower than second, she would only advance to the semis if her heat was fast, and she was a "lucky loser." Coming into the stadium, Kikkan dove inside on a steep downhill corner and moved into third, a position that she held until the finish line. She then nervously watched the next four heats, hoping her time would make her a lucky loser. She ended up advancing to the semifinals by 0.3 second.

Kikkan was not as lucky in her semifinal heat. She skied as hard as she could and moved from sixth to fourth. But it was not enough to make it to the finals. She ended up eighth overall—one place better than her sprint finish in the 2006 Torino Olympics. But she had met her goal. She had qualified for the semifinal in the classic sprint—something she had only done once before at the international level, and that was at the Canmore World Cup eleven days earlier.

"My goal was to try to make it to the semis, and I did," she said with a smile. "To qualify tenth, then to finish eighth was a huge success for me."

"It was Kikkan's best classic sprint ever and Simi's best classic sprint ever, so those are the highlights," Pete Vordenberg told USA Today.

Bjørgen ended up winning the gold medal in the final ahead of Poland's Justyna Kowalczyk, the overall World Cup leader. Slovenia's Petra Majdic, who led Kowalczyk in the World Cup sprint standings that year, was a favorite. But she crashed while warming up for the race and qualified nineteenth, then edged out Anna Olsson from Sweden for the bronze medal.

Kikkan's next race was the team sprint, a freestyle race held five days later, on a sun-splashed day that felt like T-shirt weather. She would be paired with Caitlin, and the six-leg team race was wild from the start. In their qualifying race—a semifinal of nine teams, with only the top three automatically moving on—the Norwegians and Swedes quickly skied away from the other teams. Through the first five laps, Canada, Slovenia, and the U.S. were in the mix for third place. On the bell lap, Kikkan found an extra gear and passed both Slovenia and Canada. By the final stretch through the stadium, Kikkan had so much momentum that she almost finished the semifinal in second place. It was good enough to put Kikkan and Caitlin into the team sprint final.

But at the start of the final, luck was not with them. On the first hill, Caitlin fell. She had been following the coaches' advice to stay right on the hill. But then she saw an opening and moved left. Right after she made the move, the skiers on the right fell. When one of the women stood up, she stepped in front of Caitlin and took down the American.

"It was bad luck, kind of a bummer," said Caitlin after the race. "I thought I had it done, but in the end, you learn that you should have listened to the coaches and stayed right. That pileup definitely put us back and kind of changed our game plan from being in the thick of it to having to play catch-up."

Caitlin lost the lead pack, then neither Kikkan nor Caitlin could bridge the gap to the leaders in their ensuing laps. The mishap took them out of the mix immediately, and they remained in eighth place for much of the race.

But on the final lap, Kikkan felt good and started charging after the racers in front of her. She passed Finland and Canada and crossed the finish line in sixth place behind Germany, Sweden, Russia, Italy, and Norway. It was the best American finish in an Olympic team event, one place better than the U.S. women finished in the 4 x 5-kilometer relay in the 1980 and 1984 Olympic Games. Even without a medal, Kikkan and Caitlin considered it a success.

"This is really good confidence for what we'll be able to do over the next four years," said Kikkan, with her perpetual optimism.

Three days after the team sprint—and a day after the American Nordic combined team won a silver medal in their team event—Kikkan led off the 4 x 5-kilometer relay at the Whistler Olympic Park. The course was a 2.5-kilometer loop where each skier came through the stadium twice. After starting in fourteenth position, Kikkan worked her way up to third on her first lap. On the second lap, she was feeling good, so she charged over the top of one of the hills and took the lead on the downhill.

"Holy cow, I'm leading the Olympic relay," she thought. "All this stuff I'd always watched on TV, I'm doing it!"

She tagged off to Holly in fourth and was right with the leaders. But Holly fell back to twelfth. Morgan skied the third leg and fell back one more spot. Then skiing anchor, Caitlin pulled the team back into twelfth. (In official results, they ended up eleventh after Poland was disqualified for doping.) Caitlin crossed the line alone, without her teammates at the finish to cheer, although Liz had been out on the course dressed as a superhero and cheering for her teammates. Caitlin called it the worst moment in her ski career. Kikkan, Holly, and Morgan were all racing the 30-kilometer classic race in two days. They needed to warm down properly and rest.

Despite how far back the team had finished—3:38 minutes, even farther back than at the 2006 Olympics—Kikkan was optimistic, in part because she had been so successful on her leg of the relay. "That was a glimpse that our relay has a shot," she said. "Because if I can get in there on the first leg and we develop these other girls, we can be in there."

That afternoon, in the final Nordic combined event at the 2010 Olympics, Billy Demong and Johnny Spillane won the gold and silver medals in the large hill competition—a jump off the 140-meter ski jump followed by a 10-kilometer cross-country race. It was an unprecedented triumph for a small team in a sport dominated for decades by much better-funded European teams. The American Nordic combiners had such a low budget that one year at a summer training camp in Germany, their coach had housed them in a mental institution. It was the cheapest place to stay in town. It was also a tribute to the power of teamwork. Buoyed by Todd Lodwick's World Cup wins in the 1990s, Billy Demong and Johnny Spillane grew up believing that they could do it, too. They lived and trained together for more than two-thirds of the year. And one man's triumph was the entire team's.

"If they can do it, we can do it!" Kikkan wrote in her blog for SkiTrax.

With Nordic combined's four medals, plus eight medals won by the alpine skiers, four by freestyle skiers, and five by the American snowboarders, USSA achieved its "Best in the World" vision. The twenty-one medals won by USSA athletes was more than double the amount won at the previous best Olympic Winter Games (ten medals in 2002), and it comprised over half of the thirty-seven medals won by American athletes at the 2010 Vancouver Games. The next closest country was Norway, with sixteen medals won in snowsports. With few of these medal-winning snowsport athletes retiring, it looked like USSA athletes would ride the "Best in the World" vision to the 2014 Sochi Winter Games.

Kikkan concluded her blog post by writing: "For me, this is not the end. I see this Olympics as the beginning of the next four years. I feel like the U.S. team is getting closer to the medals all the time. In Sochi, there will be another shot at a skate sprint. I hope to be competitive in the other distances as well. Along the way there are also a world championships in Oslo in 2011, a world championships in Val di Fiemme in 2013, and plenty of World Cup races to test myself against the best in the world."

It was optimism in the face of what seemed like huge odds. For an athlete with a specialty like Kikkan (the freestyle sprint), the chance for an Olympic medal comes down to one day every eight years (with the sprint alternating between classic and freestyle in each Winter Olympiad). So much can happen on that one day. And until that point, Kikkan had only competed in thirty-four World Cup and five world championship sprints, finishing on the podium in only three of them—a success rate of less than 8 percent. Her belief in her ability was unshakable, and she ended her blog post with this: "The best of the journey is yet to come!"

*   *   *

Two weeks after the 2010 Olympics concluded, Kikkan backed up her belief with results. It was a freestyle sprint in Oslo, Norway, and going by results, Kikkan was not a favorite. She had not even qualified for the heats in a World Cup sprint the previous week. And she had not qualified for a sprint final at an international race in more than a year. The closest she had come was making the semifinals at the Vancouver Olympic Games (which led to her eighth-place finish there). But she had kept the faith. On a sunny March day at a World Cup freestyle sprint held in Oslo's famed Holmenkollen stadium—which has hosted ski competitions since 1892 and is almost a shrine to cross-country skiing —she qualified eighth, then worked her way through the heats. In the final, she lined up with five other women, including Marit Bjørgen and Justyna Kowalczyk, who had won the gold and silver Olympic medals, respectively, in Vancouver three weeks earlier. At the time, Kowalczyk, from Poland, was the defending overall World Cup champion and was also ahead in the sprint standings.

Kikkan did not care who was in the final of the 1.3-kilometer sprint with her. She took the early lead. Then Kowalczyk pulled ahead on the first downhill. But Kikkan stayed with the Polish skier even after she tripped on Kowalczyk's ski on an uphill and briefly lost momentum. The two were skate skiing side by side as they climbed, and on one of her strides, Kowalczyk's ski crossed Kikkan's. The American finally moved back into the lead on a long downhill near the finish. She held the lead into the finish stretch, when Bjørgen slipped by on her left. But Kikkan held on for second place. It was her first World Cup podium in over two years and her first time back in the top three in an international ski race since the world championships the year before, when she had won a silver medal in the freestyle sprint.

The Oslo World Cup podium finish catapulted Kikkan into the 2010–2011 season—her tenth year as a fully committed professional ski racer—and she started finishing more consistently near the front of sprint races. At an early season FIS freestyle sprint in Finland in mid-November 2010, she won, beating Slovenian Petra Majdic—sprint bronze medalist at the 2010 Olympics—and Kowalczyk. A month later, she finished second in a World Cup sprint in Dusseldorf, Germany. From then until the end of the World Cup season, she finished on the podium in four more sprint races, winning twice. And she made it into the semifinals in five other World Cup sprints. The only downside to her 2011 season was the world championships, where she qualified ninth for the sprint heats. But then in her quarterfinal, she caught her ski on either Charlotte Kalla or Ida Ingemarsdotter's ski on a downhill and spun out, ending her hope for a second world championship medal.

"I'm not exactly sure what happened," Kikkan told SkiTrax magazine. "One moment everything was going fine, and the next moment I was sailing down the trail backwards. I think my ski got hooked by the Swede, and it just spun me around. There was a lot of contact out on the course today. Definitely a bummer because I was feeling really strong today and ready to go. I knew the key today was going to be staying out of trouble, and unfortunately I wasn't able to do that."

Kikkan finished the season ranked third overall in World Cup sprinting—her best ranking yet—and she won five races in the spring SuperTour series held in Sun Valley that year, in race distances from 1.3-kilometer sprints to the 10-kilometer. Winning begets winning. She belonged at the front with the world's best sprinters; it had just taken a while to get there. Patience and perseverance had paid off. That summer, she asked one of the Norwegian women if she could come train with them for a couple of weeks. On her way to Norway, she attended FIS meetings in Switzerland (Kikkan was named an athlete representative to FIS in 2009) and met a Swedish friend, who offered to host her the following summer.

Kikkan's belief began to carry over to those around her. Liz started moving up in World Cup results. After struggling through a tough 2010 Olympics, she returned in November 2010 to score her first top-thirty finish in a World Cup; in Gällivare, she finished twenty-fifth in a 10-kilometer freestyle race. A month later, she finished eighteenth in a 15-kilometer freestyle mass start. Then at 2011 world championships, Liz scored two top-thirty finishes at 2011 worlds—including sixteenth place in the 30-kilometer freestyle mass-start race—despite suffering from bursitis in her right heel. It was the best American result at that distance in international competition since Nina Kemppel's fifteenth place in the 30-kilometer classic race at the 2002 Olympics nine years earlier.

Then there was Holly Brooks, who not only believed that she could beat Kikkan Randall but had also actually beaten her—in Alaska's Mount Marathon footrace. Holly was second to the summit of Mount Marathon during the 2009 race, 2 seconds behind eventual leader Cedar Bourgeois and over a minute ahead of Kikkan, before she collapsed near the finish and ended her day in the hospital. And in the 2010 Mount Marathon—held just over four months after the Vancouver Olympics—Holly finished second for the women in a blistering time of 51:58. She was about 1:30 ahead of Kikkan, who came in third in 53:29. Those races helped Holly develop the belief that she was just as fit as Kikkan. And using the associative property, if Kikkan could beat the best skiers in the world and land on the podium, then Holly could beat them as well. She also brought with her the positivity and determination that she had tried to instill in her West Anchorage High School team, as well as the APU juniors and masters racers whom she coached. Those traits were perhaps contagious.

At age twenty-eight, Holly's elite ski career should have either been wrapping up or been well underway, not just starting. As Caitlin Compton had discovered, the U.S. Ski Team was not interested in investing in a racer that elderly. But Holly was undeterred.

"I definitely had a little chip on my shoulder because I knew I was old," she said. "I'm very familiar with the graph of the development pipeline. Most people do fall in that progression. I just happened to be the outlier. That was difficult for me, because I knew that the coaches had that development pipeline in the backs of their minds. But I feel like I hadn't really tried yet."

Although she had missed competing in the post-2010 Olympic World Cups in Europe (because she had committed to coaching the APU junior skiers at Junior Olympics in Fort Kent, Maine, in March that year, and she already felt guilty for abandoning them while she competed in the Olympics), she raced in the end-of-season national distance championships and the spring SuperTour series in Maine after coaching at the 2010 Junior Olympics. She finished third in the 30-kilometer freestyle race at distance nationals, less than 2 seconds behind Kikkan and only 0.6 second behind Rebecca Dussault. Holly wrapped up the SuperTour with three top-five finishes.

Determined to earn her way back to international competition, Holly stormed through the early season SuperTour and NorAm races in November and December 2010, winning three by decisive margins and finishing in the top three four more times. Then in January 2011, in cloudy, gray, snowless Rumford, Maine—skiing round and round on a short loop of man-made snow—Holly won her first national title. She followed up that result with two more SuperTour wins in Lake Placid, New York, in mid-January and was named to her first world championship team. With that nomination, she was granted entry into World Cup races before the world championships in Oslo. From mid-February until early April, she kept up a relentless schedule, competing in at least one race every weekend. At worlds in Oslo, she competed in three distance races, finishing in the top thirty in all three. And she finally finished in the points in the season-ending World Cup, a stage race in Falun, Sweden, in mid-March.

The 2011 season's World Cup tour may have ended, but Holly kept skiing. Working outside the umbrella of the U.S. Ski Team, she had to fund her dream on her own. And if she kept the SuperTour lead, she would not only earn a World Cup berth for the following season, but FIS would cover her travel costs for the season's first World Cups held before Christmas (known as period one). The organization covers World Cup travel costs for continental cup leaders for one (of four) periods if they are not on their country's national teams, a cost than can run up to 125 Swiss francs, or about $120, per night. If Holly could do well enough to move into the "red group" (the top thirty ranked skiers on the World Cup), FIS would continue to cover her travel costs for the rest of the season. But she knew that a place on the start line at World Cups was tenuous. Those without the support of the U.S. team were typically short-timers. So why would anyone invest time in pulling them into the team fabric?

"There's sometimes a weird vibe when you're the SuperTour leader and you come in; you're like this insider outsider," she said, two years after she retired from the team. "You're not part of the team, but you're with the team. But everyone knows it's temporary. And it's a test. If you do well, you might be invited to stay. But most people historically just flounder. They aren't able to score [World Cup] points, [and] they don't have very good races. Maybe they are racing to their potential, and they aren't used to that level of competition, or maybe they are really racing below what they would normally do. Everyone debates about that. Did you really have a bad race? If you'd had that same race in the U.S., you would have won and felt great. But here, you're racing against [the best in the world]. It was still a great race for you, but you finish sixty-seventh. You're treading lightly when you're in that position because you don't want to take too many resources from the team."

Still, Holly maintains that everyone on the U.S. Ski Team welcomed her from the start and made her feel invited. She knew that her age put her outside the graph of the development pipeline; the U.S. Ski Team wanted to invest in younger racers with years of potential, not someone who was about to turn thirty. But she maintained a good perspective and tried to focus on improving, not on what might hold her back.

"Matt's like a mother hen, for lack of a better term," she explained. "His girls are his girls. I think a lot of people go in [to their first World Cup] expecting it to be horrible, then it is horrible, and it becomes this evolving ball of disbelief in themselves. I'm used to being the weird chicken, so it was okay. Granted, I still wanted to be a normal chicken."

She returned to the United States to finish the 2011 SuperTour season. In Sun Valley, Idaho, she placed no lower than fourth in five races and held on to the SuperTour lead. It was not easy competing at the highest level in the world without the U.S. Ski Team's support. But with persistence, dogged determination, and the support of the APU team and her sponsors, including local businesses in Alaska, Holly was showing that it was possible.

"Everyone says it's so impossible, there's no route to the U.S. Ski Team [when you are older]," she said. "Yeah, there is. I'm not saying it's easy, but it's doable."

While Holly was skiing her way to the top of the American ranks, three other young American skiers were starting to show promise on the senior level: Jessie Diggins, Sadie Bjornsen, and Ida Sargent. Jessie was nineteen at the time and less than a year out of high school. Sadie was twenty-one and had almost given up cross-country ski racing a year earlier. It was a pleasant surprise when both qualified for the sprint quarterfinals at the 2011 world championships. Ida also competed at the world championships in Oslo. A twenty-three-year-old student at Dartmouth, Ida had finished fourth in the sprint at the U23 world championships the previous year. These three women had recently decided to give elite ski racing a go. Their solid finishes at their first senior world championships made the future look bright for the U.S. women's cross-country ski team. As Kikkan told SkiTrax magazine after the 2011 world championship sprint, "Great to see the younger girls getting their first taste of the big time."

TALENT

Looking back over Kikkan Randall's ascent in the ski world, many factors came together to help her create a successful ski career. She was a talented athlete born into a family and raised in a community that supported and encouraged her. She worked insanely hard with good coaches, had strong personal belief, and had the right attitude to stay on course even when results did not easily come her way. She was also a member of the APU Nordic Ski Team, and the role of this program—and others like it that formed in the twenty-first century—cannot be overstated.

The APU Nordic Ski Center started under Jim Galanes in the late 1990s as a regional Olympic training center for cross-country skiers. Now led by Erik Flora, the program accepts elite skiers who board on campus, train with the APU coaches, and travel to races—funded by the APU program (with funding coming from coaching fees paid by the hundreds of juniors, masters, and up-and-coming skiers in the club, as well as sponsors and donors).

In addition to APU, two other clubs became primary feeders for the U.S. Ski Team: the Craftsbury Green Racing Project (CGRP) and the Stratton Mountain School T2 Team (SMS T2), both located in Vermont. Founded in 2009, CGRP is based at the Craftsbury Outdoor Center, a ski touring and rowing center started in 1975 by Russell Spring and purchased by Dick and Judy Dreissigacker

An athlete cannot run with money in his pockets. He must run with hope in his heart and dreams in his head.

❋

Emil Zátopek, Czech long-distance runner and four-time Olympic gold medalist

in 2008. The Dreissigackers are both Olympic rowers who coached at the Outdoor Center in the late 1970s after they brought their company, Concept 2, an oar-building and ergometer manufacturing business, to nearby Morrisville, Vermont. Members of the CGRP live at the Outdoor Center and earn their keep by participating in projects for both the center and the community, such as gardening, running ski clinics for the public, or helping to design and build installations at the center, such as solar panels or a new ski lodge.

In southern Vermont, Sverre Caldwell, the director of Nordic programs at the Stratton Mountain School and John Caldwell's son, had long dreamed of offering a full spectrum of development programs at the school, from the local BKL programs that foster elementary-school-aged skiers, to SMS's high school program, to the elite team for postgraduate skiers who dream of competing at the highest levels. He founded the SMS T2 team in 2012 after his oldest daughter, Sophie, graduated from Dartmouth and wanted to see where skiing would take her. It's named after both the school and the T2 Foundation, an organization that began in 2008 to support promising ski racers. Like APU and Craftsbury, SMS T2 provides housing and coaching, as well as a yearly stipend to help the elite skiers pay for the cost of living. For additional financial support, skiers write proposals for sponsorships and grants. Those not yet on the A team can also receive funding from the National Nordic Foundation, a nonprofit founded in 1997 to help cover the expenses of developing Nordic skiers.

These regional ski clubs have become incubators for budding skiers and homes for the nation's top skiers in the off-season so that they can make ski racing their job. During the off-season, elite skiers train with —and are pushed by—their club teammates. It's a system based on the Scandinavian model, where home clubs foster young skiers and support their development in an endurance sport that can take skiers years to mature—the best female cross-country skiers in the world are in their late twenties and early thirties. (This model was also used in the United States in the 1970s, with the Lyndon Nordic Training Center in northern Vermont, but LNTC dissolved in 1979 due to lack of financial support.)

Key to the success of these clubs in fostering elite cross-country skiers, the coaches began to communicate and work well with the national team coaches, as if they are all in the same program. When skiers leave the clubs to attend U.S. Ski Team camps, all the athletes are on the same program working toward the same goal.

"The relationship between club coaches and national team coaches has come a long way," said Matt. "We treat each other with respect now. Rather than working exclusively toward the success of our own team or athletes, or our own careers, we work toward the success of the nation. A successful national team camp means that we all have to let go of the reins a bit, so we can create not the perfect workout for one or two athletes, but the most productive training environment for everyone. We coaches are at our best when our egos are suppressed."

Gaining entry to these elite clubs requires good results and an even better attitude. It also requires commitment to a life where everything is secondary to a focused goal. It's like going to medical school, except without the promise of a lifelong, profitable career. Despite the odds, a few dozen commit each year, determined to see where their athletic talent can take them, and the clubs have increased the pool of skiers with potential to make the U.S. Ski Team.

❋   ❋   ❋

For Sadie Bjornsen, joining the APU Nordic Ski Team saved her ski career. During the winter of 2010, she had almost given up cross-country skiing; she just wasn't having any fun anymore. Bedeviled by tendonitis, she had had a less-than-stellar collegiate season in 2009, and then she failed to make the 2010 Olympic Team—a long shot, but it still hurt not to make it. After a decade of ski racing, she wanted to move on with her life—finish her college degree at the University of Alaska-Anchorage and then start a career in business or accounting. It was a big change from her youth, when sports were the focus of her life. Her real passion back then was swimming. She grew up thinking Michael Phelps was "the greatest thing in the world." She was convinced that if she swam fast enough, she would meet the legendary swimmer one day.

But she had grown up in Winthrop, Washington, on the eastern side of the Cascade Range. It's not exactly a hotbed of swimming. Winthrop —or rather, the whole Methow Valley (pronounced "met-how")—is home to the nation's largest cross-country ski area, with nearly 200 kilometers of groomed trails. Sadie's parents—both alpine skiers—had moved to the Methow, as it's called, from Jackson Hole, Wyoming, in the mid-1980s on speculation that the area was on the verge of becoming the next big ski resort like Jackson Hole or Sun Valley. But after Sadie's older sister Kaley was born, then Sadie, then Erik, all within four years of each other, the family started cross-country skiing. It was more convenient than alpine skiing; the nearest alpine ski area was located an hour and a half from the Bjornsens' home. Besides, cross-country skiing seemed to go better with their Norwegian last name, and Sadie even looks the part—a tall blonde with Nordic heritage on both her mom's and her dad's sides of the family.

"My mom made us take a vote to see what we were going to do because it was too hard to do both alpine and Nordic," said Sadie, who smiles every time she speaks. "My older sister, younger brother, father, and I all voted alpine. But apparently, my mom's vote rules, so we did Nordic."

After the 1998 Winter Olympics in Nagano, eight-year-old Sadie watched a parade in downtown Winthrop. Laura McCabe, a two-time Olympic cross-country skier who had trained in the Methow Valley, rode on a fire truck in front of townspeople lining the streets. Young Sadie realized that she wanted to one day be in a parade, too. Shortly thereafter, the Bjornsen kids joined the Methow Valley Nordic Team. But skiing was yet to monopolize her life, and she still thought that her path to the Olympics lay in a swimming pool. In the summer, the whole family traveled to swim meets, with her mom as swim coach and her dad as a stroke and turn judge. In 2003, as a junior high student, Sadie set her goal on making it to junior nationals in skiing, running, and swimming, all in the same year. That fall, after she had just turned fourteen, she traveled to New Mexico for USA Track & Field's National Junior Olympic Cross-country Championships. She finished ninth. Three months later, she won a national cross-country ski title at the 2004 Junior Olympics in Lake Placid, New York. Squeezing in junior national swim championships that April was too much.

And another ski race beckoned. After her win at Junior Olympics, she was invited to travel to Slovenia with a group of American juniors that spring. She had never been out of the country and never traveled anywhere without her family. In Slovenia, excitement gave way to anxiety. A vegetarian, she did not know what to eat—besides chocolate. And everyone else on the trip seemed to know each other already. Warming up on the course before a race, Sadie put on her sunglasses to hide tears. As she watched the other kids ski by, she thought that she would be slower than everyone else there. Despite her fears, she did well in the race, and her emotions flipped. She decided that she wanted to be a cross-country skier—not a runner or swimmer.

It was a good choice. Back home on the Methow trails, Sadie was beating the boys. As a high school freshman, she finished first or second in just about every race that she entered, including every race at junior nationals in 2005. Encouraged by family friend Jim Bishop, who had helped coach Canadian Beckie Scott, Sadie finally realized that she had found a way to one day compete at the Olympics.

But the fall of her senior year, she came down with a sinus infection, a minor ailment but one that would have an impact on the rest of her ski career. Her doctor prescribed the antibiotic Levaquin. Common side effects of this drug include nausea, vomiting, headaches, and constipation. The drug has also been associated with tendonitis—and it hit Sadie hard. The drug attacked her Achilles tendons, and for months she could hardly ski. Entered in the West Yellowstone SuperTour in November 2007, she did not start any of the races. She made it through the U.S. nationals in January with a couple of sixth-place finishes. But unable to train much, she struggled through the rest of the season. In March, she traveled to Anchorage for the 2008 Junior Olympics but competed in only one race.

"It was a horrible time," Sadie remembered. "I hated it in Anchorage. We stayed downtown, and someone was murdered outside the window, and I remember hearing it. The whole experience was awful."

Back home, she rested her ailing Achilles and considered where she should attend college. Frustrated and rebellious, she decided to head back to the place she hated. She chose the University of Alaska-Anchorage (UAA), which lured her with an athletic scholarship. And once in Alaska, she quickly learned to love Anchorage, where the snow falls early and, like in Winthrop, ski trails loop throughout the city.

With her body on the mend, she was excited to ski again. But like many endurance athletes who return from forced downtime, she trained too hard and had another tough year. One of the few bright spots was the 2009 NCAAs, where she finished third in the 5-kilometer classic race —one place ahead of her friend Rosie Brennan, who was a freshman at Dartmouth. The only skiers who finished ahead of Sadie were a German with World Cup experience who was competing for Denver University and a Russian recruit skiing for the University of New Mexico.

With one year of college completed, Sadie returned to Winthrop that summer and decided to take a year off. She wanted to try to make the 2010 Olympic team. So she joined the newly formed Methow Olympic Development program—the MOD Squad. But again, she struggled and had another "horrible" year, vacillating between injury and fatigue from overtraining. Although she finished fifth in an early season SuperTour sprint, she struggled at the 2010 U.S. nationals, which were the last chance for skiers to earn points toward making the Olympic team. Her best result was fifteenth. She didn't finish the 20-kilometer classic race and didn't even start the classic sprint. And classic is her favorite technique. After that experience, she was done with ski racing.

"I wasn't interested anymore," she said.

Rather than quit, she decided she would use skiing to earn a college education through her ski scholarship at UAA. She told the coach that she would return to campus in the fall of 2011 and to please save her athletic scholarship.

Flying home from a racing trip in Europe that spring, she decided to stop on the East Coast and compete in the spring SuperTour races in Fort Kent, Maine. There, she ran into Kikkan and Holly Brooks, whom she had met in Anchorage. Both women had heard that Sadie planned to return to UAA. They encouraged her to join APU instead, where she could focus on skiing full time, then fit college classes around training and racing.

"Yeah, right," Sadie thought. "I'm done with ski racing."

The coach inside Holly took over. She sat Sadie down and told her that she was a very talented ski racer and questioned why she was going to return to UAA. A college athletic scholarship could limit her ski career. By accepting an athletic scholarship to an NCAA Division I school, Sadie would be obligated to compete in every collegiate race, plus NCAAS (if she qualified). With that kind of schedule, she would have few opportunities to compete internationally. Holly even asked APU coach Erik Flora to speak to Sadie.

It made an impact. Sadie realized that she wasn't ready to give up on her dream. She called the UAA coach and said that she wasn't coming back. Instead, she enrolled at APU. It was spring 2010.

An accounting major, Sadie got an almost immediate return on her investment. But it was a very big investment. Still struggling with chronic tendonitis, she could not train like her teammates—or even how most endurance athletes train. She couldn't run, and she couldn't ski. Instead, Flora backed her training way down, giving her four 30-minute workouts to do each day. "This is not going to look like the next person," he told her, "but we have to go all the way back down to the beginning." Sadie spent the whole summer aqua jogging alone in the pool.

"You end up doing a lot more mental training because all those times you're wishing you could run for three hours," she explained. "You're training your brain and convincing yourself that what you're doing looks different but is just as good."

It was just as good. She recovered and, along with Holly, Sadie tore through the early season SuperTour and NorAm races, finishing in the top three four times. At 2011 nationals, she won her first senior title in the 10-kilometer classic race. Then she traveled to Europe for the U23 world championships in Estonia, and then, with fellow world championship rookies Jessie Diggins and Ida Sargent, the senior world championships in Oslo.

Before world championships, she entered her first World Cup races in Drammen, Norway. She was in awe of the show that the Norwegians put on for ski races: the big TV screens and huge crowds. With a Norwegian last name, she was a hit with the fans; people shouted "Bjornsen!" in every race.

"Wow, this is amazing," she thought. "This is what sport is!"

The world championship races were even crazier. Tens of thousands of people showed up every day to watch their favorite skiers compete, and the stadium was so loud that Sadie couldn't hear herself even if she shouted. She was so happy to be there that she did not much care about race results. She still finished well, claiming two top-thirty finishes in both the sprint and the 10-kilometer classic. Then, paired with Kikkan in the team sprint, the duo placed ninth.

"I decided that this is the sport I belong in," Sadie said. "This is the neatest thing I could ever do."

Up in Anchorage, a benefactor with Carlile, one of Alaska's largest trucking companies, made sure that money would never limit Sadie's career. When he moved to Saltchuk, a consortium of shipping and distribution companies, he maintained his support. As her primary personal sponsor, Saltchuk would adorn the front of Sadie's hat.

❊ ❊ ❊

Then there was the phenom Jessie Diggins, whose bubbly personality and happy demeanor belie her competitive side—and her ability to handle huge volumes of pain. In 2012, she was about to take the World Cup by storm.

She was born in Afton, Minnesota, a small town in the Minneapolis–St. Paul metropolitan area—and on the border of Wisconsin—the daughter of Canadian parents, Clay and Deb Diggins. Clay played hockey in his hometown, Thunder Bay, Ontario—just north of Minnesota on Lake Superior. His friends on the team were of Finnish heritage, and they encouraged him to try cross-country skiing. When he met Deb at Gustavus Adolphus College in St. Peter, Minnesota, he taught her to ski too, taking her on ski dates with wine, cheese, and bread.

Soon after they married, Clay took a job with Slumberland Furniture and they moved to Minneapolis, then Afton. Jessie was born on August 26, 1991, and she was a bundle of energy from the start. When they took baby Jessie cross-country skiing, she rode in a backpack and pulled her dad's hair while saying, "Mush, Dad! Mush!" Or she told him that she wanted to go "super speed."

At school, Jessie was a handful. In kindergarten, she refused to nap. The rule was simple: she didn't have to sleep but she had to stay on her mat. So she would do handstands and somersaults, all within the boundaries of her napping mat. She was soon moved to a separate room and given a coloring book so she wouldn't disturb her sleeping classmates.

Jessie expended her boundless energy in the usual complement of youth sports: dance, swimming, soccer, track and field, even ice skating—because it looked like fun. The Digginses also signed up Jessie for the Minnesota Youth Ski League. Racing was not the goal. They simply wanted to cross-country ski with other families, enjoy the camaraderie, and eat potluck snacks afterward.

In seventh grade, Jessie went to Stillwater Junior High School, where she could sign up for the high school Nordic ski team (for kids in seventh through twelfth grades). But she almost skipped it. The cross-country skiers trained and raced six days per week; she wondered how she would finish her schoolwork around that kind of schedule. Peer pressure prevailed. The team had more than 120 kids, and all her friends were doing it. How could she not sign up?

The first winter, Kris Hansen, the Stillwater High School ski coach and a two-time Minnesota state champion herself, didn't make note of the new seventh grader on the team. Jessie seemed talented, but Stillwater traditionally has a strong cross-country ski team. That February (2004), at the conference championship—which would qualify the team for states—Jessie's talent showed through. About thirty minutes before the start of the first race, one of Hansen's varsity athletes announced that she was sick and couldn't race. Hansen ran inside the touring center chalet, where Jessie was eating a big candy bar and playing a video game with her friends (she was scheduled to compete in the junior varsity race later that day). Hansen walked up to Jessie and announced, "Ashley is sick. Do you want to race?"

Jessie jumped up and eagerly said yes. She finished the candy bar, then ran around the parking lot to warm up while Hansen waxed her skis. If Jessie could hang in there with the older high school students and finish mid-pack, the Stillwater Ponies would likely qualify for states. Jessie ended up winning the race. She was twelve years old, and it was her first varsity race.

"When she won that race, it was so far beyond anything that I had imagined," said Hansen. "That was when I fully appreciated what I had on my hands."

Two years later, as a high school freshman, Diggins was the Minnesota state high school champion—her first of three such crowns. She would have won four, but world junior championships interfered with the conference championship in 2009, so she missed qualifying for states. And Hansen believes that Jessie would have won the state title in eighth grade, too—except she had food poisoning and spent the entire night before the race vomiting. Jessie won every cross-country ski race that she entered in eighth grade and throughout her high school career. She became so dominant that people weren't predicting whether she would win, but by how much.

"She was in a class by herself," said Hansen. "She could ski away from any of the girls in the conference."

She could ski away from the boys as well. In one three-school conference meet, she entered the boys' field in a 10-kilometer pursuit. The boys joked about trying to break her poles, but Hansen said that they only tried that trick for the first 200 or so meters of the race. After that, Jessie was gone. She beat the entire field by a wide margin—and was never again invited to compete with the boys.

Jessie helped the Stillwater Ponies win two state titles as a team. And Hansen was amazed at how loyal Jessie was to the Stillwater team after she began traveling to races in Europe. No matter what time Jessie arrived home from a European trip, she would show up at school the next day so she could race for Stillwater, even if the race was far away in northern Minnesota.

"She would show up, and she would race hard," Hansen said.

Then after her own race was over, Jessie would pop off her skis and join her teammates cheering on other Stillwater skiers still out on the course—a school tradition of teammates cheering teammates. They called her "Sparkle Chipmunk," saying her spirit animal was an energetic chipmunk covered in glitter.

"When you have a young person who is so successful, oftentimes there's this need to separate themselves from their high school peers and be like, 'I'm so past you, I'm so past all of you people,'" said Hansen. "Jessie never did that. Our team always felt like we were even more important than the U.S. Ski Team because she was so fully engaged in our team and our team goals and what her role was in achieving those goals, not just in terms of finishing a race but in terms of lending her emotional energy to the rest of the team so we could pull off a win for the day."

On her trips to ski race races around the country and the world, Jessie began thinking about her career. In 2008, after winning her second high school state crown, she traveled to Alaska for U.S. junior nationals. Kikkan Randall was at the championships handing out autographed posters. Kikkan ran out of posters, so Jessie brought her a scrap of cardboard and asked the Olympian to sign it. Jessie still has that scrap of cardboard. Kikkan was a pro skier, and that's what Jessie wanted to do.

Back at school, Jessie filled out a survey to identify a career path. She said that she liked to work hard with others and be outdoors. The survey indicated that she should be a roofer. She asked the school career counselor why professional athlete wasn't a career choice.

The counselor replied, "Honey, not very many people make it as professional athletes," remembered Jessie, who then thought, "Well, someone has to make it, and I want to be that person."

Her parents agreed to support her ski-racer career path, but only if she had a backup plan. She had to earn an academic scholarship to a college and not an athletic scholarship, in case she either didn't make it as a ski racer or became injured. And she had to earn a living if she wanted to ski race.

"This is your life, not living at home with mom and dad," they told her. "We don't want you to be thirty years old and living at home and not paying your own taxes. If it's your job, it's your job."

Jessie graduated from Stillwater in June 2010 and earned an academic scholarship to Northern Michigan University. Her plan was to defer college for a year, join the CXC team, a regional ski club in Minnesota, and see whether she could make it as a pro skier. Jessie was the youngest and least experienced on the team and coach Jason Cork expected the nineteen-year-old to ski race for a year, then go to NMU. It's the path that most cross-country skiers took. But Jessie was about to show that she was not like most cross-country skiers. At least not in the United States.

At the first races of the 2010–2011 season in West Yellowstone, Montana, Jessie finished fifth in a sprint and was the top junior racer.

Then they moved to NorAm Cup races in Canada, where Jessie again scored a couple of top-ten finishes. "She skied pretty well, but it wasn't like she was obviously going to be crushing her competition," noted Coach Cork.

Then the CXC team signed up for a three-day NorAm race at the Black Jack Ski Club in Rossland, British Columbia—a small, hard-to-reach town about two and a half hours directly north of Spokane, Washington. It was a random race, not one that would earn SuperTour or World Cup points. But Olympian Holly Brooks would be there, plus other top skiers on the verge of making the U.S. and Canadian ski teams. Against this stiff competition, Jessie finished fourth in the sprint on the first day, second in the 5-kilometer freestyle, and won the 16.5-kilometer mass-start race, plus the 10-kilometer pursuit, giving her the overall win for the series.

"All of a sudden, it was like, 'Oh wait, you are actually pretty good,'" said Cork.

To preserve her NCAA eligibility, Jessie turned down the thousands of dollars in prize money.

Less than a month later, at the snowless national championships in Rumford, Maine, Jessie earned her first national title, winning the sprint even after falling in the final (the downhill finish allowed her to get back into the pack quickly). She was soon on her way to Europe for her third world junior championship. But the national sprint title earned her a trip to her first senior world championship, plus a World Cup sprint before world champs. At world juniors in Estonia in late January, she finished seventh and twelfth in the 5-kilometer freestyle and 10-kilometer pursuit, respectively, only seconds off the leaders.

Then at the world championships in Oslo, she was entered in two races—the sprint and pursuit. After those races, the coaches expected her to immediately return to the United States to compete in junior nationals. But Jessie had exceeded expectations for most of her short ski career. After finishing twenty-ninth in the sprint qualifier (0.05 second behind Sadie in twenty-eighth), she competed in the quarterfinals (the same quarterfinal heat as Kikkan). It was the first time ever at a major international event that the United States had more than just Kikkan competing in the sprint heats. Jessie also finished twenty-eighth in the pursuit—about 30 seconds behind American teammates Liz and Holly. Based on those results, she was invited to stay five more days to anchor the 4 x 5-kilometer relay for the American women. Kikkan led off the relay, handing off to Holly in seventh place for the second of the classic legs. Liz took over at the relay halfway and kept the team in ninth. Then Jessie skied the seventh fastest anchor leg to keep the team in ninth. It was the best relay finish for the American women at a major international championship in at least thirty years.

Then, after finishing on the podium in a few spring races, including third in the 30-kilometer classic mass start at distance nationals, beating every American except Kikkan, Jessie was named to the U.S. Ski Team's B team. She called Sten Fjeldheim at UNM and asked him what she should do: accept the team nomination or pursue her education instead. He told her to put off college and give everything that she had to skiing. School would always be there.

To support her career, Jessie put together a funding proposal, dressed up in a business suit and high heels, and walked into her parents' employer, Slumberland, to meet with CEO Ken Larson. She proposed that if he sponsored her, she would wear the Slumberland logo on her headgear (hat or headband). He liked the idea, and she landed her first sponsor.

"I'm so glad he didn't laugh at me," said Jessie, feeling awkward dressed as a businesswoman.

Then she asked Lee Stylos, owner of the Chilkoot Café in Stillwater, whether she could leave a tip jar by the cash register. Stylos asked what she was trying to do. When she explained, he said a tip jar wouldn't raise enough money. Instead, he offered to host a fundraiser at the café. Tickets cost $100, and the event sold out. Jessie's friends, high school and youth league teammates, former coaches, and race volunteers showed up. Literally powered by the community, she had enough money to compete on the World Cup for the 2012 season. Within a year, she would join the SMS T2 team.

✳ ✳ ✳

Another American also made her world championship debut in Oslo. Ida Sargent, then a twenty-two-year-old junior at Dartmouth, was proving that a talented skier could balance coursework, training, collegiate races, and international races. One of Matt Whitcomb's skiers from Burke Mountain Academy, Ida had grown up in Orleans in Vermont's remote Northeast Kingdom, skiing with her family and friends at the Craftsbury Outdoor Center, the ski touring center and elite training camp for cross-country skiers, biathletes, and rowers that sits off a dirt road near the idyllic hilltop village of Craftsbury Common. Ida always wanted to do what her older siblings, Eben and Elsa, were doing. So they dubbed her "little me too."

With a round face and an easy smile, Ida does not look like a tough competitor. But on skis, she is aggressive, sneaking in quietly behind other competitors, then passing them decisively before the finish. As a kid, she was always trying to keep up with Elsa (two years older). While Elsa and Eben talked of competing in the Olympics one day, Ida lived it. One Christmas, Ida received her first spandex racing suit. "I think she wore it the entire day," said Elsa. Soon, Ida was winning so many Bill Koch League races that she started "racing up"—competing in the next age category, which happened to be Elsa's category. Ida won those races as well (and made Elsa grumpy).

Ida attended the local public high school for one year. Then in the fall of 2003, she went to Burke, impressed with the team that Matt Whitcomb was building. From Burke, she followed her siblings to Dartmouth—but sibling rivalry was no longer an issue. "Honestly, I was happier to see her do well than do well myself," said Elsa. "I knew she was headed for a big ski career, and I was transitioning after college into new interests."

Ida thrived on the Dartmouth Ski Team. Her freshman year, she won most of the collegiate races, then went to the 2008 world junior championships, taking twelfth in the sprint. Junior year she had a breakthrough. As a twenty-two-year-old, she finished third in the sprint at the 2010 nationals, then fourth at the U23 world championships, also in the sprint. By season's end, she finished second twice to her childhood idol, Kikkan, in the Super Series spring races. It was time to put school on hold.

This is why Dartmouth is a favorite college among America's best skiers, from Olympic medalists Hannah Kearney (a mogul skier, who attended Dartmouth as a freshman) and Andrew Weibrecht (alpine) to biathletes and cross-country skiers—if they can get in. The Ivy League college's year-round quarter system allows student athletes to attend classes when their training schedules allow—for example, just the spring or summer quarters. And cross-country skiers can compete for Dartmouth when they are in school for a winter quarter. Dartmouth does not offer athletic scholarships, so if skiers are selected for world championship teams, they are not beholden to the collegiate racing schedule.

With two years of college finished, Ida decided to take off the following fall and winter quarters and race full time. In November 2010, she made her World Cup debut as a member of the relay team competing in Gällivare, along with Kikkan, Liz, and Morgan Arritola (they finished thirteenth). After returning home for the holidays and 2011 nationals in Maine, she made the U23 world championship team, where she qualified for the heats in the classic sprint but didn't advance out of the quarterfinals. She was also named to the 2011 world championship team, where she competed in the sprint and 10-kilometer classic races. She ended her season with three podium finishes, including a win, in top-level races at home in Craftsbury, then finished second again to Kikkan in a spring SuperTour classic sprint in Sun Valley, Idaho.

Back at Dartmouth for the spring quarter, she learned that she had been nominated to the U.S. Ski Team B team. She was about to embark on her first full season of World Cup racing. Soon, she would join Craftsbury's Green Racing Project.

❄   ❄   ❄

No one remembers whose idea it was. Or more likely, no one wants to take credit. Kikkan had been pushing for a women's-only team, and she suggested it again after the 2011 world championships. At the world championship in Oslo—where she had been a medal favorite in the freestyle sprint and five of the other American women who competed finished in the top thirty in at least one race—the women had gelled as a team, having fun amidst the loud, crazy chaos of a championship that was as popular as a Super Bowl in Nordic skiing's cradle. Kikkan wanted to create an identity as a women's team, with a dedicated coach. This would be a different structure than the team had used for years, where the elite skiers—both male and female—worked with a pool of World Cup coaches, and development skiers had their own coaches. As a women's team, they could do a women's-only camp in the summers, like what Kikkan had done with Chandra Crawford when they started NAWTA. And in the past couple of summers, she had trained with Norwegian and Swedish World Cup friends on their turf. These ad hoc camps had helped push Kikkan to the podium. Maybe they would help this new group of women, too.

With five women named to the U.S. cross-country ski team for the 2012 season—Kikkan and Liz on the A team; Sadie, Jessie, and Ida on the B team (Morgan Arritola had moved on to mountain running); and Holly racing with them as well—it made sense to split them off as their own team with an assigned coach. And Matt Whitcomb was a natural choice. He had worked with Liz and Ida since they were young teenagers. And he had worked with Jessie and Sadie as they prepared for the 2011 world championships, as well as several world junior championships and summer training camps in previous years. Jessie and Sadie had entered their first World Cup races, held in Drammen, Norway, the weekend before the 2011 world championships, and they were wide-eyed at the spectacle. Thousands of cheering fans lined the course, and the races were shown on huge TV screens in the stadium. It was exciting and overwhelming, and the young skiers had the usual American experience at a first World Cup—they got killed. Jessie finished the sprint qualifier, then gasped at the finish, "How did I do? Did I make it?" She finished forty-sixth, and only the top thirty qualify for the heats.

"I got my ass kicked," she said. "I remember being so overwhelmed. The cameras, the noise, the lights, the people. Everything was 'whoa.' My focus was pulled way off track."

Matt helped ease the transition to life on the road. Jessie had originally met him at a regional training camp when she was still in high school; he had come to the camp as a guest coach and talent scout. At the time, Jessie was in awe of the U.S. Ski Team, but terrified—in that young teenage girl way—of meeting anyone involved with the team. Yet here was a friendly, approachable coach.

"I'm not scared of him, and he seems so nice," she thought.

She also liked his coaching style. Rather than point out what the young junior skiers were doing wrong, he pointed out what they did well. Then he would add a skill that they should work on, saying it would make them even better.

"He was really good at giving you feedback in a way that didn't make you feel like, 'Oh my God, I suck,'" said Jessie. "He gives you feedback that makes you feel like you have a chance to get even better."

Once on the U.S. team, Jessie learned that Matt saw them as people, not just skiers. In Europe, far from friends and family, she was struggling on her first trip competing with the big guns of cross-country skiing. She was excited to be there, but just nineteen years old, she was also homesick. Matt intuitively sensed her emotions. And even if she wasn't homesick, he wanted to nip any negative emotions before they began to fester. So every night, he would check on the skiers to see how they were doing.

"He'd come in the room and act casual, and say, 'I'm not checking on you, but how's it going?'" said Jessie. "He just talked to you and made you feel like you had company."

Her teammates helped as well, especially Liz and Holly, who were both older and have personalities that lean toward emotional caretaking.

That summer of 2011, the women gathered in Alaska for their first women's-only training camp, arranged by Kikkan. They attended other camps as well, and as a team, they began to gel. They had a leader who inspired them and instilled belief. And they had a coach who not only knew how to motivate the team members but who cared about each person as well. And they had each other. At team camps, they shared a house and began to get to know each other over meals cooked together. They blared the music before training sessions and had team meetings. Matt suggested that they read a book together. Six women who all grew up in different states, with different interests and personalities but one shared goal, began to come together as a team. They brought fun to the grueling, often isolating life of the endurance sport athlete, and they began to pull together as a team in more than just uniform. As Matt often told them, "You don't have to be best friends, but you have to be best teammates." Now they just needed to show the world that the U.S. team was more than Kikkan & Company.

Sadie was the first to show the U.S. team's potential. But she almost missed the opportunity. Racing in Scandinavia in November 2011, she was scheduled to fly to Düsseldorf, Germany, for a World Cup sprint. But when she checked in at the airport, the ticket agent could not find her name on the manifest. Upon closer inspection, the agent looked at the ticket and pointed out that Sadie had accidentally booked the ticket for the following month. Already late for the flight, Sadie considered bailing out on the trip. But the agent found her a seat for $400, a large sum for a twenty-two-year-old just starting her elite skiing career. She paid. Fighting for a spot on the A team, she couldn't just skip a World Cup.

When she arrived in Düsseldorf, she found a racecourse like no other she had ever seen. To date, she had only skied on trails through the woods, not a city. The 900-meter-long course started on a snow-covered cobblestoned street along the Rhine River, where crews rowed shells in the December air. Then the tight racecourse wound through the downtown city streets on a narrow track of man-made snow. Christmas decorations hung from buildings around the course, and a circus was set up nearby—or what looked like a circus to Sadie. The racers warmed up by running on the cobbled streets, and as they skied around the course, they could smell food cooking. Kikkan won the freestyle sprint on Saturday, beating, among others, her friend Chandra. It was Kikkan's fourth World Cup win.

Behind Kikkan, Sadie missed qualifying for the quarterfinals by 0.32 second and was frustrated. She had spent $400 to fly to Düsseldorf to ski for less than two minutes. But as the top American in the sprint qualifier after Kikkan, she was chosen for the team sprint the following day. Excited for another go on this crazy racecourse, she was both petrified and motivated. She knew she could ski faster. But still new to both the APU and the U.S. Ski Team, Sadie was nervous about the race and intimidated by Kikkan. If they finished last, or near to last, surely it would be Sadie's fault. And she did not even know what to say to Kikkan.

In a team sprint, two skiers from the same country race three times each around the course, tagging their teammate after each lap. After two semifinals, the top two teams from each move on to the finals, plus the next six teams with the fastest times. With ten skiers on course at the same time, traffic is often heavy in the exchange zones, where skiers often cross in front of each other to tag their teammates. Ideally in the tag zone, the incoming skier alerts her teammate to start moving so she has momentum by the time she is tagged. But ten people yelling, "Go!" is pointless. Kikkan told Sadie that they should each yell, "It's so fluffy!" as they approached the tag zone. It's a line from the animated comedy film *Despicable Me*. Sadie laughed.

"OK, I don't have to be nervous," she thought.

Sadie skied the first leg of the team sprint. She stayed near the front of the field in the semifinal and stayed out of trouble in the first lap, then tagged Kikkan—somehow yelling "It's so fluffy" without laughing. For the next five laps, both women tagged each other cleanly and stayed near the front, and they easily qualified for the final.

In the hour or so between the semis and the final, Sadie's nerves returned. Although the day was cloudy, she put on her sunglasses to hide her tears. But Kikkan was so calm that she was sleeping in the team van. The sight of her teammate conked out on a van seat calmed Sadie.

On the starting line for the final, the nerves crept back in. All Sadie could think about was "don't fall" and "don't lose places in the pack." After the gun went off, she skated up to the front of the pack and stayed there—saying in her head like a mantra, "Don't fall, don't lose places." It worked. Every time it was Sadie's turn, she maintained third or fourth place in the field of ten. And with each turn, she gained confidence. By the final "it's so fluffy" tag-off, Sadie had done her job. She had kept the pair near the front. Now all Kikkan had to do was pass the three women ahead of her.

In the final lap, she passed everyone but Norway's Maiken Caspersen Falla and claimed the silver medal. It was the first time that Americans had ever finished on the podium in a team sprint. And it was the first time in the past thirty years that an American skier other than Kikkan and Andy Newell had finished on a World Cup podium.

After the race, Kikkan told *SkiTrax*, "I've come to Düsseldorf three or four times now, and every time I've been kind of sad to have to leave the day of the team sprint because I haven't had a partner. So it was pretty exciting to be in the mix today and come out with a good result."

❅ ❅ ❅

Six weeks later, it was Jessie's turn to pair with Kikkan in a World Cup team sprint in Milan, Italy. Jessie was only twenty years old but had spent the early season gaining confidence by racing SuperTours and NorAms in the United States and Canada, plus nationals. In a span of five weeks, she had won thirteen races and finished second in four others. No American skier had ever dominated the Continental Cup races in North American like this, and at every distance and discipline from freestyle sprints to 10-kilometer classic races.

"On the World Cup, I wouldn't have placed as well, and they didn't want me to show up and get last," said Jessie. "No one knew how I was going to place."

From nationals in Rumford, Maine, Jessie, Sadie, and Ida flew directly to Italy and were immediately hit by fierce jet lag. Excited to finally be racing World Cups again, Jessie was rooming with Kikkan, whose breathing sounds like the ocean when she sleeps, or so claimed Jessie. She remembers lying in bed trying to let Kikkan's calm breathing wash over her. But it's hard for someone as bubbly as Jessie to mellow out. By race day, she was fired up. On the bus into Milan, she and Sadie held hands to contain their nerves and excitement.

Jessie qualified twenty-first in the freestyle sprint—a great result for her third ever World Cup. But the qualifier was a race against the clock. She had not had to use race strategy to maintain position in the pack. She simply had to ski as fast as she could by herself around the racecourse. This would change in her quarterfinal heat, where she would race around the same tight course with five other women, and one of them was Kikkan. Jessie, who describes herself as a polite Minnesota girl, was not prepared for the aggression in World Cup sprint racing. The toughest races she had done were SuperTours in the United States, where competitors tend to politely say "on your left" or "track" if they want to pass. On the World Cup, competitors were elbowing her and cutting in front without saying a word. Jessie just missed moving into the semifinals in Milan, leaving her in eighteenth place. And after the race, she complained to coach Chris Grover that the other racers had pushed her.

"Yeah, you've got to push back," he told her.

While Jessie was recovering from her first sprint race, Kikkan moved on to the semis, then the finals, and finished the race in second place. It was her fifth World Cup top-three finish of the season and solidified her lead in the overall sprint standings. At the post-race press conference, Kikkan mentioned how excited she was to have three teammates in Milan with her, and that the United States would enter two teams in the team sprint on Sunday.

"It's not so often that we've had that, so it's going to be really exciting, and I hope we can challenge for a podium," she said.

Because Jessie was the top American behind Kikkan in the sprint, they would form USA I in the team sprint; Sadie and Ida would comprise USA II. While Sadie and Ida had both competed in the team sprint in Düsseldorf, Jessie had never done a team sprint in her life. As the leadoff skier, it was her job to stay out of trouble.

Jessie and Kikkan practiced tags, which helped calm her down. "OK, I've got this," she said, as if studying for an exam with multiple-choice answers. But once she was in the middle of the pack during the semifinal, she felt very small, as if she didn't belong. At any minute, she feared that the women skiing around her—Anne Kyllönen from Finland, who had won the sprint qualifier the day before, or Olympians Celine Brun-Lie from Norway or Natalia Korosteleva from Russia—would discover that she wasn't supposed to be there. But at the same time, she felt good. She was working hard but was easily staying with the pack.

Then, out of nowhere, disaster struck in the semifinal. On the final tag, Jessie approached the tag zone full steam ahead. What she did not notice was the Swedish team. The Swedish skier to her right needed to tag her teammate, who was on Kikkan's left. The only way to reach her was to cross in front of Jessie. The Swede aggressively moved in front of Jessie and swiped her skis out from under her. Already moving, Kikkan heard a squeak behind her. She looked back and stopped when she saw Jessie trying to scramble to her feet. But her skis and poles were tangled. Kikkan put down her hand, and Jessie reached up and swatted it. Then Kikkan took off and kept the Americans in contention. They qualified for the final. But guilt washed over Jessie. She feared Kikkan was mad and that this might be her last ever team sprint. But the older skier knew that team sprints are chaotic and did not blame Jessie. She was happy that Jessie had kept up with the leaders and not drifted off the back.

In the hour and a half between the semis and the final, Kikkan lay down to rest. But boisterous Jessie could not sit down. Nervously tapping around, Jessie looked up to see a big Norwegian skier by the name of Øystein Pettersen standing nearby. Nicknamed Pølse ("sausage" in Norwegian), twenty-eight-year-old Pettersen was a 2010 Olympic gold medalist in the team sprint, and Jessie was terrified of him—"because I was terrified of everyone at that point in my life," she said.

"I heard you had a rough one out there," he told Jessie.

"Yes," she nodded.

"Tell you what," he said jovially, "you stay on your feet in the final, and I'll give you my hat."

"OK," Jessie said tentatively, smiling but still scared. All she could do was hope that the final would go more smoothly.

It was not meant to be. In the final, at the end of her second leg (and the fourth leg of the six-leg team sprint), Jessie again encountered a skier who cut her off as she came into the tag zone. Again, Kikkan heard "eek!" behind her and looked back to see Jessie cartwheeling toward the tag zone. She landed on her back, and Kikkan backtracked to tag her, then took off to catch back onto the pack of ten skiers.

"I remember being like, 'Oh my gosh,' the first time," said Kikkan. "But again and again. And then having to charge out on my lap and burn all my energy to get us back in the race."

But that's as mad as Kikkan would get. In her final lap, she skied into the lead with 100 meters to go. Then in the final 50 meters, Ida Ingemarsdotter from Sweden—who had won the sprint the previous day with the same move—skied by Kikkan. The American was too gassed to hold her off. But the American duo still held on for second place—the second podium finish for the Americans in a team sprint that year.

"Jessie is young, and we were on the podium," Kikkan said. "Canada got on the podium in third with Chandra and Perianne Jones. It was all just really fun."

Jessie had mixed emotions. She was elated to stand on her first World Cup podium—a sign that she belonged racing among the world's best. But she had had two embarrassing falls, a sign that perhaps she did not belong. Kikkan had been very nice after the race, asking if she was all right after the cartwheeling fall. And none of her teammates or coaches accused her of skiing poorly.

"No one brought it up in a mean way, which was huge for me," said Jessie. "Otherwise, I might have been so mortified. I might have never wanted to do it again."

After the awards ceremony, Jessie went up to the Sausage and said, "We podiumed!"

"Yeah," he replied. "No hat."

❊   ❊   ❊

Kikkan and Jessie's team sprint finish, along with Kikkan and Sadie's second place earlier in the season, were just two of the highlights for the American women's cross-country ski team during the 2011–2012 season. Of the six U.S. women competing on the World Cup—Kikkan and Liz on the A team; Ida, Jessie, and Sadie on the B team; and Holly Brooks doing it on her own—all were having breakout years. Kikkan was on her way to winning her first World Cup sprint title, given to the skier who accrues the most points in all the sprints throughout the season. Liz scored her first World Cup points by finishing eighteenth in the season's first 10-kilometer freestyle race, on November 19, 2011, in Sjusjøen, Norway. From then on, she was consistently finishing in the points in World Cup distance races. Holly also racked up a string of top-thirty finishes in both sprints and distance races in the first part of the season and was invited to continue racing on the World Cup (although on her own dime). Ida also scored her first World Cup points in January that season. Sadie was close in all the sprints, finishing just a hair back from qualifying for the heats, and at the 2012 U23 Nordic World Ski Championships, she scored three top-fifteen finishes, including fifth in the 10-kilometer classic. And Jessie's results did not look like those of a World Cup neophyte. Less than a month after her World Cup sprint debut, she won the qualifier for a freestyle sprint in Moscow. Then she worked her way through the quarterfinal and semifinal heats all the way to the final. She finished last in the final, but that still put her in sixth place. Jessie also had three excellent distance races, including a fifth place in a 10-kilometer freestyle race in Rybinsk, Russia.

While traveling between races during the Tour de Ski that winter, the team stopped in a German town so Holly could have a wrist injury examined. While they were waiting, Kikkan and Liz wandered through a shop and found red, white, and blue striped socks that were part of a Pippi Longstocking costume. They bought four pairs. The crazy court jester socks might provide some team spirit in the relays, they thought. They did not know how much power those socks would have.

TEAMWORK

Relays have a certain power about them. With four skiers required to compete in a 4 x 5-kilometer race, they require depth and consistency for a team to do well. One strong skier does not make a medal-winning relay. It takes four, each having a good or great day, able to hang with the leaders for 5 kilometers, or about 13 minutes. The American women had yet to finish higher than ninth in a World Cup, a world championship, or an Olympic relay.

In mid-February 2012, the women—minus Sadie, who was racing U23 world championships —traveled to Nové Město na Moravě in the Czech Republic for a 15-kilometer classic race, then the season's second 4 x 5-kilometer relay. Kikkan had been waiting all season to do another relay; she, Ida, Liz, and Holly had finished ninth in the season's other relay in Sjusjøen in November. But Kikkan arrived in the Czech Republic with a bad cold and decided to sit out the races. And after the cold, miserable 15-kilometer race, no one had high hopes for the relay: Jessie had been the highest finisher—in thirty-third, almost 4 minutes behind winner Marit Bjørgen. It was one of her worst finishes all season. Liz and Ida came across the line in forty-second and forty-third, over 4:30 minutes off the winning pace. And Holly didn't finish. She had been sick, was feeling very flat, and was about to head home to

Alaska to recuperate. They would all compete in the relay the next day. But it probably would not be pretty.

"Everyone was pretty tired and we knew that without Kikkan, our chances of being near the podium were much tougher," said Jessie.

The next morning, Holly, Ida, Liz, and Jessie cranked up the music. Jessie pulled out face paint and adorned her teammates' faces with the letters "USA" and glitter. Then Kikkan and Liz passed out the striped Pippi Longstocking socks, which they pulled over the legs of their speed suits. As they approached the starting line, their more staid opponents looked at them as if they had jumped out of a clown car.

Holly led off the relay on the first classic leg. Norway I and II skied together off the front, tagging their teammates within 0.2 second of each other. Russia I was 13 seconds back, with Russia II leading a pack of six skiers another 16 seconds behind. In that pack was Holly, who managed to pull herself up both mentally and physically for the relay. She tagged Ida, who pulled ahead of three teams on her 5-kilometer classic leg: France, Russia II, and Kazakhstan. Sweden's Ingemarsdotter was the only skier to pass Ida, but the American was able to stay within 0.5 second of her when she tagged Liz, with Germany close behind.

With two freestyle legs left in the relay, Liz took off with Anna Haag from Sweden and Nicole Fessel from Germany. Haag was on the Swedish relay team that won a silver medal the previous year at the 2011 world championships, and Fessel had earned a silver medal from a World Cup relay two years earlier. Liz stayed near both of them, tagging Jessie just over 1 second behind Haag and about 0.5 second back from Fessel. Norway I was firmly in the lead, with Norway II over 30 seconds behind and working hard to hold off Finland.

Jessie flew out of the stadium, her unbounded energy focused on one task: hunting down the two ahead of her. She quickly passed and dropped the German skier. But ahead, Swedish Olympic gold medalist Charlotte Kalla was a tough target. She was trying to chase Finland and Norway II ahead, and Jessie stayed with her. Coming into the stadium at the halfway point in her lap, Jessie pulled ahead. "I'm sure I was in a lot of pain," Jessie told Fasterskier.com. "But I was so excited at the chance to race neck-and-neck with an Olympic gold medalist that I didn't feel a thing!"

While Norway I easily claimed yet another relay win, Finland and Norway II duked it out for the last two podium spots, with both women crossing in a photo finish. Twenty-two seconds behind them, Jessie and Charlotte Kalla were setting up for another photo finish. The Swede got her skis across the finish line first, giving her team fourth place. But the American women were ecstatic to finish fifth. Perhaps even more astounding, Jessie had skied the fastest anchor leg, even faster than Kalla and Norwegian legend Marit Bjørgen. As Jessie collapsed on the snow, Holly, Ida, and Liz ran over and hugged her. They were so exuberant that some of the Norwegian women took pictures of the celebration.

"It was without Kikkan, which blew our minds and everyone's minds," said Holly. "That was really a defining moment. We were fifth and we were celebrating like we won."

Matt credited Kikkan with the relay breakthrough, even though she had not skied a leg. But it was the example that Kikkan had set all those years that helped lead to the team's success. She had committed to being a professional athlete, and was not distracted by school or a job. She had raced year after year and was undeterred by lackluster results. And even though she was not competing in the relay, she was out on the course cheering for her teammates.

"Kikkan paved the way by proving to our developing U.S. athletes that there is nothing holding us back from international success except for wavering commitment," Matt said at the time.

By committing to the full World Cup schedule and making it part of their routine, the newer women on the team were no longer starstruck on the starting line. Rather than race domestically for a couple of months, then fly over to Europe for a handful of World Cups, the U.S. team now saw people like Marit Bjørgen and Charlotte Kalla every weekend. This helped them see that the mythical superstars are human. As Holly said: "The girls from Norway, Sweden, and Germany are just like us—they have good days, bad days, strengths and weaknesses. It's important for us to know that they are not unbeatable. Seeing them in the line at the bathroom or in the food tent puts faces to names, and they are no longer strangers."

And within their ranks, they were rising to the challenge. Rather than shun a brash, talented newcomer like Jessie, Kikkan welcomed her—even roomed with her. As they were getting to know each other—what they like, what bothers them, and what their insecurities are—they also began to protect each other.

"They rally around Jessie when she bursts onto the scene as if they were celebrating their own victory," said Matt. "And they'll rally around whoever is in a slump."

The first person to greet Holly, Ida, Liz, and Jessie in the finish after their historic fifth in the World Cup relay was Kikkan.

"That does not go unnoticed," added Matt, "and that attitude gets perpetuated forward."

Their performance in the Nové Město relay was just a prelude for what was to come. The rising tide was finally raising all boats.

❅   ❅   ❅

The women carried their belief from that breakthrough season through the summer of 2012. For their women's-only training camp, they invited three-time Olympic medalist Aino-Kaisa Saarinen from Finland to join them. Like any international exchange program, the Americans hoped to learn a few training tips and be pushed by such a strong and proven skier. But Saarinen also learned something from her hosts. The skiers from the Scandinavian countries tend to be reserved, and Saarinen embraced the Americans' team spirit.

"It's the fun things together," she said. "It was really nice to join them and feel that. It was totally different."

But in August, Kikkan had another setback. Her right foot started hurting, and an MRI showed a stress reaction in one of the bones—not a fracture, but a weakening of the bone from all the running and skiing. She dialed back her training, jogged in the pool rather than on the road, and wore a boot when she wasn't training. She even attended a joint training camp that the U.S. women had with the Swedish team. Over four intense days, Kikkan, Holly, Ida, Liz, and Jessie (Sadie stayed in Alaska to heal injuries of her own), as well as Canadian Chandra Crawford, went for three-hour runs through mud, rocks, streams, and a bog, followed by two hours of speed work in the afternoon, or they roller skied around Sweden for six hours. One night, they found the energy to go bowling with their Swedish hosts. Through the long hours of running with the Swedish women, they tried to learn a little of their language.

Although it was fun and intense, the camp took its toll on Kikkan's foot. She flew to the Steadman Clinic in Vail, Colorado, where a doctor advised that she back off and train only 50 percent for five weeks, and no running or skiing. She could swim, bike, and do double-pole workouts. And a nagging Achilles injury in her left foot might heal with the downtime. She flew back to Alaska and joined Sadie in aqua-jogging sessions. Kikkan even entered a swim-bike duathlon at the Bala Falls Triathlon in Ontario (her husband Jeff did the full triathlon). Then in a follow-up visit at the Steadman Clinic in early October, another image showed that the injury was indeed a fracture. She would have to log more time training in the pool.

As the season's first races neared in November, Kikkan's foot felt better. But how fit was she? She would likely have to work her way back into race shape in the early season. She hoped to contend for another medal at the 2013 world championships.

When asked about her goals for worlds, she told Fasterskier.com: "I'd like to make the final in the classic sprint. I'd like to have our team fight for a medal in the team sprint. I think we can put together a relay, the 4 x 5-kilometer in the top six. This will be the first championships where I'm almost more excited about the team goals than my own. I mean, I obviously want to race well myself, but I'm excited about what we can do as a team. That'll give me some extra motivation in rehabbing this foot injury, too, knowing that I really want to be there and competing with the team in February."

When the World Cup season opened with a 10-kilometer freestyle race in Gällivare, Kikkan realized that she had underestimated her fitness. For the first time ever, she won a medal in a distance race—a bronze, just 25.9 seconds behind Marit Bjørgen and her Norwegian teammate Therese Johaug. Perhaps rest and aqua-jogging weren't such a bad training regimen. Boring, yes, but a good way to stay fit. Charlotte Kalla finished the 10-kilometer in fourth, 1 second behind Kikkan. And Holly Brooks, in her best World Cup race to date, finished fifth, only 1.6 seconds behind Kalla. Liz Stephen also finished in the top thirty.

"You feel like you're on top of the world when you look at the results list," said Holly, who had finally been named to the B team. "I beat that person?! And that person?!"

They were excited for the season's first relay the next day and pulled out the striped socks again. With Kikkan at full strength, she was back on the relay team. But who would join her? Holly was obviously in good form, so she was a given. And same with Liz, who had finished twenty-first in the 10-kilometer freestyle the day before. Jessie and Ida had finished outside the top thirty in the 10k free, and both had been on the Nové Město relay team. The coaches chose Jessie, and Matt had to let Ida know.

"I remember calling Ida," he said. "She basically said, 'Hey, I know.' I could tell by whatever pause I just detected that she was on the verge of tears and very disappointed. She had skied a relay the year before for us and she is a great classic 5k skier."

That night, at the pre-race team meeting, Matt reminded the women to just ski like they know how to ski in the relay. "You got here because you know how to do this," he told them. "You don't have to change anything. You know how to do this, and you're really good at it."

The next day, as Holly, Kikkan, Liz, and Jessie skied through November's Arctic twilight in Gällivare, picking off skiers and pulling the team into medal contention, Ida was standing on top of one of the course's tougher hills screaming her head off for her teammates. Each American remembers skiing by her and wondering who the crazy woman was in the U.S. team coat. Normally quiet, Ida was as excited for her teammates as they were to be in medal contention.

"She had the choice," said Liz. "She could have been not fun to be around or she could get into it. She got totally into it. None of us even knew who she was cheering. I've known Ida for a long time, but I've never heard her cheer that way."

It finally hit Liz that "this is not just a bunch of girls skiing; this is a team." Ida could have been off pouting in the hotel. But she stood along the course for an hour, cheering her teammates until she was hoarse. Liz realized that Ida was as integral a part of the team as the four women skiing.

"To have the girl who should be really upset out there cheering harder than anyone, that was the moment when this became a full team," Liz added.

They started referring to the skier not competing in the relay as "the fifth leg" of the relay team.

"We might have seven athletes on a given day who could lead the team to a podium finish in a relay, but only four can compete," explained Matt. "But it's the three who aren't selected who hold the key in their hands. The tone that they set from the moment they find out they are not selected for the relay, they either add or subtract from the team atmosphere. If their reaction is one that takes away, we're done. Chemistry is everything, and Ida nailed it that day. That allowed everyone else to nail it in the race."

Soon after, Thomas Zipfel, a German illustrator and cartoonist, created a cartoon of the four women—Liz, Kikkan, Holly, and Jessie—dressed in cowboy boots, cowboy hats, and dresses, firing pistols in the air. Above the women, the cartoon reads "We Are Here!"

"It was so cool," said Holly. "It was the American revolution, us as cowboys with cowboy hats and guns."

The women signed a race bib and gave it to Matt. It's framed and hangs on the wall in his cabin in East Burke, Vermont. It's one of his most prized possessions.

* * *

Two weeks later, the World Cup tour crossed the Atlantic and convened in Quebec City. With snow trucked in from the nearby mountains, organizers created a looping sprint course in front of Quebec's Parliament Building and along the fortification wall guarding Old Quebec. With the seventeenth-century wall and architecture serving as a backdrop to the race, it could have been anywhere in Europe—except for the thousands of American fans who had driven north from New England, including a loud contingent from Dartmouth College, festooned in the school's Big Green colors. They climbed onto the light pole pedestals that dotted the 1.6-kilometer course that looped around the Parc de l'Esplanade and made the weekend feel like le Carnaval, Quebec's famous winter carnival, in December.

So close to home, the Americans had enough women to enter four teams in the team sprint, which was the first race of the weekend. Kikkan and Jessie were USA I; Ida and Holly USA II; and Sadie Bjornsen and Sophie Caldwell, a recent Dartmouth grad, were USA III. Caitlin Gregg (nee Compton), competing as a member of the CXC team, was paired with Rebecca Rorabaugh from the APU team as USA IV. Of the twenty-three teams entered in the two semifinal heats, only ten would move on to the final. USA I and II made it through.

In the final, Jessie moved to the front of the ten-woman field before the first corner. Their strategy was to sit in the pack, conserve energy, and then make a big push at the end. On the soft course made of sugary snow, Jessie skied aggressively and made clean tags with Kikkan; she had been learning how to hold her line, not get pushed around, and keep the tag zone clean. Then on her final lap, on one of the course's short uphill stretches, she shot into the lead. By the time she came into the finish stretch to tag Kikkan for the final time, Jessie held a 1-second lead on the field. She was relieved. The race also boosted her confidence. She finally felt like she was not "just the tagalong girl who's dragging us down."

"That was the moment where I was like, 'I didn't screw up, I tagged her in first like I was supposed to,'" Jessie said. "I earned my place. I felt like I was truly an equal part of the game."

Kikkan took off and did not look back. To Jessie, she looked smooth and energetic. She knew they had the win, if Kikkan stayed on her skis. And that was likely to happen. Kikkan came into the uphill finish stretch alone. With the Porte St. Louis arch in the background, she crossed the finish line in first, 0.9 second ahead of Denise Herrmann from Germany in second and Maiken Caspersen Falla from Norway —team sprint bronze medalist at the 2011 world championships—in third. It was the first time that an American cross-country ski team had ever won a team sprint, and the first time that Kikkan was not the sole woman on top of a World Cup podium.

Behind Kikkan and Jessie in the final, Ida and Holly had a tough day. Ida crashed twice during her second leg. First a Russian skier fell on her as they went over a small jump on a downhill section of the course. Ida regained her feet but her ski binding had broken and was not holding her foot firmly on the ski. She came around a corner and slid out.

After those falls, they were too far back to catch the leaders and finished ninth, 36 seconds behind Kikkan and Jessie. Holly was philosophical about their race.

"It wasn't a great race for me and Ida," she said. "But to see Kikkan and Jessie take the overall and the win, that makes it all worth it."

The next day, eleven American women entered the sprint qualifier, with a record five moving on to the heats: Kikkan, Sadie, Jessie, Rebecca, and Sophie. Kikkan easily progressed through the quarterfinal and semifinal and made the final. Then she won another World Cup race—the first time that she had ever won two World Cup races in the same weekend. After she finished, Holly handed her a big American flag, and Kikkan skied up and down the finish stretch waving the flag in front of the partisan crowd, with perhaps as many Americans as Canadians.

"I've never seen so much enthusiasm come together all at once," Kikkan told Fasterskier.com. "I was getting comments from all the other European athletes going, 'Wow, you guys really get fired up. In Sweden it's a polite clap.'"

A surprising player came close to joining Kikkan in the sprint semifinals: Sophie Caldwell, whose willowy build makes her look more like a distance skier than a powerful sprinter. Just six months after graduating from Dartmouth, Sophie had qualified for the World Cup sprint heats and then finished third in her quarterfinal heat, a ski tip back from second place (the top two move on to the semis). Her effort put her in fourteenth place in her first World Cup race. But given Sophie's background, perhaps it was not such an astonishing result.

❊　❊　❊

Unlike the other U.S. women on the team, Sophie Caldwell did not discover cross-country skiing. She was born into it. Her grandfather is John Caldwell, the "father of cross-country skiing" in the United States. Uncle Tim competed in four Olympic Games, and her dad, Sverre, is the Nordic director at the Stratton Mountain School and has coached there since 1980. Her mom, Lilly, was also a cross-country ski racer who competed in three junior world championships. The Caldwells live near the end of a dirt road in Peru, Vermont, a hamlet tucked away on a wooded plateau in the southern Green Mountains. Stratton Mountain rises from the hilly terrain about fifteen miles south, and its summit, lined with alpine ski trails, is visible from the Caldwells' house.

The eldest of Sverre and Lilly's three kids, Sophie learned to cross-country ski around the time she could walk. Before she was in school, she tagged along while her dad coached little kids once a week in the local Bill Koch League program. Once she was a little older, Sophie and her siblings—twins Austin and Isabel, who are two years and three days younger—spent their free time playing in the woods. Despite the remote location of their house, friends lived nearby—in particular, four boys within the same age range as Sophie and her siblings. In the summers, the seven kids would run through the hardwood forest, pretending a large boulder was Pride Rock from the *Lion King* or catching frogs in a nearby pond.

Snow did not deter their exploration. On winter weekends, they often skied through the meadow and woods to nearby Wild Wings Ski Touring Center, less than a half mile away. There, they continued to play around, sometimes hiding under the ski-trail bridges, pretending they were trolls. Scaring people, though, does not seem like part of Sophie's character. Although she laughs easily and often, she has her mother's quiet, thoughtful demeanor.

Racing—and training for races—was not yet the focus for Sophie, Isabel, or Austin. They belonged to the local Bill Koch League, but until sixth grade, the kids only met once a week, and the focus was on fun and games. It was a perpetuation of John Caldwell's coaching philosophy: make it fun and interesting, and get them hooked.

Besides her siblings and neighbors as playmates, Sophie also had seven Caldwell cousins, and two cousins on her mom's side. Every summer, John and his wife Hester ("Hep") would host the ten Caldwell cousins at their large old farmhouse on a hillside above Putney. They called it Camp Caldwell.

"I think they mostly made us do chores," remembered Sophie. "But we thought it was the greatest thing in the world. We were all together. We'd play, do a chore, play, do a chore."

But for Sophie, who has her dad's tall, lithe build, it wasn't all fun and games. John and Hep sent the kids out to their (cold) pond every morning for a swim before breakfast. "This is the reason I hate swimming," said Sophie with a rare grimace. She usually has her grandmother's warm, broad smile. "All my cousins would wake up at six in the morning, and I liked to sleep in until seven or eight. Then they would all watch me out the window to make sure I didn't fake dunk, which I did try to do sometimes."

Although Sophie did the usual smattering of childhood activities through elementary school—except swimming—she had narrowed her focus to soccer and cross-country skiing by the time she was in middle school. A natural athlete, she excelled at both, but she soon began excelling at cross-country skiing far beyond the Vermont borders. As an eighth grader, she won the Bill Koch League Festival, an annual event for the New England BKL programs. The next year, she enrolled full time at the Stratton Mountain School and won the junior national sprint title as a fourteen-year-old. Spring that year, Sverre took the SMS kids to Finland and Sweden to extend their season and give them a taste of racing abroad. The races in Luleå, Sweden, were stacked with some serious competition, including up-and-coming junior racer Charlotte Kalla. Sverre took one look at the competition and told his skiers, "If anyone wins one of these races, I'll give them a car."

The first race was a sprint. Sophie won.

"Luckily, we had a really old car," said Sverre, laughing and shaking his head at the memory. "We sold it for $200 and gave her the money. It was better than a Matchbox toy."

The awards ceremony in Luleå was supposed to be a celebration for Kalla, their rising star. Except a girl three years younger—and an American—had beaten her.

Back home, Sophie quickly established herself as one of the top junior sprinters in the United States. But she didn't always win races. And Sverre was happy about it. He didn't want his daughter to think that she always had to win. He wanted her to ski because she liked it. As Sverre tells his skiers, it's all practice until the Olympics.

Her senior year at SMS, Sophie finished eighth in the sprint at the 2008 U.S. nationals. She was almost a decade younger than most of the competitors who finished ahead of her. And she earned her first trip to the FIS Nordic Junior World Ski Championships. She graduated from SMS that spring and followed her father (and grandfather) to Dartmouth, not because it was their alma mater but because she had attended a couple of classes while she was touring the college and decided that she liked them—an indication that skiing would not be her sole focus. Even so, she missed classes in January and February her freshman year to attend world juniors again. She made her collegiate skiing debut three weeks late, leading teammates Rosie Brennan and Ida Sargent in a sweep of the podium at the Dartmouth Carnival in early February. In her second collegiate race a week later, Sophie won a relay (with Ida and Rosie), then finished second to Rosie in a 10-kilometer classic race.

Dartmouth opened her eyes to what the rest of the world could offer, and skiing became less of a priority. By senior year, Sophie considered enrolling in Teach America after she graduated. But that winter, she had one of her best seasons ever with her Dartmouth teammates. It culminated at the 2012 NCAA Ski Championships at Bohart Ranch near Bozeman, Montana, where Sophie finished third in the 5-kilometer classic race—her first podium finish at NCAAs. Then, in the 15-kilometer freestyle mass start, a race that favored the skiers from the western universities because they were used to skiing at altitude (Bohart's cross-country ski trails start at 6,100 feet), Sophie and her Dartmouth teammates, Annie Hart and Erika Flowers, controlled the race from the start. They wanted to ski together in the race, so Annie charged off the front from the start, took the lead, and slowed the pack down so Erika, who was typically a slow starter, could settle into the pace. One by one, the skiers from the western colleges began to drop off the pace. "You could see the western coaches getting mad beside the trail," remembered Sophie.

By the end of the race, the pack was down to seven skiers: the three Dartmouth women, three from the University of Vermont (friends whom the Dartmouth skiers had competed against all winter), and Maria Gräfnings, a Swedish skier recruited by the University of Utah. Sophie and UVM skier Amy Glen charged for the finish line. Both women lunged for the line, Amy's toe crossing an inch in front of Sophie's. Annie Hart came in fourth and Erika Flowers in sixth. The UVM women finished first, third, and fifth. It remains one of Sophie's fondest race memories.

"I was disappointed not to win when it was that close," she said. "But it was better than I expected that day, and to have the whole team on the podium, and two eastern schools up there, was awesome."

Riding a high from the great results and the teamwork it took to achieve them, Sophie realized how happy skiing made her. She knew she had natural talent. And if ever she was going to see how far she could go as a skier, this was the time. Easing her transition, Sverre was in the process of starting an elite team at Stratton—a group of the nation's top skiers who would be able to live and train at Stratton for free, while working with the younger skiers when they weren't racing or participating in training camps. Sophie was one of the SMS T2 team's first members, along with Erika Flowers, one of her best friends.

Going into the 2012–2013 ski season, Sophie's goal was to qualify for the World Cup sprint and team sprint races in Quebec City—a few hours' drive north of Stratton—in mid-December that season. To qualify, she would have to win the early season SuperTour sprints in Bozeman—again at Bohart Ranch. And to win, she would have to beat people like Sadie Bjornsen, who was competing in her second year on the U.S. Ski Team; 2010 Olympian Caitlin Gregg; and her old Dartmouth teammates Annie, Erika, and Rosie.

In the freestyle sprint final in Bozeman, she won decisively, beating Sadie by more than 2 seconds. Sadie won the classic sprint. But Sophie had earned a World Cup spot.

After Quebec City, Sophie traveled to Canmore, Alberta, for another World Cup race. She again finished in the top thirty. Although she was not on the U.S. Ski Team yet, she was on her way.

❋   ❋   ❋

As a new team traveling together, the six women and their coach settled into life on the road. With Canada hosting the World Cup in period one (November and early to mid-December), the North Americans had a rare opportunity to spend Christmas at home. Then they headed over to Europe. They would not return home for the next three months. While most of the European skiers live at home during the week, then fly to races just a couple of hours away, the Americans commit to three to four months living out of duffle bags in hotels and rented houses or condos—far from family and friends. But life on the road had changed since the days when American skiers had to call home on public phones in hotel lobbies, shouting over the line to be heard through a poor overseas connection. Or even the days of email and dial-up modem connections. With FaceTime and Skype, they could finally stay connected with friends and family at home, making the ocean seem less wide and deep.

As a surrogate family, the team members made sure that no one moped alone—at least not for long—after a bad practice or race. Perhaps it was the regular team meetings, where Matt encouraged people to share their emotions and anything that was bothering them. Or the little celebrations, like the time Sophie and Jessie made "cupcake cookies" (they molded cookie dough into a muffin pan, then filled each cookie shell with brownie and cake batter) for Matt's thirty-fifth birthday—and accidentally switched the candles to read fifty-three. Or the time Liz pulled out fake moustaches for everyone to wear on the van ride between races on Kikkan's birthday. Liz, Matt, Kikkan, Holly, and Jessie spent the three-hour drive singing and lip-synching country songs, as mustachioed troubadours, making each other laugh. Or the team's Secret Santa tradition before the holidays, where they draw a name from a hat—coaches, wax technicians, trainers, the guys on the team, etc.—and must write a poem about that person and buy a ten-dollar gift. Then each person must read the poem written about him or her and guess who wrote it.

"It's one of those things that makes our team very, very close," said Jessie. "You have to really know the person to be able to write a poem about them."

And then there's Marcel. A stuffed bunny, Marcel has accompanied Liz on the road since she was a young junior racer. With a maternal instinct, Liz loans out Marcel to anyone who is having a bad day or feels lonely. Marcel has had a humanizing effect. Once others found out about him, they pulled out their traveling companions, too. Jessie, for example, travels with a stuffed moose named Walter. One year, Matt suggested that they take a team photo, with everyone wearing their pajamas and holding their stuffed animals. Across the photo, they wrote Merry Christmahannakwanzika, or something similar, and sent it to their families.

"We realized that we are each other's family on the road," said Jessie. "On other teams, their skiers go home. We don't."

Team as family does not come naturally though, and they work at it. During downtime between races, they have also goofed around creating parody music videos, a team-building exercise made famous during the 2012 London Olympics when the U.S. swim team danced and lip-synched to Carly Rae Jepsen's pop song "Call Me Maybe." Along this same line, videos posted on YouTube show the skiers—male and female—dancing and lip-synching to songs like Taylor Swift's "I Knew You Were Trouble," with Jessie choreographing the dancing.

Matt also assigns reading to the group. One year, it was *Boys in the Boat*, about the nine men who learned to row at the University of Washington, then defeated the Eastern elite crews before beating the German eight in front of Adolph Hitler at the 1936 Olympic Games in Berlin. Matt tries to pick a book that he hopes the team will learn from, and it's also a point of reference for discussions and team meetings. For the 2016–2017 season, Holly suggested *How Bad Do You Want It*, by Matt Fitzgerald. But Matt liked *The Righteous Mind: Why Good People Are Divided by Politics and Religion* by Jonathan Haidt.

The coaches have kept themselves approachable too, partly through silliness. At one camp on Eagle Glacier, where the women, coaches, and other staff members are isolated at a small encampment for a week, with no way out except via helicopter (or a very long hike), Matt, Chris Grover, and Canadian coach Eric DeNys suggested that the group put on a talent show. The women were split into groups, and each group had to perform a skit or "something silly," explained Jessie, whose group danced. The coaches also participated, rewriting "Every Rose Has Its Thorn," by metal band Poison. Wearing sunglasses and pink buffs on their heads, they crooned lyrics like, "Every lap, has one more . . . ," while Matt played guitar.

"It's little, fun gestures that go so far in making us feel comfortable," said Jessie. "It's like they're saying, 'Hey, we're trying to go after this really hard goal of being best in the world. But if you're willing to laugh at yourself along the way, it's way more fun and doesn't feel as daunting and serious.' These guys really lead by example."

✻ ✻ ✻

After the Gällivare relay and Quebec City team sprint in late 2012, the American women truly believed that they were capable of beating the best cross-country skiers in the world. Five different women had stood on a World Cup podium at least once, and Kikkan had placed a World Cup crystal globe, given to the season's overall sprint champion, and one FIS world championship silver medal on the shelves in her living room in Anchorage. Although she could have sequestered herself with her own training program and own coach, as some of the top American alpine skiers have done, Kikkan remained part of the team, training with them at every camp, advising them on the business side of their ski careers, and traveling with them in the winter. Assured of her own talents, yet humble about her accomplishments, Kikkan motivated her teammates. Like Holly had learned at Mount Marathon, if they could keep up with her in practice, and even beat her on occasion, then when it came to cross-country ski racing, they would know that they too belonged on the World Cup tour—and near the top of results. It was the associative property of success.

Soon, Kikkan would have to add more shelving for her trophies. Her crystal globe and FIS medal were about to have company, and the Sochi Olympic Winter Games were just over a year away.

✻ ✻ ✻

Two months after the Quebec City World Cup team sprint, Kikkan and Jessie had another opportunity to be best in the world. The 2013 FIS Nordic World Ski Championships were in Val di Fiemme in the Italian Dolomites, and the sprint course was perfect for the American duo. At least that's what they kept telling themselves. They were riding the momentum from their team sprint win in Quebec City. But they also knew that they had to "ski a good clean race [and] stay out of trouble," said Kikkan. Leading up to the championships, Jessie had been visualizing the race for the past year, hoping that she would be the one picked to pair with Kikkan. The thought even motivated her on hard training days. "Do you want that spot?" she would ask herself. "Then you've got to go harder."

"It wasn't just about me," she said. "It really helps. When it's not just about me, I can dig much deeper."

Kikkan and Jessie also had been working on team tactics and had a new strategy for dealing with the chaotic tag zone. The skier waiting to be tagged would wait at the far end of the zone, in a corner. Then the skier coming into the zone could ski through the tagging carnage first before tagging her teammate. It meant that only one of them on each lap had to figure out how to best navigate the mix of skiers darting in front of each other to get to their partners. They practiced and visualized every aspect of the race. Except what ended up happening.

Jessie did not often wake up on race day and say, "This is my day." But she had that very thought on February 24, 2013. As she looked outside, she saw fresh snow. A good sign, she thought. As she and Kikkan jogged through the snow to warm up, they looked at each other and said, "Yes, this is it." They sailed through their semifinal without any problems. "In the state of flow, you don't feel pain," said Jessie. Before the final, it was the coaches who were nervous. Chris Grover kept asking Jessie if she had what she needed.

"Grover, I'm ready, I've got this," she assured him.

The final started out just like the semi—very smooth. Jessie was hyperaware. "Stay second or third, don't lead the race or get caught in the back, watch for attacks, read opponents' body language, watch for sudden aggressive moves in the tag zone," she told herself. Waiting for Kikkan to tag her for the fifth of six laps, Jessie thought, "This is it, I'm going to blow the doors off and tag Kikkan in the lead." So far, a pack of five to six had been skiing together. Jessie wanted to give Kikkan a clear lead for the final lap. So in the penultimate lap, Jessie went to the front of the group and put her head down. This is what she remembered:

I am hammering arms and legs are churning up the snow. I'm hammering as hard as I can. I barely hear the others behind me. Suddenly, I feel this yank on my left arm. My hand comes up, and there's no pole in it. The girl behind me got a little too close. I have little bird wrists, so my pole strap came off. I had half a second of being like, "Shit." Then, who cares, gotta keep going. I ski with my legs anyway.

I'm almost at the top of the hill, I can ride this out. I just started swinging my empty hand. If anything, I increased the pace because I was furious: How dare you step on my pole!

I'm going as hard as I can but yelling, "Pole, pole!" But not waving my hand because I'm using my arm to generate momentum. [APU coach] Erik Flora was at the top of the hill, and he comes running down the hill with a pole. He stops, sends up this spray of snow, I grab the pole and start going and realize it's a men's classic pole. So it's up here [way too tall]. "Oh boy."

At this point, the Finnish girl started going by me. I slipped in behind her. "This is good, this is fine, I can still pass her."

The pack is strung out behind me. "Gotta break away, gotta break away," I think. I have the mentality of a dog with a bone. I fumbled with the pole strap on the downhill and got the pole on my wrist. I get behind the Finnish girl [Riikka Sarasoja-Lilja], taking deep calming breaths. Convincing myself that I'm recovering faster than anyone else. I'm fresh, I'm ready. We go around this sharp corner, I get into my special tuck folded over at the waist and start shooting by people. Our coaches nailed the wax. I shoot around the Finnish girl and hammer as hard as I can. All I'm thinking is get to the tag zone, tag off. Don't screw up, don't trip, don't fall, get there in one piece. I started skating with no poles as hard as I could. Get to lanes, all I can think about is getting there, willing my body toward the line. I tagged off to Kikkan, thought I was going to die. I never looked at the screen. I tagged her, I did my job and know she will do hers. It was absolute confidence. I just knew we were going to win. [Kikkan crossed the finish line 7.8 seconds ahead of Sweden's Ida Ingemarsdotter. She doesn't usually collapse after a race, but Kikkan fell to the snow after she crossed the finish line as a world champion.]

Then I ran to the finish; Kikkan was there. It hits me that my parents are watching. I burst into tears. I flop on top of her, crying. We did it! She's laughing. We did it!

I realize that I can't wait to tell my mom and dad. But I won't have to tell them anything. They got up at 5:30 a.m. with a bunch of my volunteer ski coaches from Stillwater. All of them drove to the nearest McDonald's with Internet. They were in Cable, Wisconsin, for the Slumberland American Birkebeiner race. The people who watched me grow up were all there watching it. That's what really made me cry. It wasn't the feeling of yes, we did it. We did it for them.

The rest of that day was a blur. I prepared everything possible in the race but never prepared for what do we do if we win. I'd never thought about it. It was an incredible dream.

❊   ❊   ❊

Competing in her seventh world championships, Kikkan was proud of how they had skied the race, controlling it from the first lap. And she was proud of Jessie, still young in her career, for maintaining composure after she lost her ski pole. When Kikkan competed in her first world championship race in 2001, the team sprint was not even an event yet. It wasn't included in the world championship program until 2007 (Kikkan and Laura Valaas finished eleventh in the team sprint that year). Since then, the team sprint has been a classic event at world championships. In Val di Fiemme, it was finally a freestyle team sprint.

"For me, it's been a long time coming," she told Fasterskier.com. "I was here ten years ago when this wasn't even a remote possibility, so it's pretty cool to do it and do it with a teammate."

The coaches thought it fitting that the women's first world championship title would come in a team event.

"It was only two of them," Matt told Fasterskier.com, "but it's so like this team to score big at an event that relies on one another."

❊   ❊   ❊

In the other races at the 2013 world championships, the U.S. team had a couple of near misses. On the hills of Valle di Fiemme, Liz finished fifth in the 10-kilometer freestyle race, less than 10 seconds from a medal. And the U.S. women battled in the 4 x 5-kilometer relay. In the opening classic leg, Norway's Heidi Weng broke out of the lead pack on the final climb and tagged teammate Therese Johaug ahead of France and

Russia. Sadie kept the U.S. team in the chase pack, finishing the first classic leg in sixth, 33 seconds behind Norway and 23 seconds out of the medals. In the second classic leg, Polish standout Justyna Kowalczyk was the only skier to get by Norway, gaining 37 seconds by the time she tagged off. Behind Kowalczyk, Kikkan brought the U.S. team into contact with the pack battling for the bronze medal. But her efforts earlier in the championship caught up with her. Halfway into her leg, she dropped back and ended up finishing ninth, 1:18.9 behind Norway, which was back in the lead.

With her love of hills, Liz tried to make up the lost ground. Skating the fastest third leg, she gained back about 30 seconds and handed off to Jessie, 25 seconds out of bronze.

On the anchor leg, Marit Bjørgen easily extended Norway's lead over Charlotte Kalla of Sweden, leaving a battle for third between Finland, the U.S., and Russia. Yulia Tchekaleva surged from behind to take the bronze medal. Jessie tried to stay with her, but the Russian was too fast. Then in the final climb, Jessie passed Finland for fourth place. It was a historic best finish in a relay for the United States at a major international championship.

"We hoped for a medal, but fourth feels like a medal to me today," Liz said after the race. "Everyone skied their heart out today. Jessie could have easily decided that fifth was good enough, but on that last climb she decided, 'I'm getting fourth,' and to me that's a medal."

With the 2014 Sochi Winter Olympics less than a year away, there was reason for hope. In her one-hundredth World Cup race, in March 2013, Kikkan sealed her second consecutive World Cup sprint title, and she finished third overall.

"My fitness gets a little stronger every year, the experience gets a little sharper, I can handle being on the road for a long time, and I know when I'm going to peak," Kikkan said at season's end. "It's all coming together. I have to say, it's quite fun. You think you've hit the top, and you keep finding another level."

For Erik Flora, Kikkan's coach at APU, the season far exceeded expectations. "She achieved more than we thought was possible after she got through the stress fracture in the fall. A lot of it has to do with her, who she is and her strength as a person and her persistence and all the training, and lots of attention to detail in training over the last ten years. It's all building on itself. Each year, she has success, and I think okay, we hit a new level. And then she takes another step up."

Flora also credited her teammates with Kikkan's success. "It's been an incredible help for her to have training partners on a daily basis when she's on the World Cup, and teammates to share the experiences with. I think it's been a really important piece of her success. There's so much good positive energy. The ladies on the team are all really supportive of each other but also really competitive."

Going into the Olympic year, Kikkan would be a favorite to win Olympic gold in the sprint—a freestyle event after Vancouver's classic. And now Kikkan and Jessie would be favorites in the team sprint. Liz was looking good in the distance races. Holly and Ida were both ranked in the top thirty in distance and sprint events, respectively. And although she was ranked outside the top thirty, Sadie had cracked into the top thirty in a few races.

But mostly, they wanted to win a medal in the 4 x 5-kilometer relay. Matt considered a relay medal as the ultimate measure of a team's success, even more than winning the Nation's Cup, which is the combination of skiers' points throughout the season, or even a World Cup title. An Olympic medal is flashy, he said, and would bring attention to cross-country skiing, a fringe sport. But mostly it would show the depth of this team.

As Matt likes to say: "If you are having success in the women's four-by-five relay, there's a good chance that you're having success in other events as well. There's also a good chance that it involves more than four women."

THE
POWER
OF
TEAM

SOCHI

This was it. This was the thirteenth year in Kikkan's ten-year plan to win an Olympic medal. And all systems were good. Finally, after eight years, the Olympic sprint in Sochi would be in the freestyle technique—Kikkan's forte. Although she had won medals in classic sprints, she was a stronger skate sprinter. And unlike the previous season, she had remained healthy over the summer with no nagging overuse injury or lingering illness. Her World Cup sprint titles in the previous two years gave her confidence, as did her world championship win in the team sprint. She knew that she could be strong in any condition and on any course.

"I was so excited about the opportunity in Sochi," she said.

The media came calling, intrigued by this blonde with pink highlights in her hair who had once sat in for then-Governor Sarah Palin at a fish-recipe judging contest in Alaska. In September 2013, at a pre-Olympic media event organized by the U.S. Olympic Committee, she sat for hours on a stool in a convention center in Park City answering the same questions over and over. And she fielded interview requests—from *USA Today* and the *Wall Street Journal* and local newspapers and magazines around the country who all wanted to tell Kikkan's story to their readers. Many of them would call in January, just as Kikkan and her teammates were trying to peak for

> Victory is in having done your best. If you've done your best, you've won.
>
> ✳
>
> Bill Bowerman, American track and field coach and cofounder of Nike

the Games. It was tiring. But it was the kind of exposure that she had always hoped cross-country skiing would receive.

Despite all the demands, Kikkan's racing did not seem to suffer. She finished second in one of the season's first sprints (a classic) in northern Finland. Then Kikkan, Sadie, Liz, and Jessie—dressed in the red, white, and blue striped socks and with U-S-A painted on their cheeks—finished on the podium at the Lillehammer World Cup. In falling snow and below-freezing temperatures, Kikkan led the relay for most of her classic leg, tagging off to Sadie in third. While Norway's Therese Johaug took the lead, Sadie held on to third place, about 1 second behind Finland. On the first freestyle leg, Liz tried to drop Finland but couldn't. The hard work took a toll, and she almost fell as she approached the tag zone in the stadium. She tagged Jessie about 15 seconds behind Finland. With Marit Bjørgen far off the front, almost assuring Norway yet another victory, Jessie began waging battle with Finland's Krista Lähteenmäki. Over the 5-kilometer lap, they exchanged the lead. But when they hit the final downhill, Jessie was out front. Matt was standing beside the trail swinging a ski pole over his head like a cowboy and yelling, "This is what you live for!" Jessie got a surge of adrenaline. It looked like the U.S. women were about to win their first silver medal in a relay.

Until Jessie caught a ski in some loose snow and fell. Lähteenmäki skied by as Jessie scrambled to her feet. She recovered in time, although without one of her ski poles ("one-pole skiing is becoming my thing," she quipped afterward). Norwegian coach Vidar Lofshus handed her a pole (despite the fact that Norway's second team would likely finish on the podium if Jessie could not keep her position in the race with only one pole). With a new ski pole, Jessie was able to remain in third. If the Americans could finish third even after a mishap, it was a good sign for Sochi.

"We're far from being in our peak form right now, so to put together a solid day here is great and we know we're just going to keep getting better and better," Kikkan said after the race.

"When your teammates win medals, it's exciting," said Sadie, who had won her first relay medal. "But when you actually experience it and feel it, then you truly one hundred percent believe in it. For me, that was amazing because it was the year of the Olympics. I was like, we can do it! We can do this at the Olympics."

An even better sign: the Americans had fielded two relay teams in Lillehammer. Sophie, Ida, Holly, and Rosie Brennan, racing as USA II, had been in contention until the falling snow slowed them. They came in twelfth.

By the time the U.S. women flew to Sochi, Kikkan was leading the World Cup sprint standings for the third year in a row; Jessie had finished top five in two World Cup races, plus won a silver medal in the sprint at the U23 world championships held in January 2014; and Liz, Sadie, Ida, and Holly had all finished in the top ten at least once. Then there was Sophie Caldwell, who, in her first year racing full time on the World Cup, had qualified for the heats in every sprint, made the semifinals twice, and made the finals once. As the team dressed in their crazy patchwork Team USA sweaters for the Opening Ceremony in Sochi, they were giddy with the possibilities.

❄   ❄   ❄

In Russia's Caucasus Mountains above Sochi, the Laura Biathlon & Ski Complex—named after the nearby Laura River—was built on the Psekhako Ridge plateau high above the mountain village of Krasnaya Polyana. Situated at 1,500 meters (about 4,900 feet) above sea level, it was considered one of the most difficult cross-country and biathlon venues in the world, with steep descents, long climbs, and—because of Sochi's more southern latitude—the potential for big temperature fluctuations. The only way for spectators to reach it was via a twelve-minute gondola ride followed by a long walk to the stadium. The area was renamed Gazprom Mountain Resort Laura after the Olympics and is one of four alpine ski resorts near Krasnaya Polyana.

The first official competition day of the Sochi Olympic Winter Games dawned sunny and warm, and the U.S. women's cross-country ski team was just looking to shake out the Olympic jitters. The first race on the program was the skiathlon. A version of the pursuit, the format was changed to resemble a triathlon. In the skiathlon, female skiers race 7.5 kilometers in the classic technique, then change their equipment (longer poles and shorter skis) in a transition zone before racing

7.5 kilometers in the freestyle technique (men race 15 kilometers in each technique). The mass-start event is appealing to spectators who can watch their favorites catch (or get dropped by) the competition in the freestyle part of the race. In the Olympic skiathlon, each country could enter up to four skiers. Skiing for Team USA would be Liz, Holly, Jessie, and Sadie, who had been sick for over a month before arriving in Sochi. It was the second Olympics for Liz and Holly, and the first for Jessie and Sadie.

As the sixty-one women started the skiathlon, the Americans—dressed in dark blue speed suits with red and blue stripes and stars on the left leg, and the matching pattern on the right arm—held on in the classic leg. Sadie was the first American into the transition, in twenty-second place and 45 seconds behind race leaders Marit Bjørgen, the defending Olympic champion in the event, her teammates Therese Johaug and Heidi Weng, and Charlotte Kalla, who was trying to win another Olympic gold medal for Sweden. Jessie was another 4 seconds behind Sadie, and Liz came into the transition over a minute behind the leaders. Now racing freestyle, their favorite technique, Liz and Jessie took off after the leaders. Neither was expecting to win a medal in this race, but a top-twenty result would boost their confidence.

While Bjørgen and Kalla duked it out at the front of the race, and the thousands of fans lining the course and in the stadium cheered loudly (including family members of the American skiers), Jessie and Liz steadily made their way through the field. By the finish, Bjørgen —a statuesque Norwegian with dark hair and a chiseled frame—had won her fourth Olympic gold medal, while Kalla collected silver and Weng won bronze in a photo finish with Johaug. Behind them, Liz had skied the seventh fastest freestyle leg, Jessie the eighth fastest. Their efforts in freestyle moved them into eighth for Jessie and twelfth for Liz—the best results ever for female American cross-country skiers in distance events at the Olympics. It was a huge improvement for Liz, whose top result at the Vancouver Olympics was forty-ninth in the 10k free.

"Hopefully, the rest of the races go just as well because it felt awesome and definitely came as a surprise to have such a good race," bubbled Jessie after the competition. She was so excited to compete for her country that she dyed her blonde hair red, white, and blue—except the red turned into pink.

"It's nice because my parents can always find me," she joked.

Although they had finished over a minute and a half behind Bjørgen, the Americans seemed content with their own races and happy for their Norwegian friends.

"We're finally catching up to where they're at," said Liz, of the Norwegians. "It's been really fun to get to know the girls and talk about what they do for training and even train with them. It's been really fun at the World Cup having friends from every nation. I feel like we're a big family here."

The American women planned to carry their momentum into the next race: the freestyle sprint scheduled in two days. It would be Kikkan's first race in Sochi and—she hoped—the culmination of her plan to win an Olympic medal.

❄   ❄   ❄

Ski wax plays an important role in cross-country skiing—perhaps even more so than in alpine skiing because, except for the few downhills encountered on the cross-country trails, speed is generated by human effort. The easier that skis glide over snow, the less effort that a skier must exert to go fast. For skate skiing, skis need glide wax. For classic, they need kick wax underfoot. Whereas many recreational skis have fish scales or mohair strips underfoot that serve the same purpose as kick wax, most race skis are smooth and require a special wax that will provide cohesion with the snow when the skier pushes down before kicking off to move forward (some new race skis are now waxless and have the mohair strips). Whether waxing for skate skiing or classic, it's a combination of chemistry and physics, where the right chemical combination and structure of a ski base helps a skier glide forward at the fastest speed possible.

Just like the Eskimos have fifty words for snow, skiers can encounter fifty (or more) different types of snow conditions in temperatures from sub-zero to almost tropical. New falling snowflakes are sharp, pointy crystals that cause abrasion and scrape, poke, and grab at ski bases, whereas wetter, warmer snow packs more easily, flattening out the pointy edges. But wetter snow can melt and create suction under a ski. Man-made snow, with its angular crystals, presents a different kind of surface, as does old snow that fell days earlier. And so on. Each different type of snow at different temperatures creates different levels of friction. For example, anyone who has walked (or driven) on new snow in cold temperatures knows that it has a different coefficient of friction than in warm temperatures. It's squeaky underfoot, not slippery and greasy. Skiing on snow in sub-zero temperatures is very slow and can feel like skiing on sand.

Ski wax serves as a lubricant to overcome this friction. Early waxes in the 1800s, referred to as Black Dope or Sierra Lightning to the California miners, were made of fats and oils. For instance, one recipe called for 1 pound of spermaceti wax (derived from sperm whale blubber), 3 ounces each of balsam fir tar oil and spruce oil, 2 ounces of pine pitch, and 1 ounce of camphor. Ski waxes are now made from hydrocarbons, with hard waxes providing better lubrication on cold snow and soft waxes working better on warm snow.

But wax isn't the only secret to better glide. Wax technicians also grind structure—or micro-channels or patterns—into ski bases that are made from polyethylene and graphite. These structures or grinds also help overcome mechanical and wet friction, with different structures working better in some conditions than in others. Because cross-country skiers can encounter every condition from new falling snow in cold weather to warm, slushy spring snow, elite skiers usually have large quivers of skis, each with a different structure and flex (or stiffness of the ski, with stiffer skis working better in cold snow). Most skiers on the U.S. team have around thirty pairs of skis each.

Adding to the complexity, wax techs do not just look at the temperature and apply one type of wax. They are modern-day alchemists, finding combinations of waxes that work for very specific snow conditions, and sometimes mixing in their own additives. Fabric brightener, newspaper ink, and metal shavings were once used as secret ingredients. Other secret sauces are concocted now, and wax techs guard their recipes as if they were CIA agents.

Finding the right combination of grind and wax is as much art as science, and it requires time, experience, and wizardry. A specific ratio of yellow to red wax on a day when temperatures hover just below freezing could be spot-on, as long as it's the right ratio. Miss the wax and skiers lose time on the course, going downhill more slowly than other competitors and/or slipping on the uphills in classic races. When skiers say they had fast skis, it means that their team's techs nailed the wax. If their skis are slow, skiers rarely cast blame on the overworked and unheralded technicians.

The big teams (Norway, Russia, Finland, Sweden, Germany) travel to European races in giant tractor-trailer trucks with pop-out sides and roofs that are built specifically for waxing and have at least a half dozen wax techs on staff. Smaller teams rely on the local race organizing committees to provide them with waxing trailers. Until recently, the American coaches helped the small wax staff prepare skis on race days. But the U.S. Ski Team now has five wax techs traveling the cross-country World Cup tour (more for world championships and the Olympics), and starting in November 2017 will have its own wax truck. It will help the team stay competitive in the Wax War.

As the Olympics eased into the first week of competition, the sun remained high over the Caucasus range, and the teams knew that wax would be a challenge. The snow was plentiful at all the Olympic venues. But under the warm sun, it turned slushy during the day. While spectators slathered on sunscreen, wax techs did their best to find the right formula for glide (and kick in the classic races). But how often had anyone, even the most seasoned technicians, waxed for summer temperatures? In the coming two weeks, even the Norwegian skiers would struggle. On the U.S. team, the skiers never complained about their skis; they knew that the wax techs were doing their best. Some teams' techs nailed the right wax for some of the races. Others seemed off, with skiers either slipping on the climbs in classic races or going downhill a little more slowly than the rest of the field.

✳ ✳ ✳

As Kikkan prepared for the sprint qualifier in Sochi, she was excited to get going. It had been thirty-eight years since Bill Koch won an Olympic medal for the United States in cross-country skiing. That was long enough.

Kikkan's plans remained on track during qualification. On the 1.3-kilometer course that started in the stadium, looped up a hill on the far side of the stands before doing a 180-degree turn to a downhill, then two more 180-degree turns to the finish, Maiken Caspersen Falla won the qualification round in just over 2:30 minutes, and four American women would also move on to the quarterfinals. Sophie qualified seventh, Jessie twelfth, Kikkan eighteenth, and Ida twenty-sixth. It was surprising that Kikkan was 4.6 seconds off the Norwegian's pace, but American fans figured that she was saving herself for the heats.

Less than two hours later, the five quarterfinal heats began. Ida competed in the third heat, Sophie and Jessie in the fourth. In the fifth heat, Kikkan would face five other skiers, including Bjørgen, the defending Olympic gold medalist in the sprint (albeit the classic sprint), and Denise Herrmann, the German who had finished on the podium in just about every sprint that season. In order to move on to the semifinals, Kikkan would have to finish first or second in that heat or have a fast enough time to move on as a lucky loser.

In the third quarterfinal, Ida was first off the line and third coming into the stadium. But she finished fourth and because the heat was slow, had no chance of moving on as a lucky loser. Sophie and Jessie competed in the fourth quarterfinal, and Jessie came into the finish stretch with Katja Visnar from Slovenia. But with a late surge, Sophie got by her teammate and finished second in the heat. She would move on, but in another slow heat, Jessie likely would not make the semifinals. Then the crowd in the stands stood for what would likely be the fastest quarterfinal of the afternoon.

From the gun, Kikkan took off with Bjørgen and Herrmann. The pack of six stayed together until the climb, when Kikkan attacked and created a gap. But they caught her on the descent. She came around the second hairpin turn off the downhill into the stadium area in first with the group right behind her. On the final turn before the finish stretch, she felt good. But there was a perceptible shift. Bjørgen and Herrmann kicked it up another level and surged by Kikkan. The three women dashed toward the finish. Coming up behind Kikkan, Italy's Gaia Vuerich lunged her foot forward at the line. Kikkan lunged too. But it wasn't enough. Kikkan's toe crossed the finish line fourth, 0.05 second behind Vuerich. The cheering crowd stopped. Many stared at the finish line, blinking and disbelieving what they had just seen. Vuerich and France's Aurore Jéan, who finished third in the first heat, moved on to the semifinals as lucky losers. Thirteen years of preparation, and Kikkan had missed her dream by the length of her big toe.

Kikkan stood in the finish area in disbelief. Even Jeff and coach Erik, who were in the finish area, were speechless. What had just happened? She had skied as hard as she could, had executed her strategy to lead the heat, and had prepared as well as she could have for the Olympics. She knew that she would relive those last few meters of the quarter-final for a long time. But for the moment, she could not dwell on it. She put her feelings aside, smiled, and ran over to Sophie. The two women hugged, and Kikkan shared her strategy with Sophie, who was the only American left in the sprint.

Skiing in the second semifinal and with her teammates cheering wildly on the sidelines, Sophie surged from fourth in the homestretch and lunged her foot forward again at the line, finishing second in a photo finish with Ingvild Flugstad Østberg from Norway. In only her first full year racing on the World Cup, Sophie had made the sprint final at the Olympics. She would finish no lower than sixth in her first Olympic Games and had a 50 percent chance of winning an Olympic medal, as three of the six in the final would go home with hardware and the other three would not.

The sprint final started, and on the climb out of the stadium, Sophie tucked in behind Caspersen Falla and Flugstad Østberg from Norway, and Vesna Fabjan from Slovenia.

"She's right where she needs to be," said her dad, Sverre, who was watching the race on his computer at home in Vermont with Lilly and their neighbors, Bill Koch and his wife Kate.

But then the six racers disappeared behind a clump of trees and into the big turn. They were out of sight from the spectators in the stadium and the TV cameras. When they came back into view, there were only four women. And Sophie was not one of them. Going into the turn, Norway's Astrid Jacobsen had been behind Sophie and had tried to cut the inside of the corner. The two became tangled, and Sophie fell. She got up but could not catch the leaders. At the front of the race, Falla won the sprint gold medal, with Østberg taking the silver medal and Fabjan the bronze. Sophie skied across the line 12 seconds later in sixth place. It was the best Olympic finish for an American cross-country ski racer since Bill Koch's silver medal in 1976.

After the race, Sophie was a mix of emotions—thrilled to have made the final and finish higher than any American woman ever in an Olympic cross-country ski race, disappointed not to have won a medal, and sad that Kikkan had not made the final as well.

"We were all a little heartbroken [that Kikkan missed the final]," she said. "But she's a tremendous competitor and teammate, and she was extremely supportive. She came up to me beforehand with a smile on her face and gave me a big hug."

Kikkan took a few minutes to gather herself before talking to the press and, as usual, did not dwell on disappointment.

"I've been thinking about this race for a long time, and we've been planning it out and showed up today ready to go. I was really happy with the way the preparation has been coming into these Games. I felt really strong and ready to go today. I've always said my number one goal was to come in ready to go and ready to fight for the medal and give it everything I had, and I did that today."

"If the last four, eight, or twelve years really hinged on today, I would be bummed, I would be really sad," Matt told reporters after the race. "I'm fine with the result. Everybody on the team—Kikkan, her coaches, the entire staff—did a phenomenal job. Today's result is just what happens."

Kikkan knew that the Olympic sprint was just one day—out of thirteen-plus years—and that she couldn't wallow in disappointment. That's sport, she said. Athletes prepare their whole lives for a two-minute performance. There is no guarantee of success. The team sprint and 4 x 5-kilometer relay were yet to come. She had a chance to win a medal in those races, and perhaps even more important, her teammates would count on her in those races.

That night, everyone except Kikkan—who was out with her family—went for a walk, the entire team and staff. They threw snowballs and joked around, celebrating Sophie's result. It wasn't an all-out celebration. How could it be? Sophie had done very well, especially in her first Olympics. But their view of ski racing for the U.S. team had shifted. The strongest woman on the team had not won the event in which she was favored. It rattled everyone—perhaps the Olympic veterans Liz and Holly more than Olympic neophytes Jessie, Sophie, and Sadie, who were still just thrilled to be there.

The craziness of the Sochi Olympics continued two days later, when the women skied the 10-kilometer classic race in temperatures that hit 70 degrees. Wearing only their sports bras under their race bibs and the bottoms of their speed suits, Sadie, Sophie, Ida, and Holly struggled up the course's tough climbs on skis with wax that wouldn't stick, giving them glide but no kick. It was demoralizing. Sadie had the best result, crossing the line in eighteenth, 1:41.9 behind winner Justyna Kowal-czyk from Poland.

The night before the 4 x 5-kilometer relay, the team gathered for a meeting. They were feeling a bit battered by the Games so far. But Matt focused their attention on the goal ahead: a medal in the relay. They discussed three goals for the relay: never say die and fight until the end, believe in their teammates, and believe in themselves. "We can use that fuel better than any team in the world, I believe," said Matt, who also encouraged the women to "get their sparkle on."

On relay day, they woke up to another warm, sunny day in Krasnaya Polyana. Some teams wore short sleeves, but not the Americans. They put on their race suits, painted their cheeks with glitter, and applied red, white, and blue face paint. And they pulled on their lucky striped knee socks.

"The relay socks are a mentality," Liz explained. "You put them on, and it's relay day. It's about the team, and you go out and fight until you bleed, and that's what we do every time we put them on."

This would hopefully be the race that would turn around the team's Olympic fortunes. They were favored to medal, if not a gold, then per-haps a bronze. Just a year earlier, at the 2013 world championships, they had finished fourth in the relay. Then three months before Sochi, they had finished third in a World Cup relay in Lillehammer. Norway was the clear favorite; they had not lost a relay since 2009, and their four skiers, with Bjørgen as the anchor, were each ranked in the top four in the world. The Norwegians had become so strong that everyone else was essentially racing for second place.

"We train together, and we are at a high level," explained Bjørgen. "To be together and push each other, it's making the whole team better."

But in the past couple of years, the U.S. women had shown that they could vie for the podium spots with traditional favorites Sweden, Finland, and Russia.

With bib 4, Kikkan lined up at the start, and as the race began, she looked strong, moving into second position behind Finland up the first climb. On the first of the two classic legs, Kikkan's skis slipped a couple of times on the first climb, disrupting her stride. But the slips did not seem to faze her. She maintained her position. Skiing in front of a home country crowd, Julia Ivanova from Russia began to push the pace. About halfway through her 5-kilometer leg, Kikkan could no longer hang with the leaders. As six women dueled at the front—including skiers from Russia, the Czech Republic, Sweden, Norway, France, and Germany—Kikkan began losing ground. In her words, her body could not find that top gear needed to ski with the leaders. When her body tried to shift up a level, it wasn't there. By the time she handed off to Sadie, she was in twelfth place, almost 40 seconds behind. There were only fourteen teams in the race.

As Russia would soon learn, one good leg does not make a relay. Nor does one bad. Sadie took off and caught three teams ahead of her, including the Czech skier, who was in second place after the first leg. Ahead of her, Finland's Aino-Kaisa Saarinen was having the relay of her life. Ninth when she started, Saarinen stormed through the field and had pulled ahead of everyone except Sweden. And Stefanie Boehler from Germany had gone with her. Sweden, Finland, and Germany had a 13-second gap on the next three teams, one of which was—shockingly—Norway. Therese Johaug was struggling as well. Even farther back in the race, the Russian skier had dropped off the leaders and was only 30 seconds ahead of Sadie.

Liz and Jessie, who were about to ski the final two relay legs, watched the race unfolding from the start area. Making up a minute on teams like Norway, Finland, and Sweden wasn't going to be easy. But they were not going to give up. Liz and Jessie locked hands and said, "Let's go hunting." Sadie tagged off to Liz in ninth place, right on Italy's tails. But the hunt was futile. Liz and Jessie went after it, but skiing their relay legs alone, far off the lead pack, they couldn't make up time on the teams ahead.

At the front of the race, Charlotte Kalla was having a great day, bringing Sweden from a 25-second deficit to win in a sprint finish against Finland and Germany. It was Sweden's first Olympic relay medal since 1968 and first gold since 1960. For Finland, it was the team's first medal in a major championship since 2011.

Jessie crossed the finish line in ninth, more than 2:30 minutes later, then vomited.

"Not what we were hoping for, but we could not have tried any harder," she said after she recovered.

Once Kikkan lost touch with the leaders in the first leg, it was too large a gap for the others to close. They were mostly skiing their relay legs alone, and it's difficult to make up time on a lead pack, where the skiers push each other and draft off one another.

"We knew that there were probably five or six teams in the hunt for those medals," said Kikkan. "We knew we would be in the hunt if we put it together. It was tough to feel that already starting to slip away on the first leg. I tried to dig and tried to get it back but couldn't find that gear."

Immediately after the relay, the U.S. women did not appear devastated. Either it had not hit them yet, or it was a testament to their perpetual optimism. Talking to reporters, they were philosophical about defeat.

"That's how we ski relays," Jessie said. "Sometimes that means we're in the hunt for medals, and sometimes that means we're at the back of the pack. We prepared as well as we could, we pushed ourselves as hard as we could, and we believed in each other. And that's what matters."

The women also claimed that the pressure of expectations did not weigh on them in the relay, and Matt agreed. The team has two sports psychologists with them—a norm at big events. They help the athletes keep expectations in perspective and try to ensure that nerves do not become paralyzing. But this group of women did not need professionals to help them maintain psychological equilibrium in Sochi. They had each other. As Matt said, "We have hardly used them because the team chemistry and stability of the team is so great."

Although Kikkan was off her game in Sochi, the rest of the team had personal bests: Jessie's eighth in the skiathlon with Liz in twelfth, and in her first year on the U.S. Ski Team, Sophie made the sprint final, finishing sixth.

"We're at the Olympic Games and everybody's at their top shape," Sadie said. "If you're off a little bit, you're off. That's part of it. Our team is capable of winning medals. We've done it before, and I think we will again. Today was just not the day."

That night as Sadie walked back to her room in the Olympic Village from dinner, she ran into Aino-Kaisa Saarinen, who had just won her fourth Olympic medal as a member of Finland's relay squad. The normally reserved Finnish skier was bouncing up and down, excited by the silver medal that her team had won in the relay and happy to greet her American friend.

"The only reason we won a medal today is because of the lessons I learned from you in Alaska two summers ago," Saarinen told Sadie. "We were in the game room until late last night, and we were playing karaoke and having fun and doing all the things that you girls taught us."

When Sadie got back to the American's lodging, she told her teammates what Saarinen had told her. They all cried.

"Hey, we can't be disappointed," Sadie told them. "It didn't go perfectly, but we have the core to do something amazing. The Finnish team learned something from us. We're right there. We just have to figure it out."

The rest of the Sochi Games did not go much better. In the team sprint, Sophie put the team in fourth on the first leg, but Kikkan again struggled, and they finished eighth—two places lower than Kikkan and Caitlin (Compton) Gregg had finished in Vancouver. On the second to last day in Sochi, Liz, Holly, Kikkan, and Jessie raced the 30-kilometer mass-start freestyle race. At the 8-kilometer mark, Jessie was in sixteenth and Holly was in twenty-first, just a few seconds off the three leaders: Johaug, Bjørgen, and one of their Norwegian teammates, Kristin Størmer Steira. Liz and Kikkan were also within 15 seconds of the Norwegians. But then the American skiers switched skis partway through the race—on the theory that their wax would wear off during the long race on another warm day. They could never regain the seconds that they lost in the transition. Liz was the top finisher in twenty-fourth, just over 3 minutes behind Bjørgen, Johaug, and Steira. It was Bjørgen's tenth Olympic medal and sixth gold, putting her in a tie with Raisa Smetanina (Soviet Union) and Stefania Belmondo (Italy) as the most decorated female Winter Olympians.

＊　＊　＊

Looking back, Kikkan realized that she had made some small but crucial errors before the Sochi Winter Olympics. As a medal favorite, she had faced much more media attention in the months leading up to the Olympics than she had ever faced before. These interviews and sponsor obligations meant less rest as she prepared for her fourth Olympics. She also tweaked her back in early January. Rather than push it, she decided to rest her back and withdrew from the Tour de Ski, the World Cup event that was created to mimic the Tour de France, where skiers participate in races every day for eight days, with one day off. The winner is the skier who has accumulated the lowest time. An exhausting event, it can also give a big fitness boost to those who compete in it. And over the past three years, Kikkan had used it for that purpose. Racing every day for a week made her strong.

 Once her back felt good again, she resumed training. But with only a short window of time before the Sochi Games started, she focused on sprinting. She was really fast for 30 seconds, she said, but when it came to accelerating to the front of the pack, she had lost that high end of fitness that allowed her to shift into top gear. When Bjørgen and Herrmann surged by her at the end of their quarterfinal heat, they had—like a Lamborghini accelerating out of a corner—shifted down a gear and found that extra power. Kikkan didn't have that gear.

"Going into [the Olympics], I was so psyched at how confident I was," she said. "I was finally in a position where I could win an Olympic gold medal. I promised myself before the race that as long as I did everything I could leading up to it, then I would be satisfied. That was the most important thing. Of course, when you're going to win the gold medal, it's easy to say that."

Ironically, the racing that Kikkan did in Sochi helped her regain her fitness. She won a World Cup freestyle sprint in Lahti, Finland, a week after the Games closed. Sophie finished third, giving the Americans their first double podium in thirty-one years—since Sophie's uncle Tim Caldwell and Bill Koch finished second and third in a 15-kilometer World Cup race in Anchorage, Alaska, in 1983. Kikkan also finished the 2014 season with her third consecutive overall sprint title—another crystal globe for her living room shelves.

"Overall, I don't regret the [Sochi] experience at all," Kikkan said. "It will always be something I'm a little frustrated by, but it also kept me motivated to try for one more. If I'd won a gold medal in Sochi, it would have been a little easier to go, 'Well, geez, that's the top, I've hit everything I wanted, time for a family.' It left me a little bit hungry."

Looking back at Sochi, Matt realized that the sprint was one of the most memorable moments in his career. Kikkan, the team's stalwart, did not advance to the final and Sophie, the newest member of the team, did. It marked a shift in "the way everyone had seen things," he said. Kikkan was no longer the only person on the team who was capable of winning a medal.

Matt was not even sad about the team missing out on a relay medal. The Germans ended up winning the relay bronze in Sochi—the Olympic medal that the Americans had hoped would be theirs. In the years after the Sochi Games, Matt would see this very same medal when he visited his girlfriend, Stefanie Boehler, who skied the second leg of Germany's relay in Sochi, just as Sadie did for the U.S. team.

"She literally has the actual medal that Sadie would have won in her tool drawer," he said. "It's crazy looking at it. It trivializes it to see it. It's so not about this actual thing."

For Matt, the reward is not about winning medals. The reward comes from the journey of creating a team that can win. He does not even really enjoy medal ceremonies. To him, they are a letdown. His peak moment of excitement and satisfaction occurs during the race, when the women are doing well and he realizes that the hard work is paying off.

"I'm not someone who powers myself through life on winning," he said. "But I do power myself through life on trying to win."

ONWARD

Every athlete knows that failure is part of the game. The risk of failure is what makes sport exciting. And disappointment is a normal reaction to failure. It's a healthy emotion that can, if steered properly, lead to a positive outcome —if the goal not achieved is a stepping-stone to the ultimate goal. Disappointment can motivate an athlete to train harder, focus better, and work on overcoming any perceived weaknesses that led to failure. As sports psychologists and coaches say, disappointment is not what matters. What matters is how an athlete responds to disappointment.

But what happens when the goal that's missed is the ultimate goal—like an Olympic gold medal that an athlete has worked toward her entire career, especially if that athlete was fully prepared and was favored to do well? Even the most positive, optimistic athlete can feel kicked in the gut. At times like this, it can be difficult for an athlete to remember that sport's true reward is the journey because the outcome is never guaranteed. As Kikkan told reporters after the sprint in Sochi, "That's sport, right? You prepare your whole life for something like this, and it's over in two and a half minutes."

Then she let out a deflated "puh" sound before adding, "But I gave it everything I had, and my career up to this point has been amazing. So even to come in to these Games as a medal contender is incredible." It was as if she were reminding herself.

But for Kikkan, winning an Olympic medal was about more than her own dreams. She felt as if she were carrying the weight of the sport and her country on her back. An Olympic medal would have looked nice next to her two world championship medals and three World Cup crystal globes on her trophy shelves back in Anchorage, and it would have been a shiny treasure to cap a historic career. But more important, it would have brought attention to a fringe sport in the United States and increased participation the same way that it did after Bill Koch won a silver medal at the 1976 Olympic Winter Games. With increased participation, more money would have likely flowed to the team, and it would have been easier for skiers to attract sponsors. It was more pressure than any one person should bear.

Over the next year, Kikkan managed to use disappointment as prescribed—to fuel her training for another run at an Olympic medal in 2018. She started off the 2014–2015 season full of optimism and was motivated to win a fourth sprint globe and more medals at the 2015 world championships. But she did not race like the Kikkan everyone knew. She struggled through the entire season feeling fatigued, yet with no apparent cause. She only managed to finish on one World Cup podium—a third place in a sprint in Lahti, Finland, at the end of the season. After a dozen years on a mostly upward trajectory, it was her first real downturn in results. She took a six-week break that spring and spent a lot of time with her coaches trying to figure out the causes of her fatigue. In her blog, she wrote:

> Our analysis determined that I had been under a lot of extra stress during the training season and that extra load in addition to the training load I was trying to sustain led to the overtraining-like fatigue and lack of gears. The extra stress was probably due to a combination of carrying some delayed emotion from the disappointment of the Sochi Olympics, the extra load of doing work for sponsors, leading the FIS Athlete Commission, and working to get Fast and Female USA officially incorporated and off the ground as a nonprofit

Onward

[the nonprofit started by Chandra Crawford in Canada and run by Kikkan in the United States to empower young girls through sport]. All great things that I absolutely love to do, but probably too much time spent not recovering from a heavy load of training.

✳ ✳ ✳

Even when channeled properly, disappointment can be an exhausting emotion to bear. It can overcome you, undermining belief and confidence, then leave you in a state of existential despair, questioning life's choices and purpose. It's also a difficult emotion to shake, especially when you've worked so hard for a goal for so long. But like always, Kikkan was determined to move on. The next Olympics were three years away, and her job was not finished.

✳ ✳ ✳

While Kikkan was struggling, the team that she had helped build began to thrive on its own. Throughout the season, at least one American woman made the quarterfinal heats in almost every World Cup sprint, and often one or two moved on to the semifinals and finals. Ida came close in the first classic sprint, making the final, and finishing fifth behind winner Marit Bjørgen. At the Tour de Ski in early January 2015, Liz finished fifth overall after eight days of racing. It was the best ever finish for an American in the Tour de Ski. For a skier who thrives skiing on tough courses, especially uphill—and admits that she is not wild about downhills—Liz called the Tour "the race that's built for me."

She carried the confidence earned from that result forward and, two weeks later, earned her first World Cup medal in an individual race— second place in a 10-kilometer freestyle in Rybinsk, Russia. Liz had picked that race over the summer as one in which she wanted to aim for the podium. No unnerving downhill on the 10-kilometer course, and it's usually cold in northern Russia in January, making the snow slow and the race tougher. The top-ranked skiers also usually skip the Rybinsk World Cup because it requires a lot of long travel. Throughout her career, Liz had had trouble envisioning herself on the podium. It was an indication that belief had not thoroughly permeated the team. But with most of the Norwegians sitting out the race, Liz had a chance.

"[In most World Cup races] the [podium] steps are already taken by Therese Johaug and Marit," she said. "Then you had that random third one. You have to really work to get on that third step on the podium."

She knew that once she could make her first podium in a distance race, then she could start seeing herself up there with the big guns from Norway. In her mind, she was going to win the Rybinsk 10k. When she finished second, she was pumped.

"It was a different mind-set than I've ever been able to come through with," Liz said. "It was utter confidence. That has always been a struggle for me. I see everyone else as a little bit better than me, except for on an uphill. That's the one place where I can see myself on the podium. But [in] a normal race, it's very, very hard for me to think that I'm the best one out there."

In mid-February, eight women from the United States traveled to Falun in south-central Sweden for the 2015 world championships. For Kikkan, Liz, Jessie, Ida, Sadie, and Sophie, worlds would be a chance to exorcise the demons that remained after Sochi. They were joined by Caitlin (Compton) Gregg and Rosie Brennan, who had graduated from Dartmouth in 2011 and had been training with APU since then. Falun would be her first world championship.

For Caitlin, now a thirty-four-year-old veteran skier, making the 2015 worlds team was a goal after she missed making the Sochi Olympic team the previous season. She had not raced much internationally since the 2010 Vancouver Games. International racing was too expensive, and she had had to pay off $3,000 in debt from the 2010 Olympic season. The following year, she had qualified for the 2011 world championships but declined the berth.

"I finally said I need to get my feet beneath me; I can't come out of the year wondering if I can pay my rent," she said.

Instead of competing at worlds that year, she entered the American Birkebeiner, a 50-kilometer freestyle race from Cable to Hayward, Wisconsin. She won, crossing the line 3 seconds ahead of former U.S. Ski Teamer Morgan Smyth. Caitlin collected the $7,500 prize for first place, plus a $2,500 bonus for the first American across the finish line. That spring, she married Brian Gregg, also a cross-country ski racer, and they used Caitlin's winnings to buy a house in Minneapolis. Their house cost $10,500. With the Birkie win, Caitlin attracted more sponsors, and she and Brian learned how to market themselves, creating Team Gregg. With more sponsors, plus her work with In the Arena, a nonprofit that partners elite athletes with underserved youths, and manageable expenses (no more rent to pay), Caitlin finally felt as if she could be a full-time athlete.

During the winter of 2014, she took the SuperTour lead and earned her way back onto the World Cup—but still not the U.S. Ski Team. Racing Stateside (she won her fourth national title in the 20-kilometer freestyle in January 2014) and on the World Cup, she was competitive with some of the women on the U.S. team. After winning her fifth national title in January 2015 (in the 10-kilometer freestyle), she earned another trip to world championships.

❊ ❊ ❊

The 2015 FIS Nordic World Ski Championships began in Falun, Sweden, on February 19 with a classic sprint. And from the qualifier, it looked as if this championship might be a repeat of the Sochi Olympic Games. Kikkan's lackluster year continued, and she missed qualifying for the sprint heats. Only Sophie and Ida competed in the quarterfinals, with Sophie moving on to the semis but not making the finals, where Marit Bjørgen won her thirteenth world title.

Then in the team sprint—a freestyle event at 2015 world championships—Jessie entered as the defending world champion and was paired with Sophie this time, not Kikkan. Sophie finished her first 1.2-kilometer leg in sixth place, and even though she skied the second-fastest second leg, Jessie could only pull the team into fifth. By the end of their six laps, they finished eighth, more than 30 seconds behind the Norwegian duo of Ingvild Flugstad Østberg and Maiken Caspersen Falla.

After the race, emotions caught up with Jessie. She had had high hopes for the team sprint—to defend the title that she and Kikkan had won two years before—and she had felt "crazy pressure" as a defending champion. She and Sophie had given it their all, but the race did not go as planned. The previous week had been an emotional roller coaster for Jessie, and she felt drained. She climbed into her bed, curled into a ball, and started to cry. She had the 10-kilometer freestyle race the next day, but she could not fathom unfurling her body or her emotions for the race.

Then Liz walked into the room, saw Jessie crying, scooped her into her arms, and told her it would be all right.

"I understand you're feeling bummed out," Liz told Jessie. "You're feeling like there's a lot of pressure on you. But now you're free, you can do whatever you want. You have no more pressure, no more titles to defend."

That night, Matt gathered the team together and tried to re-instill confidence. He talked about skiers who count themselves out before the race has even started, who think that they can't win or finish on the podium. "Why not you?" he asked. "You have to go out there and think, 'Why not me?' You have as good a chance as anyone."

Snow was forecast for the day of the 10k, and new snow accumulating on the course would make it soft and slow. It would be a tough race in these conditions. But they also knew that it would be tough for everyone. When the race started at 1:30 p.m., the snow had yet to start falling. Unseeded in the 10k, Kikkan and Caitlin would be among the first five skiers to start—Caitlin was wearing bib 3, so she would start 30 seconds ahead of Kikkan in bib 4. Jessie would start 17 minutes later (bib 37) and Liz 8 minutes after Jessie (bib 53). The big guns like Bjørgen and defending 10k world champion Therese Johaug would start about 30 minutes after Caitlin and Kikkan—near the back of the seventy-one-women field, the fastest seeded skiers chasing the slower ones.

Caitlin started out well, skiing the first 1.5 kilometers in 4:09.2, about 3.5 seconds faster than Kikkan. It started to snow while she was on course, but the snow had not yet started to accumulate significantly. By the halfway point in the race, she held about a 20-second lead on those who had started around her. She was meeting her goal to hold an early lead. She crossed the finish line in 25:55.7 and was directed to the leader's chair. She expected to sit there through the next dozen or so skiers, then relinquish the leader's chair to someone ranked higher in the World Cup standings. But thirty skiers later, Caitlin still sat in the leader's chair.

"My goal was to try to come in, be the leader, and put in a good time," Caitlin told Fasterskier.com. "I think it took maybe another twenty or thirty skiers before I started realizing that it was actually a really, really good time."

Out on the course, Jessie was powering through the new snow on brand-new, untested Salomon skis. When she and coach Jason Cork had tried them out that morning, they had a certain zing, a pop that her old skis lacked. They gambled and decided to go with the unproven skis. But even with fast skis, it wasn't easy. She kept telling herself that it was hard for everyone, not just her.

"I'm not going to give up, and I'm going to stay on my feet," she told herself over and over.

For much of the race, she was virtually tied with Caitlin—7.5 seconds ahead of her at the halfway point, then a few tenths behind her at the 6.3- and 7.8-kilometer splits. At that point, Jessie—who has an extraordinary ability to tolerate pain (a trait inherited from her father, who once broke his foot while running in a park and ran 8 miles back to the car without complaining)—told herself that she was now racing a sprint qualifier, not a 10k. She only had 2 kilometers left to race, and that's just a little longer than a sprint.

"A lot of my racing has to do with lying to myself in positive ways," she said. "I was able to convince myself that I was fresh as a daisy, and I was doing the sprint qualifier, and I needed to move. I just went after it."

Jessie crossed the finish line and collapsed. Her time of 25:49.8 moved Caitlin off the leader's chair and into the runner-up spot. Neither American expected to stay there long. The Norwegians had just started and were clocking fast times at the first split. But as the two Americans waited, skier after skier crossed the line with a slower time. Jessie looked at Matt and made a funny face in disbelief.

Six minutes later, Charlotte Kalla stormed across the finish line in 25:08.8—the first skier to make it through all the splits faster than Jessie and Caitlin. The three sat in the leader's chairs, first, second, and third. Would this be the podium? Out on the course, the Norwegians looked like they were slogging through the new snow. Fast at the 1.5-kilometer split, they all slowed significantly by the 5-kilometer mark.

By the finish, Heidi Weng was the fastest Norwegian, crossing the line with a time of 27:00.7 for twenty-second place. Kalla won the 10-kilometer gold medal, with Jessie and Caitlin taking silver and bronze. For the first time in U.S. ski history, two Americans had won medals in a world championship race—and it was a distance race, not a sprint.

"It felt like it was a dream, like it was happening to someone else," said Jessie. "I had trained hard, I had confidence in my career, felt like I belonged on the World Cup, but I hadn't yet felt like I could win. It was something I had never thought to myself. I knew I had won one leg of the team sprint. I knew I was a competent skier, but my best events were always the team events. My individual races, I didn't have people to push for besides myself. Until that point, I wasn't able to unlock everything. I had to learn how to decide that it's okay to care about my own race as I care for the team race. I didn't think it was okay to want it for myself."

"Also I'm part Canadian," she added, a half-joking explanation for her polite competitiveness.

For Caitlin, the medal was a huge reward after a long battle. Her smile was so big, it looked as if her face might burst. Eleven years after graduating from college, she had proven what she knew all along— that she was good enough to win a medal among the best in the world. It had been an eight-year fight to get there, and now she wanted to enjoy it.

"When you feel like you're the underdog, and it actually happens," Caitlin said, "you're so excited and on top of the world."

Her excitement was muted by the reception she received from some in the ski community, as well as the press. A U.S. Ski Team "outsider" winning a medal at world championships had caused tension, and many were quick to point out that weather conditions during the 10k had played to Caitlin's favor. She had started early in the interval-start race and had not faced the same amounts of heavy snow on the course that the favorites had. In fact, the five unseeded racers who started in the first 3 minutes of the race all finished in the top fifteen. But upon closer inspection, results were all over the place. Katja Visnar, a top sprint skier from Slovenia, started tenth, shortly after Caitlin, but finished thirty-sixth. And Liz Stephen, a distance skier starting fifty-third, came in tenth. As Matt said, it just happened to be the United States' day. And Sweden's.

At the end of the championships, Caitlin received a bill for her expenses at worlds. The National Nordic Foundation covered it.

✳   ✳   ✳

As part of her commitment to In the Arena, Caitlin Gregg works with inner-city youth who live in the poorest parts of Minneapolis. For years, she has told the kids that they "can transcend this place where you think you're going to remain," that they can be successful. She has reminded them to believe in themselves and to go for it.

"Don't hold back," she's told them, "and don't let others tell you where you belong."

On November 22, 2015—fifteen days after her thirty-fifth birthday—Caitlin Gregg was named to the U.S. Ski Team. The B team, not the A team. But she had figured out the business side of a ski career and could make it work. And she hoped that as a member of the team, not just an adjunct player added to a championship roster, she would feel like part of the group. Although she had been excited to join the close team at worlds the previous season—and the team had welcomed her—she had felt like an outsider in the close-knit group that had traveled and trained together for the past two to three years.

"One of the hardest things is when you're outside of the national team, you are competing against the national team, even when you're at an international competition representing the United States," she said.

After helping the American women finish fourth in the relay at the 2015 world championships, Rosie Brennan was also named to the U.S. Ski Team's B team for the 2015–2016 season. It was her second time on the team and first time since she was dropped during her sophomore year at Dartmouth. Her previous experience made it harder for Rosie to fully commit to the team dynamic. She had felt very let down by the team when she was not renamed back in 2009 and approached the new nomination with caution. And even though she had been on the team before, she still felt like the new girl. She had known Sadie since their high school days racing together. And she had been on the Dartmouth Ski Team with Sophie and Ida. But she was new to this particular team

The Power of Team

dynamic and had to find where she fit in the group. The core of her team was still her two APU teammates, Sadie and Kikkan.

With eight women on the team now, six of whom were veterans, they were no longer upstarts on the world stage. At every World Cup and world championship race, they felt like any one of them could win a medal—and several had. Of the eight women on the A and B teams in 2016, six of them had at least one World Cup or world championship podium finish on her resume. And in practice, they now had the talent and depth to push each other at the pace that they would experience at the highest levels. It was helping the entire team improve. At races, expectations were high, but they had to have perfect—or near perfect —days to meet those expectations. Kikkan was there to cheer on their triumphs and console them in defeat, sometimes having to remind her teammates how long it had taken her to perform consistently on the World Cup.

"Because I had set the bar up here, and they got results close to it, they felt like they should be right there all the time, that that was the expectation," said Kikkan. "I had to say, no, no, no. What you don't see behind the curtain is the ten years it took for me to get here. I would get one [good result], then I might go two years without that next one."

She reminded them to give it their best in each race, to think about finishing consistently and building to the next level. Then the good results would start coming more often. She reminded them to find something to celebrate in every race and something to learn. And she reminded them to be patient.

"I was worried it would bog them down because they would feel like they had to be at this level or they were failing," she said. "[I would tell them,] 'You don't understand, the level you're at is so far ahead of where I was. You're going to get where I am. It's just a matter of time.'"

And then Kikkan wasn't there—at least not physically. In October 2015, Kikkan announced that she was pregnant and would sit out the season (FIS listed her status as injured in her bio on their website, an indication that the organization is still trying to catch up with women's athletics in the twenty-first century). She and Jeff had wanted to start a family, and it was a good break, a chance to reset after the disappoint-ment of the Sochi Olympics and the subsequent frustrating year. After consulting with her doctor, Kikkan still trained with her teammates in the fall and kept in touch with them throughout the winter. As her pregnancy progressed, she was home in Anchorage, riding her fat-tire bike, skiing, lifting weights—much like her normal training routine, minus the racing. Breck Stuart Randall Ellis was born at 7:47 p.m. on April 14, 2016, a healthy 8-pound, 11-ounce baby boy.

In her absence, her teammates looked as if they were carrying on as usual. Rosie, Sadie, Liz, and Jessie collected another third place in a World Cup relay in December 2015. Then in the Tour de Ski over the New Year's holiday, Sophie won a World Cup classic sprint—the first win for an American skier ever in that discipline. Three days later, Jessie won a Tour de Ski stage—the 5-kilometer freestyle in Toblach, Italy. She had asked the coaches to lie when they gave her split times out on the course; she told them to tell her that she was in the top five or tied for the lead. She figured it would motivate her to ski faster. So when head coach Chris Grover jumped up and down and said, "Diggs, you're winning the race!" she laughed to herself thinking what a good actor he was. "He was really living the lie," she thought. Except she really was winning.

It was the race where Jessie's true talent and versatility began to show through. Except for the world championship silver medal in the 10-kilometer freestyle race, all of her other podium finishes had come in team events—the team sprint and relays. Now she was showing her individual strength, and at a variety of race distances. She was twenty-four years old—the youngest member of the team—and had already finished on the podium in World Cup or world championship races eight times. At the same age, Kikkan had only finished on two World Cup podiums.

Later in January 2016, Jessie finished third in a 10-kilometer free-style race in Nové Město, then anchored the relay to the team's first-ever second-place finish. In February, she finished second in a freestyle sprint, then came to North America in March for the Ski Tour Canada, where she collected two more podium finishes and finished fifth over-all in the eight-race Tour. Also during the Canadian Tour, Sadie won a sprint qualifier and finished eleventh overall. And Rosie finished twenty-fourth overall.

On paper, it appeared as if the U.S. women's cross-country ski team was not missing a beat with Kikkan sitting out the season. But Matt noticed a subtle change. Without their longtime leader, the team was having to readjust the pecking order. Although he would not name names, jealousy crept into the team dynamic.

"It was fine if you were the fourth fastest or the second best in the race as long as it was just Kikkan who was winning," said Matt. "Then all of a sudden, Liz or Sophie or Jessie or Sadie wins, and Jessie becomes the dominant skier. Things really shifted on the team."

So who was the leader in Kikkan's absence? Was it the person who had the best result? Or the person who had been on the team the longest? Or the oldest person? Or the person who was checking in on everyone? Or the person—people—who kept the team on an even keel emotionally? Or the one who kept the team energized and motivated? Or was each of these roles important?

It was a subtle shift, though. The women did not fight or argue. As Sadie said, "We aren't that group." It was more a shift in the team's equilibrium. The balance had shifted, and they needed to readjust.

"When your teammates are having success, when there's a leader there, everyone feels super good about it," said Sadie. "We all felt good about Jessie and Sophie standing on the podium. But we also were all like, aw, we kind of wanted to be that person. 'Kikkan's gone, what about me?'

"Before, it was so easy. Kikkan was the winner, we knew it. We weren't fighting for that place. It was amazing when we got to be there with her. We knew she was the best, it was easy. Now when she was gone, there was a new best. And it's hard not to want to be in that position. I feel like we still operated very well as a team, superior to many other teams around us. But there wasn't that special leadership and vibe when she was gone."

And it was this special leadership that had really made this team. Kikkan's leadership style had defined how the team operated. She was a leader, but she was also the consummate teammate, as happy for her teammates' successes as she was for her own.

"What makes Kikkan such a great leader is she doesn't capitalize and horde all the control," Matt said. "She allows others to lead. She had it in her power to really never be beaten by anybody. There are subtle ways of intimidating your teammates into not beating you. She just chose not to practice that. For a lot of athletes—I don't know if it's women, it's just humans—other people's success casts a larger shadow on you. And Kikkan welcomed other people's success and saw it as a wind at her back. She truly wanted her teammates to succeed. I do think it was probably hard for her the first time one of her teammates skied faster. But she didn't change her philosophy, and I think that's something very defining of who she is."

Her leadership had helped create a road map for the team going forward. Maybe they didn't need one team leader. Like Matt had experienced when coaching at Burke, the team didn't need a team captain because everyone was expected to be a leader—no leader, all leaders. On the U.S. women's team, each person had taken on a leadership role—a role that they created based on their personalities and strengths, be it team mom, or emotional counselor, or intellectual sounding board, or team motivator, or team organizer. And each role was equally important, whether they were at a race or in training camp. By caring for each other and supporting each other like family members, and fulfilling their own individual roles in the "family," they could be the same strong team.

At a team meeting during the fall, Matt confronted the group. He told them that he did not think that they had an environment that was going to produce a medal in 2018, let alone 2017. The team had been coasting on its good reputation—becoming more "talk than walk," said Matt. Communications had slipped, insecurities allowed to fester. He took some of the blame. After eleven years with the U.S. Ski Team and five years as women's coach, he had set his coaching on cruise control for a little too long, taking a little extra time for himself. During the meeting, everyone cried, including Matt.

"It's so emotional because it's your family, it's your job, it's your best friends, they are literally the people I care about the most aside from my family and boyfriend," explained Sadie. "You forget how important it is to all be supporting each other and all be understanding of each other and all be lifting each other. It's a very emotional thing because it's so important."

A big pull has been technology, Matt said—blogs and social media profiles that need to be updated, along with the addictive nature of Facebook, Instagram, SnapChat, and Twitter. The team might be together in a room, but if everyone is spinning through their phones and connecting with friends at home instead of gelling with teammates, then they can become isolated from each other. By recognizing the problem, Matt opened the gates of pent-up emotion, and they refocused on being a team again.

"I credit Matt completely," added Sadie. "Without someone who opens the door so people can talk, it would never be possible. He sat us down and said, 'I don't think we have the magic that we once had. We're still amazing, but we're not there.' That's when the doors started opening, people said what they could be better at, what they need, and how to go forward with what they need. Things were talked about."

To keep communication open, Matt reinstated the team rule of no cellphones at the lunch and dinner table. The team also brainstormed other team-building ideas. Sadie suggested taking a team photo every Monday, but not posting it to social media, to just keep it on each of their phones. Then over the season, they could look back at the photos and remember funny instances from the time when each photo was taken.

"It's a constant reminder that team is what we first take care of," said Matt. "Then everything else has this foundation, this great life preserver that keeps us floating high in the water."

* * *

Soon after Breck was born in April 2016, Kikkan was back outdoors, first walking, then jogging. By early July, she joined her teammates for their annual Alaska training camp. She worked steadily to recover from pregnancy and childbirth, and by the end of October 2016, she looked like she was flying. In a mock sprint on roller skis along the paved trails at Soldier Hollow—site of the cross-country ski races during the 2002 Salt Lake City Olympic Winter Games—Kikkan accelerated past her teammates on a downhill and flew into the lead, winning the mock final. It looked like she was back to full strength.

But once World Cup racing started in late November, it was apparent that she still needed to find her race gears—that high-end pace and the ability to handle the intense suffering brought on by competition. In the season's first race, a classic sprint in Ruka, Finland, she finished fifty-second, 8 seconds back from qualifying for the quarterfinal heats.

"My results were pretty disappointing and not the start I had hoped for," she wrote in her website's blog. "However, I recognize that I am in unchartered territory as I navigate this return back to racing after having a baby. I could feel that the right ingredients are in my body, and now I just need to sharpen my race gears with more hard efforts."

The coaches took a gamble and entered Kikkan in the 2017 FIS Tour de Ski, then in its eleventh year. The U.S. team did not have enough start spots for all seven women on the team, and Kikkan would take Ida's spot.

"We felt that we needed to invest in Kikkan and unfortunately at someone else's expense," said Matt. "We felt like Kikkan's great result potential was still inside her, perhaps double-padlocked in her post-pregnancy year."

The Tour de Ski proved to be the turning point in Kikkan's recovery. In the first race of the eight-day Tour, she qualified for a sprint quarterfinal. It was her thirty-fourth birthday (December 31). She raced in four more stages, finishing in the points (top thirty) in three of them. By the end of January 2017, she had made it into her first sprint final, taking fifth.

Then at the FIS 2017 Nordic World Ski Championships, held in Lahti, Finland, in late February, Kikkan finished tenth in the freestyle sprint qualifier and moved on to the heats. In the quarterfinals, she squeaked into the semis as a lucky loser—thanks in part to Jessie, who led her quarterfinal heat and kept the speed under control to allow Kikkan to remain the second-fastest lucky loser. Then in the semis, Jessie, Kikkan, and Sophie all qualified for the final. It was the first-ever sprint final at a major international race with three Americans. A sprint final has six competitors, so the United States had a 50 percent chance of winning a medal. But those chances were skewed by the caliber of the other racers in the final: Norway's Maiken Caspersen Falla, the sprint gold medalist from Sochi; Sweden's Ida Ingemarsdotter, a six-time world championship medalist; and Sweden's Hanna Falk, ranked third in the sprint standings in 2017.

Prior to the final, the three American women discussed strategy with their coaches. Like roller derby, sprint heats can be chaotic, with crashes and obstructions often dictating the outcome. Kikkan, Jessie, and Sophie were adamant that they all needed to watch out for each other.

In the final that evening, held under the lights in Lahti's packed Nordic stadium, Caspersen Falla set the pace from the start, with Falk and Ingemarsdotter skiing close behind. Halfway into the 1.4-kilometer final, the Norwegian and two Swedes held the lead, with Jessie, Kikkan, and Sophie strung out in fourth, fifth, and sixth positions. But then on the second climb out of the stadium, Jessie and Kikkan moved aggressively into third and fourth. On the downhill back into the stadium, Jessie took over second place and held the silver-medal position for the rest of the race. Behind her, Kikkan passed Ingemarsdotter in the final 100 meters and held off an accelerating Falk to win the bronze medal. Caspersen Falla was way out front and won the gold medal. Sophie finished sixth.

Jessie's silver and Kikkan's bronze were their third world championship medals each—with Jessie having won a gold medal with Kikkan at the 2013 world championships in the team sprint and a silver medal in the 10-kilometer freestyle in 2015, and Kikkan having a gold from 2013 and a silver in the sprint from 2009. Although the sprint is an individual race, both American women credited the team for their performances in Lahti.

"That's for sure the most fun I've ever had in a final," said Kikkan. "Before we went to the start, we did a team cheer. We had such a good energy among the three of us and all of our team that is supporting us. It was a really magical day for our whole team."

Their pre-race cheer was not a typical team cheer. It was "shout whispered," so as not to distract other racers or draw attention.

For Jessie, it was the start of a historic world championship. Three days later, in the team sprint (a classic event at the 2017 world championships), she won another medal. Paired with Sadie and dressed in their lucky striped socks, the two women skied most of the six-lap team event in fifth and sixth place, until the final leg when Jessie slingshot by Sweden's Stina Nilsson in the final curve. As she charged up the straightaway for the finish line with Nilsson on her tails, Jessie kept thinking, "I can, I can, I can, because Sadie needs me." She lunged for the line and beat Nilsson by a boot length. The pair won a bronze medal. It was Sadie's first world championship medal and Jessie's fourth. Only a handful of American skiers—in alpine and moguls skiing—have won more.

"I never could have done that if this girl wasn't waiting for me at the finish," Jessie added, referring to Sadie. "That's the power of team. When we put on our relay socks, we have the energy of the entire Team USA with us, supporting us. We know everyone is there. It takes a huge team to support just two people on the track."

It was the first medal for the United States in a classic event at world championships. And it capped a phenomenal season for Jessie, who racked up an unprecedented series of top-ten finishes in every World Cup race she entered from December until world championships, including two wins in 5-kilometer freestyle races, a second-place finish in a skiathlon, and fifth overall in the 2017 Tour de Ski.

"My goal for a while had been to become an all-arounder," Jessie said. "I want to come to every race ready to play no matter the distance or format, and I'm chipping away, I'm making progress. I have some technique things that I know I can improve for next year, which is good because I want every season to go like this."

During the 2016–2017 World Cup season, Jessie had company on the podium, too. In the Tour de Ski skiathlon in early January, Sadie finished fifth, her best skiathlon finish yet. Two days later, Jessie and Sadie shared the podium in the 5k in Toblach, Italy. Jessie was happy to win the race but seemed even happier to have a friend and teammate on the podium with her. It was the first time that two U.S. women shared a World Cup distance podium (Kikkan and Sophie were on a sprint podium together in March 2014 after the Sochi Olympics). It was also the eighteenth World Cup win for the American women—nineteenth counting Alison Owen-Spencer's win in 1978.

"I knew she was going to do it this year. I had such belief in her, and to see her up here is just making me so happy," Jessie told the TV commentators after the race.

For Sadie, she had to push through the mental hurdles that sprang up on the relentless course, where any skier who lets off on the down-hills or easier sections finishes far off the podium. During the 13-minute race, she continually ran two phrases through her mind: "Stay strong, Sadie" and "What would Jessie Diggins do?"

"There is so much work on the second half of the race, and Jessie is just amazing at being strong on that section," Sadie explained. "So I was imagining her the whole second half in front of me, and it seemed to have worked."

Gaining her first podium in an individual race (not a team event) was emotional for Sadie, and it harkened back to how important belief is to this team.

"All the girls on this team are an inspiration to me," she said. "We are dreamers. But we are also believers. It's crazy how much confidence you can get from a teammate's success if you allow yourself to stand beside them."

A month later, Ida Sargent and Liz Stephen stepped onto the podium in the classic sprint and skiathlon, respectively, on the 2018 Olympic course in Pyeongchang, South Korea. It was Ida's first World Cup podium. Two days later, Ida and Sophie finished third in the team sprint.

❆   ❆   ❆

Of all the races during the 2016–2017 season, the one that best illustrated the story of the U.S. women's cross-country ski team was the 4 x 5-kilometer relay at the 2017 world championships. On a team with seven strong women, how would the coaches select four for the relay? As Kikkan said after she won the sprint bronze medal, "It's a position we've never had coming into a world championship. [In the past], it was pretty clear who was going to be on the relay and team sprint teams. It's a new reality for our team, but it's a good problem to have. You have to fight for your spot."

The fight for a spot on the 4 x 5-kilometer relay team at the 2017 world championships began two days before the actual race. Jessie and Liz are two of the fastest 5-kilometer freestyle skiers on the team, if not the world, and they had skied the two freestyle legs in every relay but one for the past five years. They would likely ski the freestyle legs of the world championship relay. But the classic legs have been more up for grabs. It's a trickier discipline, requiring more finesse than brute power, particularly in warm or damp weather when the ski tracks can become slick, or "glassy," as the skiers say. The skiers, like the Scandinavians, who have classic skied since they could walk tend to do the best in these conditions, relying on muscle memory and technique so ingrained that they do not have to think, kicking off the ski with just enough force to move forward but not enough to slip back, then gliding for as long as possible on that ski. Pushing harder in classic skiing can make it more difficult—and slow. As Kikkan described, classic skiing "is really about the timing and finding that efficiency and rest-recovery in between strokes." Sadie was typically the fastest classic skier on the American team. This left Kikkan, Rosie, and Ida to fight for the final spot in the relay. The 10-kilometer classic race would be a test. The woman who skied the fastest would likely be chosen. And that woman was Kikkan, who edged Rosie by a few seconds. Fighting illness, Ida finished farther back.

The morning of the world championship relay dawned warm (in the mid-30s) and damp and stayed that way until midafternoon, when the race started. The American women put on their relay socks and glitter, and Kikkan led off the relay. Halfway into her 5-kilometer leg, she was gapped by the women from Norway, Sweden, Finland, and Poland. She tagged Sadie in fifth. In the second classic leg, Sadie made up time on the four women ahead of her, quickly passing Poland. But then the Scandinavian trio of Norway, Finland, and Sweden dropped the hammer and began to pull away, and the Americans would ski alone in fourth for the remainder of the relay. Anchoring the relay, Jessie crossed the finish line just over 30 seconds from a medal—and more than 1:30 minutes behind Norway. For the second consecutive time at world championships, Norway, Sweden, and Finland went one-two-three. And the Americans finished in fourth for the third time in a row. They all hugged each other at the end.

Even without a medal, it was evident the impact that the Americans have had on the relay—and perhaps the entire women's World Cup tour. The Swedish women each had Swedish flag temporary tattoos on their cheeks, and more than one team sported team-colored ribbons in their hair and glitter on their cheeks. After the race, the Norwegians

—who had won their one hundredth world championship medal in the relay—talked about how special the relay is, winning medals for their whole team and their country. Marit Bjørgen credited her team for the success that has put ten Olympic and twenty-six world championship medals in her trophy cabinet. Her teammates have pushed her, she said, and each other. This intra-squad competition has helped them become the best team in the world. The Norwegians swept the women's world championship gold medals in Lahti, and four of the seven who competed in the 2017 world championships won at least one medal. The team also swept the World Cup titles in 2017 (the overall title, plus the titles for sprint and distance). And that was without Therese Johaug, who won the overall World Cup title in 2016 but was serving a fourteen-month suspension for doping (she claimed that she inadvertently used a performance-enhancing substance in medication given to her by a team physician to treat sunburned lips).

Although the Americans finished far behind Norway in the relay (and the other world championship races as well), they felt as if they had come a long way since Sochi. Their fitness had improved and their belief had grown. They still have to have a near-perfect day to get on the medal stand in the relay. But those days were becoming more frequent.

"I think that each year, we are getting closer and closer to that place where we can fight for a gold medal in the relay," said Sadie. "I think we're figuring it out."

For this group of women and their coaches who bucked the odds and built a team, an Olympic medal would be a nice reward for their effort. But they have also come to realize that it's not the primary driver.

"We're knocking at the door," Liz said after the relay in Lahti. "I think we can all admit that we wanted this medal today. But I feel like I have won gold already with this team. I am inspired to be part of the U.S. cross-country ski team. I don't need a medal to show that. It would certainly be nice. I'd take it. But it's more about these friendships and these inspiring teammates who I'm around every day. They are why I ski, and I couldn't be happier to just be a part of this team."

ACKNOWLEDGMENTS

Writing a book is like training for a marathon—or a very long cross-country ski race. It takes dogged day-to-day work and vast amounts of time away from other endeavors (such as paying work and even a breath of exercise). If it were not for the generosity and patience of my husband, Andy, I would not have been able to write one word. He has always supported me, keeping the roof over our heads, offering humor and companionship, and preventing me from "overtraining." He is also a great traveling companion, and "Finland Finland" would not have been the same without him. He's pretty good with a camera, too.

Then there was my "coach" and editor, Phyllis Deutsch at UPNE. I am forever grateful for the many times she steered me back on course. Her kind encouragement kept me moving forward, and her genius at editing kept the story from spinning in circles. And many thanks to Karen Levy for her meticulous copy editing (oh right, the pluperfect!).

When it came to delving into ski history, I would like to thank Marty Hall, John Caldwell, Jim Balfanz, Peter Ashley, Alison Bradley, Trina Hosmer, Betsy Haines, Sverre and Lilly Caldwell, Cami Thompson Graves, Nina Kemppel, Wendy Wagner, and Rebecca Dussault for the hours that they spent sharing their stories. I could have listened for days. I am also indebted to Peter Graves, John Fry, Seth Masia, and Kathleen James for catching my mistakes. No book on skiing in the United States could be written without the help and insight of these people. They are all champions of snowsports and generous with their time and knowledge. To this list, I must add the late Paul Robbins, whose spirit has carried me through sports writing for the past decade (and in person for a decade before that). His Nordic coverage in old issues of *Ski Racing* was invaluable. I like to think he's up in heaven cheering on the women of the U.S. cross-country ski team—and a book about them, too. Here's to you, Paul. Onward.

The passionate and diligent ski writers at Fasterskier.com took over where *Ski Racing*'s coverage left off. Their detailed coverage helped jog my memory about key races, and they deserve big thanks for continuing to cover races, even in the face of challenging economics.

At U.S. Ski & Snowboard, Tiger Shaw, Tom Kelly, Luke Bodensteiner, and Robert Lazzaroni patiently explained the inner workings of the organization and their involvement in skiing. Now retired, Bill Marolt also shared what he saw in the cross-country program while he was at the helm of USSA. It's an organization that really does strive to be Best in the World—and not just in competition. I also want to thank Pete Vordenberg, who took time away from his kids to help me fill in important blanks.

In Alaska, Ronn Randall took a morning off work to provide insight into his daughter and the family and town that raised her. His storytelling could have filled this book, and I enjoyed every minute listening to him. Deborah Randall was equally willing to give me a glimpse into the Randall and Haines families.

And of course, I want to thank the women on the U.S. cross-country ski team. Their schedules are packed full with training, recovery, sponsor obligations, and other tasks. Yet they always had time to sit down with me, even after running for three hours in the mountains or while packing for a winter's worth of travel (thanks, Jessie!). And even with a new baby in the house, Kikkan Randall was always generous with her time. Thank you!

Finally, this book would not have been possible without the help and passionate commitment of Matt Whitcomb and Chris Grover. They too were always happy to answer my many questions. They adroitly coach and manage a team in a sport that keeps them away from home for over half the year, and they do it with keen insight, unlimited patience, good humor, humility, and openness. They are a rare breed, and they and the skiers they coach have showed the world what a well-functioning team can do.

❊   ❊   ❊

To Donate to the U.S. Cross-Country Ski Team

The U.S. Ski Team derives 40 percent of its budget from private donations. The U.S. Ski & Snowboard Foundation was founded in 1964 as the nonprofit fundraising arm of the U.S. Ski Team. Donated monies help support year-round athlete training, development, competition, and educational needs. To donate, log onto foundation.ussa.org. Or contact the organization by mail:

U.S. Ski & Snowboard Foundation
PO Box 100
1 Victory Lane
Park City, UT 84060

Athletes with their eye on making the U.S. Ski Team rely on funds from the National Nordic Foundation, which was founded in 1997 to help develop up-and-coming cross-country skiers, Nordic combined athletes, and ski jumpers. In the second decade of the twenty-first century, the NNF stepped up fundraising and now provides thousands of dollars to unfunded and underfunded cross-country skiers, particularly promising junior skiers, and Nordic combined athletes competing internationally, as well as athletes like Caitlin Gregg who qualify for world championship teams but are outside the U.S. team's funding umbrella. For the 2016–2017 season alone, the organization raised $190,088, with $158,787 earmarked for cross-country skiers (the remainder helps fund the nation's Nordic combined athletes and ski jumpers). To donate to the NNF or for more information, log onto www.nationalnordicfoundation.org. Or email nnf@nnf.ski.

GLOSSARY

Cross-country Ski Techniques

Classic The traditional kick and glide technique, where skis move parallel. The skier thrusts one ski and his/her body weight forward with the rear leg and ski extended behind.

Freestyle or skate skiing The skier moves like a speed skater, with the skis alternately gliding out in a diagonal direction. The skier moves forward by pushing off the inside edge of alternating skis.

Cross-country Ski Races

Sprint A cross-country ski race of 1.0 to 1.8 kilometers in length. The winner is determined through a series of quarterfinals, semifinals, and a final. Six skiers compete in each of five quarterfinal heats, with the two fastest in each heat moving on to the two semifinal heats, plus two "lucky losers." ("Lucky losers" are the next two fastest competitors in the quarterfinal and semifinal heats.) In the two semifinals, the fastest two skiers in each heat qualify for the final, plus two "lucky losers." The sprint can be contested in either the freestyle or the classic technique.

Sprint qualifier A time-trial race held the morning of a sprint race. Each racer skis the sprint course (in the specified technique) against the clock, starting at 30-second intervals. The thirty fastest skiers move on to the sprint heats, with the quarterfinals divided into five heats of six skiers.

Distance races In World Cup, world championship, and Olympic races, women participate in races that vary in length from 5 to 30 kilometers. Races are either interval start or mass start. In interval-start races, competitors head out onto the course at a set interval (e.g., 30 seconds). The winner skis the course in the fastest time, calculated after every competitor has finished. In mass-start races, competitors all start together, with the highest ranked skiers starting near the front. The first person across the finish line is the winner.

Pursuit The pursuit race combines classic and freestyle skiing. Skiers ski the classic leg first, then start the freestyle at the same time interval that they finished behind the leader in the first leg of the race. The winner of the first leg starts last. The pursuit winner is the first skier across the finish line.

Skiathlon A mass-start race with a 7.5-kilometer classic leg followed by a 7.5-kilometer freestyle leg. The exchange zone resembles a triathlon, where skiers exchange their skis and ski poles as fast as they can (freestyle skis are shorter and poles longer than classic).

Team sprint Two skiers alternate skiing the sprint course three times each, for a total of six laps. With each exchange, skiers must physically touch their teammate. The winning team is the first team to cross the finish line after the completion of all six laps. To determine the ten teams competing in a team sprint final, two semifinals are held, with the top five teams moving on to the final.

Relay Teams of four ski the first two legs of the relay using the classic technique, and the last two legs using freestyle technique. The women ski four 5-kilometer legs for a total of 20 kilometers while the men ski four 10-kilometer legs for a total of 40 kilometers. The relay begins in a mass-start format with teams lined up in rows. To exchange between legs, skiers must make physical contact. The winning team is the first across the finish line after the completion of the fourth leg.

Ski Races and Race Series Descriptions

Junior Olympics U.S. national championship for skiers under age nineteen. Now called junior nationals. Held once each year in January.

NCAAs The National College Athletic Association sanctions alpine and cross-country ski racing as part of Division I skiing. The colleges and universities in the Eastern Intercollegiate Ski Association participate in weekly Carnivals in January and February. The Rocky Mountain Intercollegiate Ski Association schools compete in weekly Invitationals. The two conferences meet every year in March for the NCAA Ski Championships. The Division I schools include the Universities of Alaska-Anchorage, Colorado, New Hampshire, New Mexico, Utah, and Vermont; Denver University; and Dartmouth and Middlebury Colleges, among others.

U.S. Championships or Nationals Held annually in January. The races for women typically include a 10-kilometer individual start (classic or freestyle), a 20-kilometer mass start (classic or freestyle), and sprints (classic and freestyle).

SuperTour USSA's premier cross-country ski race series in North America, with prize money provided. The series starts in late November and concludes in March. The overall SuperTour winner is determined by the best cumulative total of a skier's SuperTour points.

NorAm Short for North American Cup, these are high-level ski races in the United States and Canada (but not races that are part of the SuperTour). They are held from late November through March.

World Cup FIS's premier ski race series in all snowsport disciplines. For cross-country, the World Cup tour typically begins in late November, with races of varying distances held almost every weekend until World Cup Finals, held in mid-March. The overall World Cup winner is determined by the best cumulative total of a skier's World Cup points in all cross-country races. A World Cup sprint or distance winner is determined by the best cumulative total of a skier's World Cup points in either sprint or distance (5 kilometers or longer) races.

World Championships The FIS Nordic World Ski Championships are held every other year on odd years. For women, world championship races now include a sprint (alternating freestyle and classic), team sprint (if sprint is classic, team sprint is freestyle, and vice versa), 10-kilometer individual start (alternating freestyle and classic), 30-kilometer mass start (freestyle if 10 kilometer is classic, classic if 10 kilometer is freestyle), skiathlon (7.5 kilometer classic, 7.5 kilometer freestyle), and a 4 x 5-kilometer relay.

Junior World Championships Annual world championship event for skiers under age nineteen.

U23 World Championships Annual world championship event for skiers under age twenty-three. Held in conjunction with Junior World Championships.

Olympic Winter Games Held every four years, on even years and alternating with the Olympic Summer Games.

Note: Races at the Olympics are like the world championships. Techniques alternate from one Olympic Games to the next, so if a sprint is freestyle in 2014, it will be a classic sprint in 2018, and so on.

Other Terms

All-American A skier who finishes in the top ten at the NCAA Division I Skiing Championships.

Blowing up When an athlete surpasses his or her physical limit in a race or in practice and either has to measurably slow down or stop.

FIS The International Ski Federation (or Federation International du Ski). Founded in 1924, it is responsible for the Olympic disciplines alpine skiing, cross-country skiing, ski jumping, Nordic combined, freestyle skiing, and snowboarding. The FIS is also responsible for setting the international competition rules. The organization now has a membership of 118 national ski associations and is based in Oberhofen am Thunersee, Switzerland.

Nordic Refers to all forms of free-heel skiing (where the skier is only attached to the ski with a toe binding, leaving the heel to move up and down), including freestyle and classic cross-country skiing, ski jumping, backcountry touring, Telemark skiing, and Nordic combined (a competition that begins with ski jumping followed by a cross-country ski race).

Podium The top three finishers in a race. It also refers to the actual steps on which the top three competitors stand to receive their awards.

Roller skiing When snow is not available, cross-country skiers often train on roller skis, short skis with wheels attached on both ends.

USSA United States Ski & Snowboard Association, the national governing body for alpine, Nordic, freestyle, and snowboarding (but not biathlon). Rebranded as U.S. Ski & Snowboard in 2017.

Wax Two types of wax are used for classic and freestyle skiing. In classic, kick wax provides grip. It is applied like a crayon to the middle section of the ski and rubbed into the ski base using a cork. Glide wax is melted and ironed onto a ski base to reduce friction with the snow. For classic skis, it is applied on the tip and tail. On freestyle skis, it is applied along the entire base.

SUGGESTED READING

Allen, E. John B. *From Skisport to Skiing: One Hundred Years of an American Sport, 1840–1940.* Amherst: University of Massachusetts Press, 1996.

Beauchamp, Mark R., and Mark A. Eys. *Group Dynamics in Exercise and Sport Psychology.* New York: Routledge, 2007.

Bodensteiner, Luke. *Endless Winter: An Olympian's Journal.* West Bend, WI: Alta Press, 1994.

Burfoot, Amby. *First Ladies of Running: 22 Inspiring Profiles of the Rebels, Rule Breakers, and Visionaries Who Changed the Sport Forever.* Emmaus, PA: Rodale, 2016.

Caldwell, John. *The Cross-country Ski Book, 6th Edition.* Brattleboro, VT: The Stephen Greene Press, 1981.

Hooke, David O. *Reaching That Peak: 75 Years of the Dartmouth Outing Club.* Canaan, NH: Phoenix Publishing, 1987.

Lombardi, Vince. *Coaching for Teamwork: Winning Concepts for Business in the Twenty-First Century.* Bellevue, WA: Reinforcement Press, 1996.

Miller, David. *Athens to Athens: The Official History of the Olympic Games and the IOC, 1894–2004.* Edinburgh: Mainstream Publishing, 2003.

Vordenberg, Peter. *Momentum: Chasing the Olympic Dream.* Williamston, MI: Out Your Backdoor Press, 2002.

Walker, Sam. *The Captain Class: The Hidden Force That Creates the World's Greatest Teams.* New York: Random House, 2017.

Wallechinsky, David, and Jaime Loucky. *The Complete Book of the Winter Olympics, 2010 edition.* Vancouver: Aurum Press, 2009.

Waterhouse, Stephen L. *Passion for Skiing: The Story of Alumni, Staff and Family of One Small College in New England (Dartmouth College) Dominating the Development of Modern Skiing for Over 100 Years . . . And They Still Are!* Lebanon, NH: Whitman Communications, 2010.

❆　❆　❆

Articles on Fasterskier.com; the International Skiing History Association's website, www.skiinghistory.org, and its magazine, *Skiing History*; *Sports Illustrated* (available in www.si.com/vault), *Skiing Magazine* (available on Google), and in *SkiTrax Magazine*.

Other sources: Conversations with members of the U.S. Ski Team (current and alumnae) and U.S. Ski & Snowboard coaches and administrators, as well as conversations with friends and family members cited in this book.